More Than Daisies -

a hidden history of Namaqualand and the Richtersveld

by

David Fleminger

Copyright © 2020 by David Fleminger

All rights reserved. This book or any portion thereof may not be reproduced or used in any manner whatsoever without the express written permission of the publisher, except for the use of brief quotations in a book review.

First Edition 2020

DogDog Publishing
P.O. Box 1816
Highlands North
Johannesburg, South Africa, 2037
www.dogdogpublishing.com

www.davidfleminger.com
davidfleminger@gmail.com

Cover Design and Maps by Ilan Mizrachi
Cover Photographs by David Fleminger

Disclaimer: while the author and publisher have made every effort to ensure that the information contained in this book is accurate and up to date, they cannot accept any liability whatsoever arising from errors or omissions, however caused. Readers are encouraged to do their own research and confirm details before they visit any venues or make use of any services mentioned in this book. The views and opinions expressed in this book are the author's own and do not necessarily reflect the official policy or position of any other agency, organisation, individual or company. The author and publisher accept no responsibility for any loss, injury or inconvenience sustained by anyone using this book. Some material in this book was previously published in 2008 under a different title.

Maps

- Namaqualand and the West Coast -

- Namaqualand in Context -

- Springbok, the Richtersveld and Surrounds -

- Nieuwoudtville, Cederberg and Surrounds -

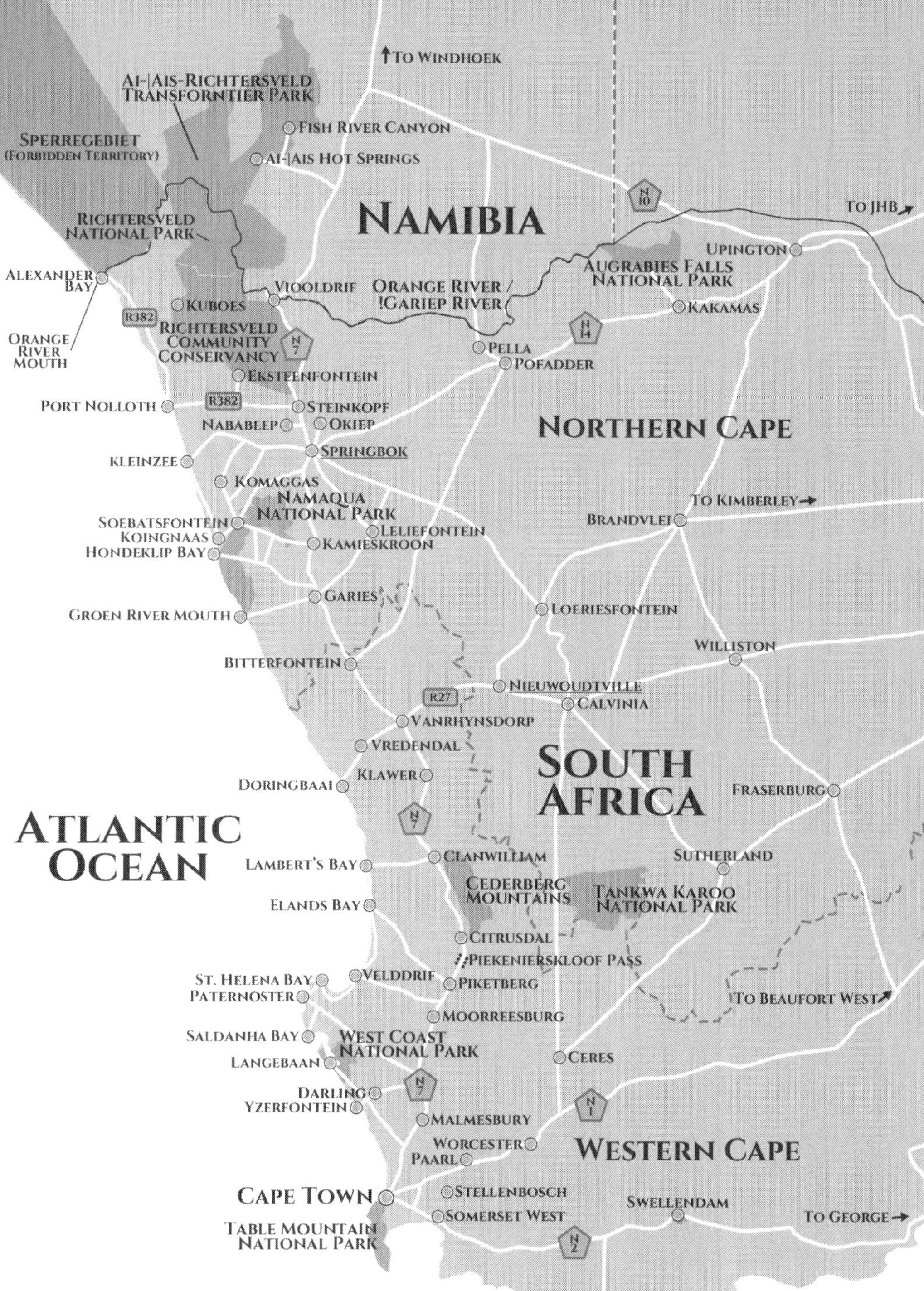

To Windhoek
Ai-|Ais-Richtersveld Transforntier Park
Sperregebiet (Forbidden Territory)
Fish River Canyon
Ai-|Ais Hot Springs
Namibia
N10
To JHB
Richtersveld National Park
Upington
Augrabies Falls National Park
Alexander Bay
Viooldrif
Orange River / !Gariep River
Kakamas
Kuboes
R382
Richtersveld Community Conservancy
N7
N14
Orange River Mouth
Pella
Pofadder
Eksteenfontein
Port Nolloth
R382
Steinkopf
Northern Cape
Nababeep
Okiep
Springbok
Kleinzee
Komaggas
Namaqua National Park
To Kimberley
Soebatsfontein
Brandvlei
Koingnaas
Leliefontein
Hondeklip Bay
Kamieskroon
Garies
Loeriesfontein
Groen River Mouth
Williston
Bitterfontein
Nieuwoudtville
R27
Calvinia
Vanrhynsdorp
Vredendal
South Africa
Klawer
Doringbaai
Fraserburg
N7
Atlantic Ocean
Sutherland
Lambert's Bay
Clanwilliam
Cederberg Mountains
Tankwa Karoo National Park
Elands Bay
Citrusdal
Piekenierskloof Pass
St. Helena Bay
Velddrif
Piketberg
Paternoster
To Beaufort West
Moorreesburg
Saldanha Bay
West Coast National Park
Langebaan
Ceres
N7
Darling
Yzerfontein
N1
Malmesbury
Worcester
Western Cape
Paarl
Cape Town
Stellenbosch
Swellendam
Somerset West
To George
Table Mountain National Park
N2
Agulhas National Park
Map not to scale

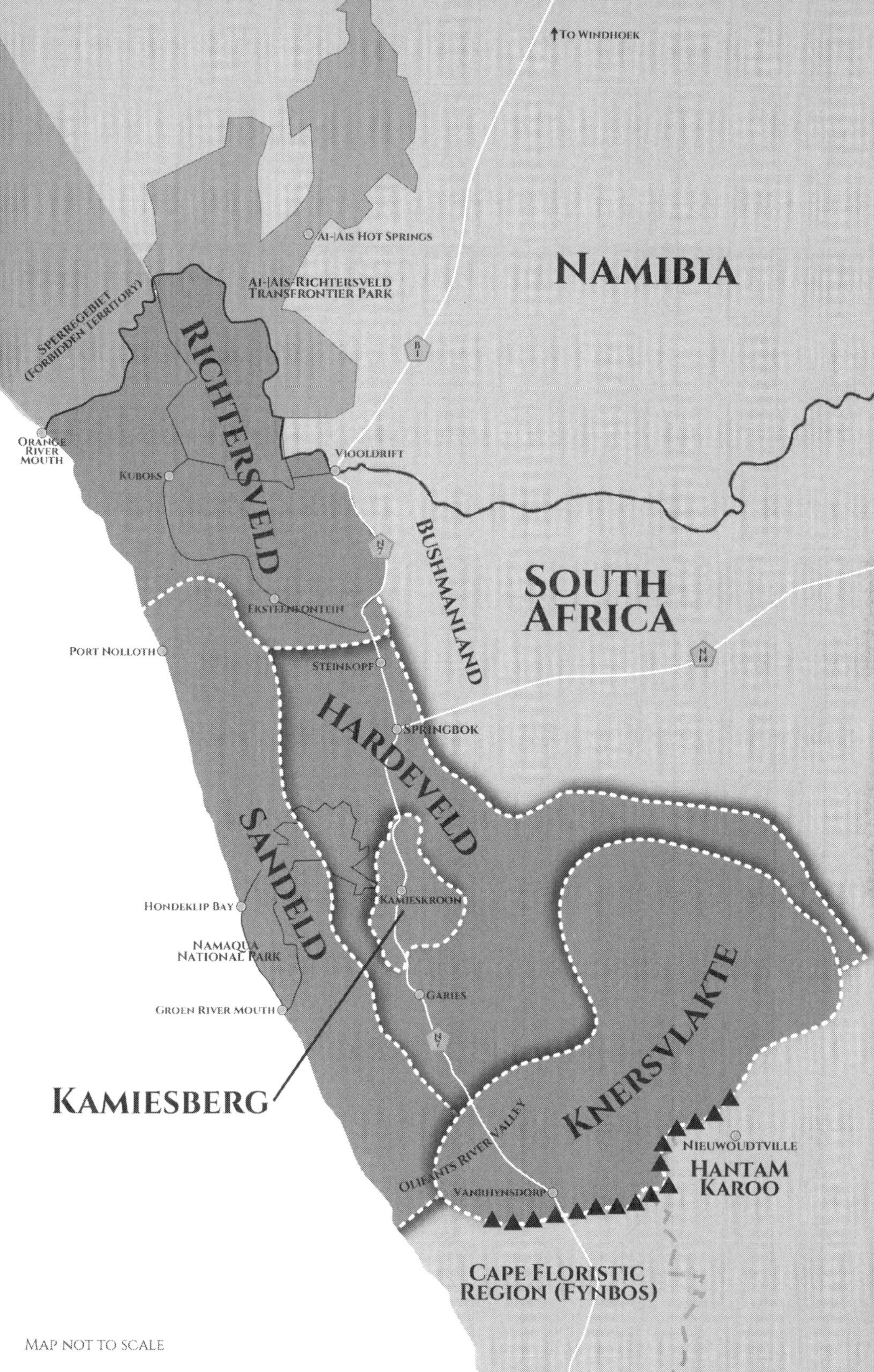

To Windhoek
Ai-|Ais Hot Springs
Namibia
Ai-|Ais-Richtersveld Transfrontier Park
Sperregebiet (Forbidden Territory)
Richtersveld
B1
Orange River Mouth
Vioolsdrift
Kuboes
N7
Bushmanland
South Africa
Eksteenfontein
Port Nolloth
N14
Steinkopf
Hardeveld
Springbok
Sandveld
Kamieskroon
Hondeklip Bay
Namaqua National Park
Knersvlakte
Garies
Groen River Mouth
N7
Kamiesberg
Olifants River Valley
Nieuwoudtville
Hantam Karoo
Vanrhynsdorp
Cape Floristic Region (Fynbos)
Map not to scale

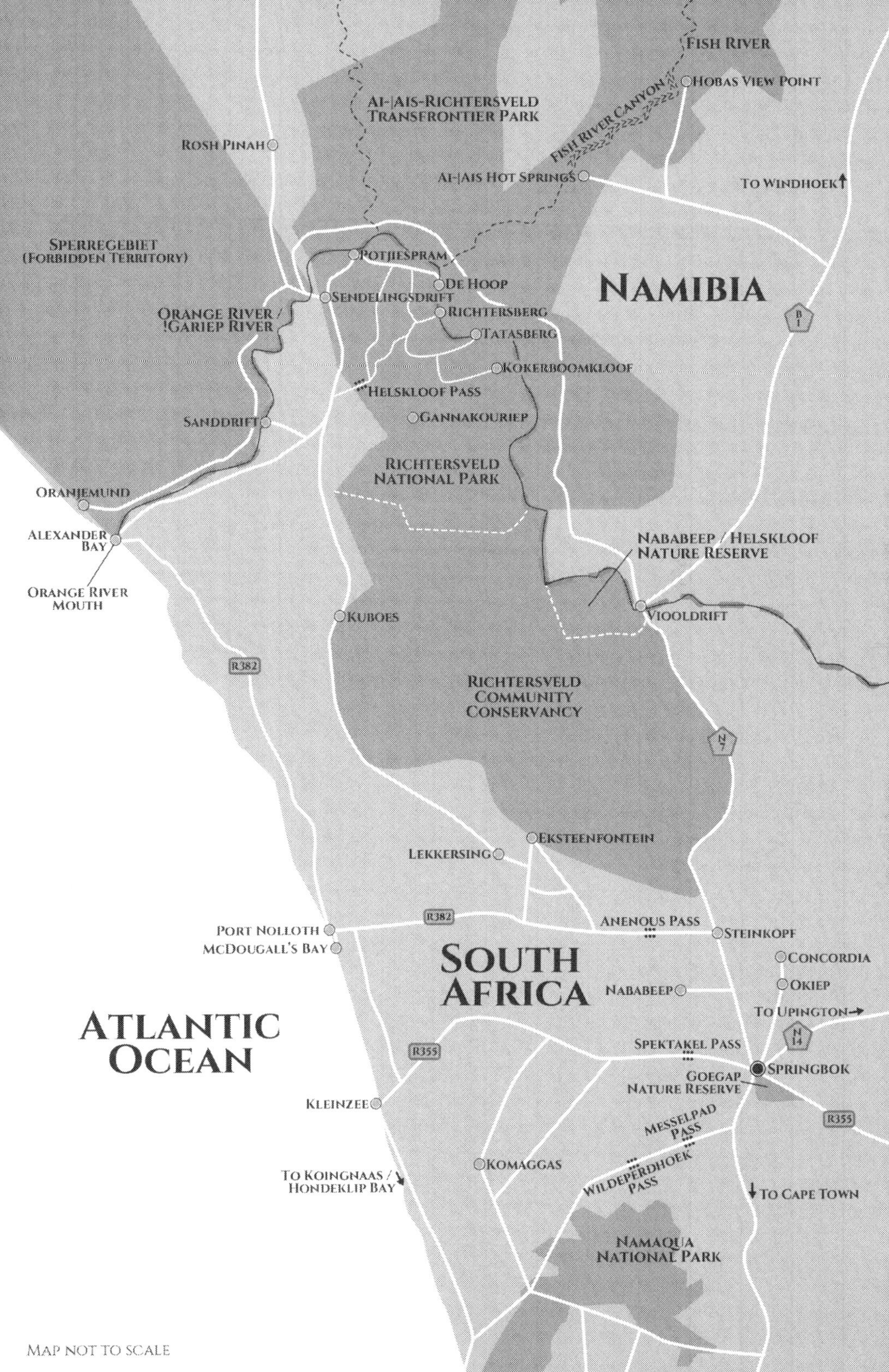

Fish River
Hobas View Point
Ai-|Ais-Richtersveld Transfrontier Park
Fish River Canyon
Rosh Pinah
Ai-|Ais Hot Springs
To Windhoek
Sperregebiet (Forbidden Territory)
Potjiespram
De Hoop
Namibia
Sendelingsdrift
Orange River / !Gariep River
Richtersberg
Tatasberg
B1
Kokerboomkloof
Helskloof Pass
Sanddrift
Gannakouriep
Richtersveld National Park
Oranjemund
Alexander Bay
Nababeep / Helskloof Nature Reserve
Orange River Mouth
Kuboes
Viooldrift
R382
Richtersveld Community Conservancy
N7
Eksteenfontein
Lekkersing
R382
Anenous Pass
Port Nolloth
Steinkopf
McDougall's Bay
Concordia
South Africa
Nababeep
Okiep
To Upington
Atlantic Ocean
N14
R355
Spektakel Pass
Goegap Nature Reserve
Springbok
Kleinzee
R355
Messelpad Pass
Komaggas
To Koingnaas / Hondeklip Bay
Wildeperdhoek Pass
To Cape Town
Namaqua National Park
Map not to scale

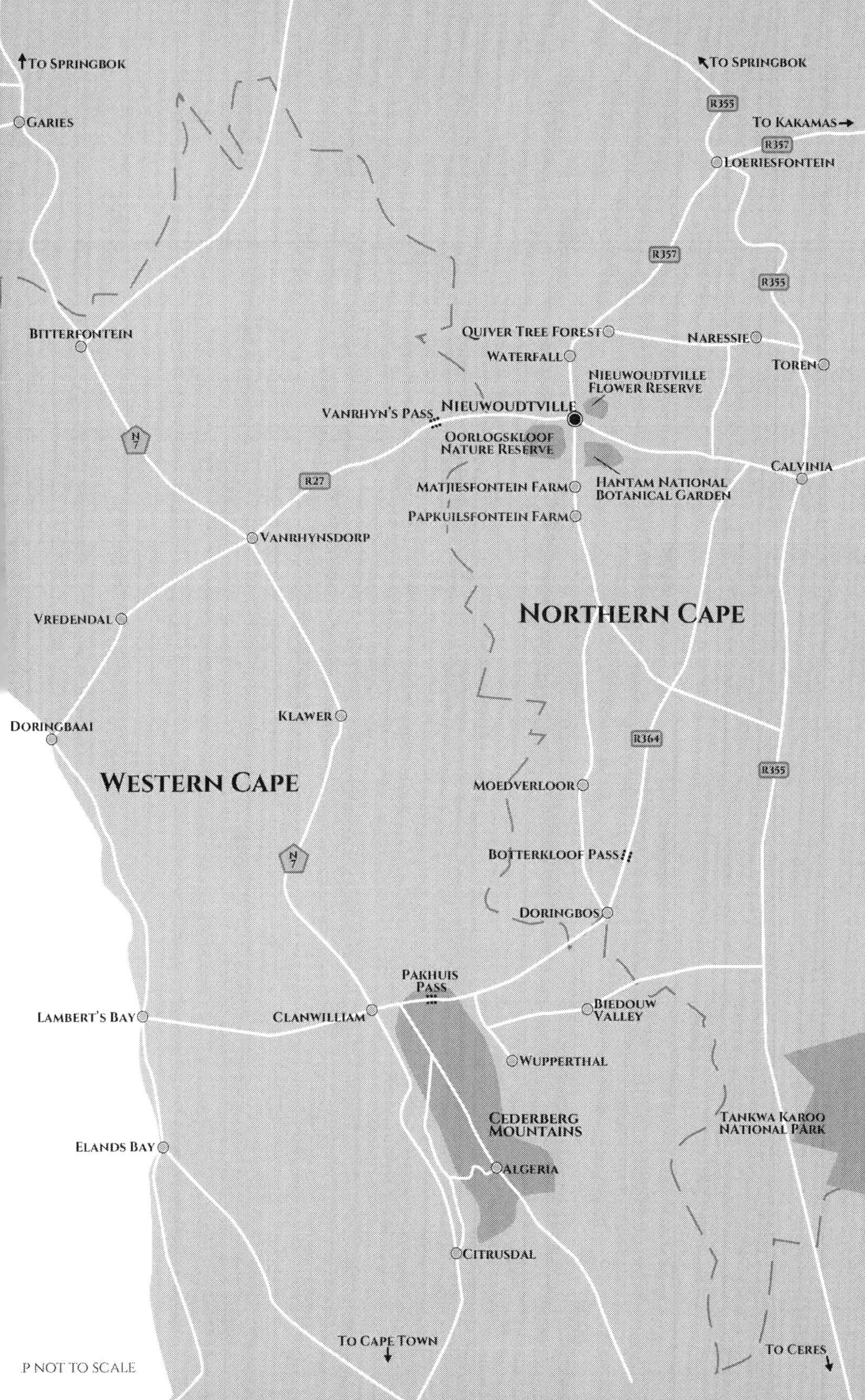

To Springbok
To Springbok
R355
Garies
To Kakamas
R357
Loeriesfontein
R357
R355
Bitterfontein
Quiver Tree Forest
Naressie
Waterfall
Toren
Nieuwoudtville Flower Reserve
Vanrhyn's Pass
Nieuwoudtville
N7
Oorlogskloof Nature Reserve
Calvinia
R27
Matjiesfontein Farm
Hantam National Botanical Garden
Papkuilsfontein Farm
Vanrhynsdorp
Vredendal
Northern Cape
Klawer
Doringbaai
R364
R355
Western Cape
Moedverloor
N7
Botterkloof Pass
Doringbos
Pakhuis Pass
Lambert's Bay
Clanwilliam
Biedouw Valley
Wupperthal
Cederberg Mountains
Tankwa Karoo National Park
Elands Bay
Algeria
Citrusdal
To Cape Town
To Ceres
P NOT TO SCALE

Books by David Fleminger

Fair Game – a hidden history of the Kruger National Park

More Than Daisies - a hidden history of Namaqualand and the Richtersveld

Coming Soon

A hidden history of Mapungubwe National Park

A hidden history of Swaziland/Eswatini

A hidden history of Lesotho

A hidden history of Robben Island

Back Roads of the Cape

TABLE OF CONTENTS

Introduction

The first incarnation of this book was published in 2008 as part of a series of pocket guides about South Africa's World Heritage Sites. Now out of print, that initial volume (by definition) focussed on the Richtersveld Cultural and Botanical Landscape - a UNESCO World Heritage Site since the previous year.

Located in the arid north-west of South Africa, hemmed in by Namibia, the Great Karoo and the cold, dark waters of the Atlantic, the Richtersveld is a remote and peculiar part of the world - two of my favourite things. A subsequent research trip further confirmed that the Richtersveld is indeed worthy of its World Heritage status, thanks to a unique botanical diversity and its small, resident population of nomadic NamaKhoi farmers - the world's last living connection to a traditional lifestyle pattern that dates back millennia.

But, because I'm a maddening completist, it quickly became clear that the Richtersveld couldn't be discussed on its own. It's also an integral part of the wider Namaqualand region that runs up the rugged west coast of southern Africa, roughly from Vanrhynsdorp to beyond the Orange River (which forms the international border with Namibia).

Then, obviously, you can't write a book about Namaqualand without mentioning the famous Spring Daisies - an annual display of wildflowers that transforms dusty fields into spontaneous, dazzling carpets of colour for a few weeks each year.

These imperatives expanded the scope of both my research trip and the resulting book, which grew from a short pocket guide about the little-known Richtersveld into a somewhat sprawling story of greater Namaqualand in all its glory.

Now, 12 years later, I thought it's time to revisit Namaqualand and the Richtersveld. After all, I can't find any equivalent book on the area that's been published in the intervening decade and, since we are currently in the throes of a strict lockdown precipitated by the Covid-19 pandemic, I've got a bit of time on my hands...

Regrettably, I haven't been able to return the region since my original research trip of 2007 and much has changed since I was there - both for the good (the Namaqua National Park has grown substantially, for example) and the bad (many of the diamond mines in northern Namaqualand are now closed or closing, depriving the local communities of income). On the other hand, my armchair research over the last couple of months suggests that many things haven't changed at all in this timeless corner of the world.

In any case, I've taken this opportunity to polish the text, fill in some extra details, add new stories, and update relevant information where possible. The result is this latest volume in my Hidden Histories series, and I do hope that you'll find the journey contained in the pages that follow to be both enlightening and engaging.

More specifically, this book is roughly divided into three sections: Natural History, Human History and a Planning Guide that will encourage you to get out there and experience this remarkable part of the world for yourself. And, if you ever get the opportunity, you really should make the effort because Namaqualand is offers much more than just 'daisies'.

For the sake of expedience, at this stage I have kept the book text-only (apart from a few custom maps). If you would like to browse through a selection of my Namaqualand and Richtersveld photographs, please visit the appropriate Gallery on my website: www.davidfleminger.com.

Oh, and if you spot any mistakes or oversights please let me know by writing to davidfleminger@gmail.com. The pages that follow might sound authoritative but errors are inevitable and I'm always open to correction!

Orientation

Before we begin in earnest, let's take a moment to familiarise ourselves with the geography of the area, starting with the Richtersveld and zooming out.

The greater Richtersveld region can be said to form a rough square in the top left-hand corner of South Africa. The region is named after Rhenish missionary inspector, Dr. E Richter - for no good reason, to be honest, other than he went there on an inspection trip in 1830.

The western boundary is the Atlantic Ocean coast, roughly from Port Nolloth to Alexander Bay (where the Orange River meets the sea). The Orange River (or *!Gariep,* meaning 'great river' in the Nama language) is a major watercourse, originating in the highlands of Lesotho, that in its lower stretches marks the northern edge of the Richtersveld and the international border between South Africa and Namibia.

In the east, the N7 highway from Steinkopf to the Namibian border post at Vioolsdrift nominally separates the Richtersveld from parched Bushmanland, which in turn blends into the oxymoronic 'Green Kalahari'.

The southern edge of the Richtersveld can be said to be the R382 road that runs from Steinkopf to Port Nolloth, over the Anenous Pass. Steinkopf is about 50kms north of Springbok, a dusty oasis that functions as the major urban centre in the region (although that is a relative term).

Politically speaking, southern Namibia is not part of the Richtersveld, but from an ecological perspective, it's very similar. To that end, the Richtersveld National Park (a true natural wonder) has now been united with conservation areas in Namibia to create the |Ai-|Ais/Richtersveld Transfrontier Conservation Area (incorporating the Ai-Ais hot springs and the staggering Fish River Canyon - one of the largest on Earth).

The Richtersveld Community Conservancy (the actual World Heritage Site) is located in the middle of this square, bounded by grazing lands to the south and west, the N7 highway and the Nababeep/Helskloof Nature Reserve in the East, and the Vandersterr mountains to the north. Beyond the Vandersterr mountains lies the Richtersveld National Park (RNP), which extends to the banks of the Orange River. The RNP should not be confused with the Conservancy for several reasons that we'll get to in a moment. The land between the coast and these two conservation areas is held in private hands and is (or was) used mainly for mining activities.

If we widen out a bit, we will see that the Richtersveld is located in the top-left corner of the greater Namaqualand region; a maddeningly imprecise term that can be defined in several different ways. As Willem Steenkamp recounts in his memoirs, *Land of the Thirst King:* "The place is like a concertina. If you want to live inside its borders you stretch it out all the way to Vredendal. But if you don't fancy being called a Namaqualander you squeeze it flat till it ends at Garies, and that's that."

Botanically speaking, Namaqualand can be roughly defined as "the part of the Succulent Karoo that is strongly influenced by winter rainfall and fog". Following this description, the southern boundary of Namaqualand extends from the mouth of the Olifants River, near Vredendal, to the edge of the Matzikama mountains at Vanrhynsdorp (part of the Cape Fold mountain range). The eastern boundary then follows the Bokkeveld Escarpment and plateau between Nieuwoudtville and Loeriesfontein and thence into the north-west, all the way to the coast at Lüderitz in Namibia.

From a political point of view, the Namaqua District Municipality (covering over 26 000 square kilometres) includes several environmental units that are quite distinct from the Succulent Karoo biome. In the north, the district runs along the twisty course of the trusty Orange River from Alexander Bay to Pofadder. In the west, it follows the Atlantic shore to a point some 35kms south of Garies. From here, it extends eastwards and somewhat south into the Hantam Karoo (including the towns of Loeriesfontein, Nieuwoudtville, Calvinia, Sutherland and Fraserburg). Bushmanland and the Hantam Karoo are both part of the Nama Karoo biome.

Stepping back further, thanks to an ancient migration of NamaKhoi north of the Orange River, Namaqualand in its widest sense extends far along the west coast into Namibia, covering a total area of around 440 000 square kilometres. In this context, Little Namaqualand *(Klein Namakwaland* in Afrikaans) is in South Africa and Great Namaqualand lies in what is now the ǁKaras region of Namibia. In Afrikaans, Great Namaqualand translates as *Groot Namakwaland,* which has nothing to do with Guardians of the Galaxy.

Finally, in terms of the legendary Namaqualand wildflowers, these occur throughout the region including the seemingly barren Richtersveld. You also get wildflower displays south of Vanrhynsdorp, in what is technically the Cape Floristic Region (or Fynbos biome). Depending on conditions, the wildflowers bloom for a few weeks in August or September each year.

Although they are several hundred kilometres apart, the towns of Springbok and Nieuwoudtville are the de-facto centres for the springtime wildflower experience. The Namaqua National Park, near the town of Kamieskroon, is another reliable flower spotting destination.

The most notable flower sites outside of Namaqualand can be found in the Cederberg mountains, along the west coast around Elands Bay, and in the West Coast National Park at Langebaan (the closest location to Cape Town).

The Richtersveld World Heritage Site

As we've seen, the Richtersveld is located in the extreme north-west of South Africa, on the border with Namibia. Effectively, that means it's far away from everything; isolated by the frigid Atlantic Ocean in the west, the Namib Desert in the north, and the arid Nama Karoo savannahs to the east.

This is a very dry region, technically a desert, with an average annual rainfall below 220mm. It's also very dramatic. Mountains of bare rock rip through the hot plains. Succulent plants with thick leaves cling to the boulders and hide in the meagre shadows. Summer temperatures can soar to over 50 degrees and winter nights can be freezing. The only perennial water source is the doughty Orange River that flows obliviously through the barren landscape, granting a narrow strip of verdancy among the stone and sand. And yet, for all this ecological hostility, the Richtersveld is one of the most biologically diverse deserts in the world.

Despite the low annual rainfall, several climatic conditions are present in the Richtersveld that allow an amazing variety of botanical life to proliferate. 350 plant species are endemic to the region and it contains the world's most diverse lichen fields (found near Alexander Bay). And that's not counting the broader Succulent Karoo biome that covers the western coastal regions of South Africa and southern Namibia. This wider botanical region contains over 5000 plant species and around 40% of these are endemic, including many rare succulents, making it the only arid bio-diversity hotspot on Earth. The Succulent Karoo, incidentally, is on the road to becoming a World Heritage Site in its own right (currently listed on the UNESCO Tentative List).

The Richtersveld also has a long and valuable cultural history that stretches back, unbroken, for over 2000 years. More specifically, the Richtersveld Community Conservancy is home to the world's last population of Nama stock farmers who still maintain a nomadic lifestyle, moving with their small flocks from post to post as they have done for countless generations.

This special form of 'transhumance' involves small family groups who move with their herds of sheep and goats from one seasonal grazing area to another. Significantly, some of them still live in traditional dome-shaped *matjieshuise* (reed huts), known as */haru oms* in the Nama language.

Both the natural and cultural riches of the Richtersveld are therefore priceless, and it's probably the geographical isolation of the region that has ensured its relatively pristine condition to this day. In other words, it's so hard to access that the various colonising forces who generally mucked things up in the rest of Africa simply couldn't find a way to profitably exploit the Richtersveld.

Even now, in terms of human development, there are few roads and fewer people. Only a handful of small towns offer any form of social or tourism infrastructure, and economic activities are limited. There's a bit of commercial agriculture on the banks of the Orange River, but the main earner in the area is (or was) diamond mining, which still seems to be controlled by a handful of all-powerful companies operating under an impenetrable veil of secrecy - even though the supply of gems is rapidly drying up.

In any case, the Richtersveld's esoteric beauty and hidden depths encouraged a State Nominating Party to propose the site to the UNESCO World Heritage Committee, based on both the natural and cultural criteria that make it unique.

Interestingly, it was the cultural significance of the Nama stock farmers and their ancient lifestyle that most impressed UNESCO and its investigating committees and, in their final report, it was found that the site had a high degree of integrity and authenticity in this regard. The traditional system of seasonal migration is still functional, the stock posts and */haru oms* are being used as part of daily life, and the nomadic form of herding practised by the Nama is testimony to an ancient form of land management that has helped maintain the fragile Succulent Karoo ecosystem for centuries.

In light of these findings, the Richtersveld Cultural and Botanical Landscape was admitted onto the World Heritage list in 2007 under criteria iv and v, viz.:

(iv) to be an outstanding example of a type of building, architectural or technological ensemble or landscape which illustrates (a) significant stage(s) in human history.

(v) to be an outstanding example of a traditional human settlement, land-use, or sea-use which is representative of a culture (or cultures), or human interaction with the environment especially when it has become vulnerable under the impact of irreversible change.

These criteria have been interpreted by UNESCO as follows:

(iv) the rich diverse botanical landscape of the Richtersveld, shaped by the pastoral grazing of the Nama, represents and demonstrates a way of life that persisted for many millennia over a considerable part of southern Africa and was a significant stage in the history of this area.

(v) the Richtersveld is one of the few areas in southern Africa where transhumance pastoralism is still practised: as a cultural landscape [implying a significant interaction between humans and their physical environment] it reflects long-standing and persistent traditions of the Nama, the indigenous community. Their seasonal pastoral grazing regimes, which sustain the extensive biodiversity of the area, were once much more widespread and are now vulnerable.

As indicated above, however, the integrity of the Richtersveld World Heritage Site is fragile. There are currently only a couple of hundred individuals who still practice this traditional form of stock farming, and most of these are elderly. The area has also become overgrazed - mainly because private land ownership has encroached on the Nama over the last couple of hundred years, limiting the wider migration patterns of the stock farmers.

Mining activity along the Orange River and in the Richtersveld National Park is also potentially damaging as this destroys both the physical environment and the cultural traditions of the Nama, who would often leave their villages to work on the mines and in the nearby towns.

In view of this, the actual World Heritage site has been limited in size to what is called the Richtersveld Community Conservancy (RCC). This is an area of 160 000 hectares of grazing land, surrounded by a 398 425 hectare buffer zone, controlled by the *Sida !hub* Community Property Association (CPA). For more info, visit the Richtersveld page on UNESCO's website: whc.unesco.org/en/list/1265.

At this stage, the spectacular Richtersveld National Park (located north of the Conservancy and managed by SA National Parks) is excluded from the World Heritage site because there is still mining going on within the reserve's boundaries. There is a possibility that World Heritage status will be extended to the park once the mines are shut down and the land has been rehabilitated.

This may happen sooner rather than later as most of the diamond mines in the region are nearly exhausted, and there are already agreements in place which allow the Nama stock farmers to graze within the national park's boundaries. However, for the last 15 years, effective leadership in the RCC has been crippled by corruption and in-fighting on a number of levels (especially after a huge, diamond-laden land claim came into the picture). As we shall see in the chapters that follow...

UNESCO and the World Heritage List

UNESCO (the United Nations Economic, Scientific and Cultural Organisation) was formed shortly after the Second World War when it became clear that, as a species, we don't really get along.

The newly formed United Nations therefore set up an organisation that would encourage cooperation between nations by sharing knowledge and promoting culture. But, after the horror of two world wars in which millions of lives and many irreplaceable global resources were lost, it was apparent that building classrooms, mounting festivals, and publishing obscure scientific papers would not be enough. So, the UN created UNESCO and tasked this specialised agency with a most ambitious goal: to build peace through international cooperation in Education, the Sciences and Culture.

In 1972, UNESCO's mandate was significantly enlarged at the *Convention concerning the Protection and Preservation of World Cultural and Natural Sites.* The original impetus for this worthy endeavour came about several decades earlier because, as is often the case, a valuable site was about to be destroyed in the name of progress. In this instance, it was the Abu Simbel temples in Egypt, which were going to be flooded by the soon-to-be-completed Aswan Dam. The year was 1959 and, thanks to international pressure and funding, the threatened temples were quickly dismantled and re-assembled out of harm's way before the damn dam was built.

Soon, authorities in charge of other endangered sites applied to the UN for protection and assistance and, in 1965, the United States proposed a 'World Heritage Trust' that would identify, promote and protect "the world's superb natural and scenic areas and historic sites for the present and the future of the entire world citizenry".

In 1968, the International Union for Conservation of Nature (IUCN) developed similar proposals for its members and, eventually, a single text was agreed upon by all parties concerned, which resulted in the adoption of the above-mentioned convention of 1972.

And that's not all. UNESCO's programmes also contribute to the achievement of the UN's Sustainable Development Goals as defined in Agenda 2030, adopted by the General Assembly in 2015. These goals include a comprehensive list of 17 global outcomes that include the eradication of poverty and hunger, good health and well-being, quality education, gender equality, clean water and sanitation, affordable and clean energy, decent work and economic growth, reduced inequalities, sustainable cities and communities, responsible consumption and production, climate action, and the promotion of peace, justice and strong institutions.

As their current vision statement declares: "Political and economic arrangements of governments are not enough to secure the lasting and sincere support of the peoples. Peace must be founded upon dialogue and mutual understanding. Peace must be built upon the intellectual and moral solidarity of humanity.

"In this spirit, UNESCO develops educational tools to help people live as global citizens free of hate and intolerance. By promoting cultural heritage and the equal dignity of all cultures, UNESCO strengthens bonds among nations. UNESCO fosters scientific programmes and policies as platforms for development and cooperation. UNESCO stands up for freedom of expression, as a fundamental right and a key condition for democracy and development. Serving as a laboratory of ideas, UNESCO helps countries adopt international standards and manages programmes that foster the free flow of ideas and knowledge sharing.

"UNESCO's founding vision was born in response to a world war that was marked by racist and anti-Semitic violence. Seventy years on and many liberation struggles later, UNESCO's mandate is as relevant as ever. Cultural diversity is under attack and new forms of intolerance, rejection of scientific facts and threats to freedom of expression challenge peace and human rights. In response, UNESCO's duty remains to reaffirm the humanist missions of education, science and culture."

So, if the latest pandemic, the climate crisis, an asteroid strike and/or nuclear Armageddon don't get us first, UNESCO is working together with its 190 member states to make sure that our planet's precious and collective heritage resources are maintained for future generations. As UNESCO acutely points out, "by regarding heritage as both cultural and natural, the Convention reminds us of the ways in which people interact with nature, and of the fundamental need to preserve the balance between the two".

That's some good thinking right there and World Heritage List continues to grow. But how does a site gain access to this exclusive list?

The first step in the process is for state parties to make an 'inventory' of their heritage assets - known as the Tentative List. Then, when they're ready with all the supporting documentation, local stakeholders can submit sites on their Tentative List to UNESCO's Nomination File. According to UNESCO's website: "Each nominated property is independently evaluated by two Advisory Bodies mandated by the World Heritage Convention: the International Council on

Monuments and Sites (ICOMOS) and the International Union for Conservation of Nature (IUCN). The third Advisory Body is the International Centre for the Study of the Preservation and Restoration of Cultural Property (ICCROM), an intergovernmental organization that provides the Committee with expert advice on conservation of cultural sites as well as on training activities.

"Once a site has been nominated and evaluated, it is up to the intergovernmental World Heritage Committee to make the final decision on its inscription. Once a year, the Committee meets to decide which sites will be inscribed on the World Heritage List. It can also defer its decision and request further information on sites from the States Parties.

"To be included on the World Heritage List, sites must be of outstanding universal value and meet at least one out of ten selection criteria. The criteria are regularly revised by the Committee to reflect the evolution of the World Heritage concept itself. Until the end of 2004, World Heritage sites were selected on the basis of six cultural and four natural criteria. With the adoption of the revised Operational Guidelines, only one set of ten criteria exists."

But don't think of the World Heritage List as a big, fuzzy group-hug. If a declared World Heritage Site is neglected or compromised, the relevant State Party will be alerted that their site has been put on the 'The List in Danger'. And if things continue to deteriorate, as a last resort, sites can be removed from the List entirely.

South Africa's World Heritage Sites

Since South Africa ratified the World Heritage Convention in 1997, we have become particularly well-endowed in this regard. We currently have ten sites on the World Heritage list, which is quite a lot considering the relatively small size of our country (not to mention all those lost years when we were out of the UN fold during the dark days of our Apartheid-induced international isolation).

South Africa's ten World Heritage Sites are (in order of declaration):

- iSimangaliso Wetland Park - formerly the St. Lucia Wetlands Park (1999)
- Robben Island (1999)
- Fossil Hominid Sites of South Africa - including the Cradle of Humankind (Sterkfontein, Swartkrans, Kromdraai and Environs), the Makapan Valley, and the Taung Skull Fossil Site (1999, extended 2005)
- Maloti-Drakensberg Park (2000, extended 2013)
- Mapungubwe Cultural Landscape (2003)
- Cape Floral Region Protected Areas - including Table Mountain, the Boland Mountain Complex (incl. Hottentot's Holland, Limietberg, Jonkershoek,

Assagaaibosch, Kogelberg), the Groot Winterhoek Wilderness Area, the Cederberg Wilderness Area, Boosmansbos Wilderness Area, De Hoop Nature Reserve, Swartberg Nature Reserve, and Baviaanskloof Nature Reserve (2004, extended 2015)

- Vredefort Dome (2005)
- Richtersveld Cultural and Botanical Landscape (2007)
- ǂKhomani Cultural Landscape (2017) - coinciding with the Kalahari Gemsbok National Park
- Barberton Makhonjwa Mountains (2018)

FYI, South Africa's Tentative List currently includes the following sites:

- Succulent Karoo Protected Areas (2009)
- Liberation Heritage Route (2009)
- Early Farmsteads of the Cape Winelands (2015)
- The Emergence of Modern Humans: The Pleistocene occupation sites of South Africa (2015)
- Human Rights, Liberation Struggle and Reconciliation: Nelson Mandela Legacy Sites (2015)

More information about all these fascinating locations can be found on the South Africa page of UNESCO's World Heritage Site portal: whc.unesco.org/en/statesparties/za.

Natural History

Full confession: I'm a bit useless at natural history. I do my best, truly, but there's something impossibly intricate about floral, faunal, climatic and geological knowledge that keeps full understanding just beyond my reach. Nevertheless, even though I find it all a bit recondite, I humbly offer this overview of the natural processes that make the deserts of Namaqualand and the Richtersveld such incredible ecological treasures.

For more detailed information about this side of things, please refer to the resources and technical guides listed in *References / Further Reading* at the end of this book.

A Rocky Start

The business of geology is a complicated and rather arcane affair. Moreover, the Namaqualand boasts a particularly long and convoluted geological timeline which, quite frankly, sets my mind a-boggle. Personal shortcomings notwithstanding, however, the peculiar landscapes, plant life, mineral deposits and cultural riches of the region are all directly connected to the rocks on which they rest. So, here's a quick overview of the story...

The earliest identifiable rock layers in the Namaqualand region date to around 2 billion years ago. Known as the Orange River Group, these are mainly igneous rocks that are volcanic in origin. The lavas of the Orange River Group were then overlain by some sedimentary rocks (sandstone and shale). These strata can still be seen in the Rosyntjieberg formation, located in the Richtersveld National Park.

There followed a long period of intrusion events during which molten rock from the Mantle was pushed up through cracks in the Earth's crust to cool close to the surface. This resulted in the formation of several granitic suites that formed an 'basement' that stretches from the Knersvlakte (north of Vanrhynsdorp) to Steinkopf. This area is now known as the Namaqualand Metamorphic Complex or Province, as the heat from these subterranean intrusions transformed (metamorphosed) the surrounding rocks.

Thus, volcanic rocks were transformed into schist, shale turned into slate, and sandstone became quartzite. In the Richtersveld, these intrusions include the Vioolsdrift Suite (emplaced 1.9-1.75 billion years ago), the Richtersveld Igneous Suite (dating back 1 billion years) and the Gannakouriep Suite (a series of north-south tending black dykes that were emplaced between 870 and 540 million years ago).

An important element of these intrusion events is the presence of a series of discontinuous 'mafic bodies' that contain deposits of copper and other valuable minerals. These isolated outcrops of ore are found in distinctive 'steep structures' and are known collectively as the Koperberg (Copper Mountain) Suite. The erratic copper deposits of Namaqualand would go on to play an important role in the development of the region.

Then, around 850 Ma (million years ago), the super-continent of Rodinia began to split apart (or rift). This caused an ocean trough to form in a north-south orientation across much of present-day Namaqualand. Material was subsequently eroded from the hinterland and deposited into this trough, consolidating into the various formations of the Gariep Group.

In the Richtersveld, some of these sediments are thought to have collected at the foot of an ancient mountain range. This caused calcium carbonate to precipitate out of the water, forming limestone and dolomite. These rocks were subsequently subjected to heat and pressure, causing them to metamorphose into the erosion-resistant quartzites and marbles of the Stinkfontein group. Another element of the Stinkfontein group is the Kaigas Formation: a collection of tillite rock, thought to have been deposited by glaciers that once crept through the region. Recent thinking, however, has moved away from this interpretation.

The Vandersterr and Stinkfontein mountains (the so-called backbone of the Richtersveld) are part of this group and contain some of the highest peaks in the area. Ecologically, these two ranges are important because they act as a barrier that prevents the moisture-bearing clouds that roll in from the Atlantic Ocean from reaching the interior. This creates several distinct micro-climates within the Richtersveld, which is one of the factors that contribute to its high botanical diversity.

Next, around 570 Ma, there was a period of sedimentation that created the Nama and Numees Groups, which consist of dolomite, limestone (the Hilda Suite), shale and sandstones. 540 Ma, this group of flat-lying rocks was intruded by the Kuboos-Bremen suite of granites, which occur in a rough line that runs northwest-southeast. The Ploegberg mountain (near the village of Kuboes) and the granitic Tatasberg pluton (located in the Richtersveld National Park) are part of this suite.

Plutons are large domes created when volcanic (or igneous) material rises up from the Mantle and cools in underground chambers, only to be exposed when the softer rocks above it are eroded away. Another example of a pluton is the famous Paarl (Pearl) Rock, located in the south-western Cape.

Around 450 Ma, the various landmasses were once again coming together to form the supercontinent of Pangaea. This continued continental rifting caused a large basin to open in the vicinity of what is now the south-western Cape, causing the erosive forces eating away at the Namaqualand plateau to shift south, transporting sediments into the new basin. These would eventually form both the great Cape Fold Mountain ranges and the nutrient-poor soil of the Cape Floral Kingdom (also known as the Fynbos biome).

Incidentally, the idea that the planet's continental landmasses are involved in a constant process of slowly drifting together and then splitting apart was initially proposed by Alfred Wegener in 1912. Using the analysis of fossil remains, geology and other scientific intricacies, this concept has now been developed into generally accepted theory of Plate Tectonics.

Skipping forward 100 million years, the edge of Pangaea (the most recent supercontinent) was now drifting slowly across the southern polar region and the land was covered with thick ice sheets. The grooves scoured by these glaciers can still be seen at Grasdrift, close to the Richtersveld National Park, and in the vicinity of Nieuwoudtville.

By 270 Ma, however, the land had moved out of the polar region and things were starting to heat up. The glaciers began melting, leaving behind glacial deposits that became the Dwyka group of tillites. This marks the start of the Karoo Supergroup, which extends over much of South Africa's current interior. These deposits are distributed unevenly in the Namaqualand region, lying on top of the Nama Group of rocks.

Around 200 Ma, the entire region was subject to an extended period of geological turbulence caused by the splitting apart of Pangaea into Laurasia and Gondwanaland (with the latter later splitting again into the South American, African, Australian and Antarctic continental landmasses we know today). This caused dramatic folding of the rock layers and considerable orogenic (mountain building) activity across the region.

As part of this upheaval, a large basin was formed across the Karoo region and the south-eastern parts of Namaqualand. The Ecca and Beaufort groups were subsequently deposited into this basin, forming the basement of much of the Nama-Karoo biome.

As part of this process, the sea level also receded to expose the coastal plains, which the rivers running down to the new coastline proceeded to erode. This caused, amongst other things, the formation of the Fish River Canyon (one of the largest in the world). By this time, the Namaqualand region was already quite dry, and the newly exposed marine terraces began to get covered by sandy deposits.

Diamonds Are Forever

The next important geological phase occurred around 120 Ma (million years ago), when a series of volcanic pipes pushed their way up from the Mantle towards the surface. These funnel-shaped pipes, characterised by a crumbly rock type later named 'Kimberlite', carried with them considerable quantities of diamonds formed at a depth of up to 250km below the surface.

Significant diamond pipes would emerge at various locations across South Africa - most notably at Kimberley's Colesberg Kopje (now a Big Hole). But not all diamonds are found at 'dry diggings' like Kimberley. Over the ages, these diamondiferous pipes were eroded by rivers (most notably the Orange River) and the glittering gems were slowly washed along various watercourses on their way to the sea.

A steady stream of diamondiferous gravel was thus deposited along the banks of the Orange, with the thickest layers dating to between 20 and 15 Ma. At the river's mouth with the Atlantic, the diamonds were either pushed up the shoreline by currents or carried a short distance into the ocean before dropping to the sea floor. Both these 'onshore' and 'marine' diamonds continue to play a major role in the region, for better and for worse.

By 100 Ma, South America and Antarctica had separated from the African landmass and the African sub-continent (which had once been in the centre of Gondwana) was surrounded by water. This caused the rim of the subcontinent to 'buckle', resulting in the creation of a low-lying coastal plain that was separated from the high interior plateau by a sharp escarpment that runs almost unbroken in a great horseshoe around South Africa.

By now, the river that would become the Orange (or *!Gariep*) was already the major watercourse in the region. As mentioned previously, the Orange (named after the Dutch royal House of Orange and not the fruit) originated in the highlands of Lesotho and flowed in a westerly direction to enter the Atlantic Ocean near present-day Alexander Bay.

Then, around 65 Ma, a little geological hiccup caused the Orange to change its course and shift to the south through the Koa Valley, to reach the Atlantic near the mouth of the present-day Olifants River near Klawer. This meant that the diamond-bearing gravel was now getting transported up the coast from further south, carried along by the nascent, north-flowing Benguela current.

50 million years later, another subterranean glitch caused the Orange to revert to its original course through the Richtersveld to Alexander Bay. The result of all this back and forth is that the entire north-western shore of South Africa, as well as the southern coast of Namibia, is literally laden with diamonds - both on land and beneath the water.

The western coast of South Africa now grew steadily drier over the next couple of million years and the Namib desert, one of the world's oldest, was established between 40 and 25 Ma. Finally, by 5 Ma, the cold Benguela current (which originates in the Antarctic) had become the dominant climatic driver in this arid region, which saw Namaqualand shift from a summer rainfall area to a winter rainfall area.

The last major geological development started around 5 Ma, when the Namaqualand coastal plain was uplifted. This exposed several marine terraces that were gradually covered by a variety of sand types (collectively called the Sandveld). Mixed in with the sand, however, were millions of those gem quality diamonds mentioned above and, in modern times, these gravel beds have been voraciously mined.

One last thing to mention: the most recent rocks in the region are found along the banks of the Orange River where thick layers of silt have accumulated as a result of flooding. Some of these banks are 30m higher than the current water level, signifying the biggest floods in southern Africa's history. Dating of these rocks has shown that these deluges took place as recently as 700 years ago, which suggests that they could occur again!

We should also note that the Earth's crust in this part of the world has remained relatively intact for millions of years, with no recent earthquakes or volcanic activity, etc. This has given the plants plenty of time to adapt to their specific environments as they slowly evolve in symbiotic harmony with the prevailing climatic conditions.

And so we come to end of this part of the story with the evocative Namaqualand landscape that we see today: a rugged, cold shoreline with a wide, sandy coastal plain separated from a hot, dry interior by several ranges of jagged mountains. It is indeed a strange land of contrasts, resting on a jumble of igneous, sedimentary and metamorphic rock formations riddled with volcanic intrusions containing valuable minerals.

How Does the Garden Grow?

Amid this patchwork of rock and sand, against every expectation, a remarkable botanical biodiversity took root with a wide variety of plants eking out a living in the most precarious and ingenious ways - proving that no matter how harsh the conditions may be, life will find a way.

Less poetically, there are several climatic conditions that have conspired to create this unlikely Eden. The first important element to consider is the cold Benguela Current that flows in a northerly direction up the west coast of the sub-continent.

The Benguela originates in the Antarctic region, where the warmer water of the Atlantic mixes with the icy Southern Ocean. This mingling causes the warmer water to cool and sink, resulting in an 'upwelling' of cold, nutrient-rich water from the depths. Powerful winds from the South Atlantic anticyclone system then drive this stream of cold water up to the Cape of Good Hope and along the west coast.

The Benguela finally peters out along the shores of Angola, where it meets with warmer equatorial currents.

The Benguela Current has a major impact on the environment of southern Africa supporting large stocks of pelagic fish, which in turn support seals, water birds and other marine life. On the surface, the water is cold - about 5 degrees cooler than off-shore waters at equivalent latitudes. This limits the amount of evaporation that can occur and, as a result, the rainfall along the west coast is low. In short, the current is said to have an 'aridifying' effect on the region.

But the Benguela Current also stabilises the climate of Namaqualand. Cool winds that blow in off the sea moderate the temperature of the coastal belt, so summers aren't too hot and winters aren't too cold. By comparison, because there is effectively a line of mountains running parallel to the coast, these sea breezes do not penetrate far into the interior and summer temperatures inland can soar well above 40 degrees.

Crucially, the Benguela Current is also the source of thick, moisture-laden fogs that regularly roll in from the coast. These heavy mists, known as *malmokkies* or *!hurries* by the locals, are created when humid air blows in from the west and is cooled down by the cold surface water. This forces the warm air to condense into a thick fog that creeps over the coastal plains, covering the plants with a fine haze of moisture. Occurring mainly in the autumn months when wind speeds are low, these regular *malmokkies* are a vital component of the region's relative fertility.

The reliability of the *malmokkies* is supplemented by a surprisingly predictable rainfall pattern that means, unlike other desert regions, Namaqualand does not suffer prolonged periods of drought. So, while rainfall is low, it's reasonably consistent and this allows plants to perpetuate their life cycles. The reasons for this regular precipitation cycle are not well understood (by me, at least).

The last important climatic condition that sustains the Namaqualand ecosystem is the Berg Winds, which blow down from the interior every winter. This phenomenon is caused by a high-pressure cell of dry air which descends on the high plateau. This air is then drawn towards low-pressure systems along the coast, causing it to rush down the slopes of the steep escarpment.

As it descends through the valleys, the air is heated and becomes turbulent. The result is a series of hot, dry winds that blow across the coastal plains several times a year. In Namaqualand and the Richtersveld, these Berg Winds create sporadic warm winter temperatures that allow the plants and animals to develop and reproduce.

Breaking It Down

So, there are several environmental conditions that allow life to thrive in Namaqualand. But we still have some way to go before we can understand the full botanical context of this amazingly biodiverse region. To get the full picture, let's widen our perspective before zooming in, step by step, to describe the various components that come into play. Bear with me now...

Namaqualand is a small part of the much larger Karoo-Namib botanical region, which extends from southern Angola all the way to the western Free State and into the Eastern Cape midlands. This large 'province' is made up of three biomes. Briefly put, according to Cowling and Pierce, these break down as follows:

	Rainfall Type	*Characteristic Vegetation*
Namib Desert	Summer, unpredictable. Less than 100mm inland, less than 25mm at the coast.	'Sand-sea' with sparse vegetation, mostly Ephemerals (short lived herbs and grasses) and a few perennials (e.g. *Welwitschia mirabilis)*
Nama-Karoo	Summer, sporadic. 100mm to 300mm	'Karoobossies' - hardy, low shrubs adapted to extreme temperatures.
Succulent Karoo	Winter, regular. Around 150mm per year	Dwarf shrubs with succulent leaves or stems that store water.

In other words, the Namib is a 'proper' dune desert while the Nama Karoo and Succulent Karoo contain a mix of plant types suited to their respective rainfall patterns. The latter two biomes also share a similar soil composition that is rich in lime and 'weakly developed', with 'pseudo-nutritious' and well-drained soils ensuring that the succulents don't rot away. The name 'Karoo', BTW, derives from the Khoi-San word meaning 'land of thirst'.

OK. Now, zoom into the Succulent Karoo. Despite its extreme summer aridity and low winter rainfall (between 20 and 290mm per year), this region has an extraordinary biodiversity containing between 5000 and 6000 plant species, around 2400 (40%) of which are endemic. A total of 18% of the plant species found here are endangered, thanks to their limited habitats. In an area measuring roughly 100 000 square kilometres, less than 1% of the Succulent Karoo biome is currently under formal protection.

The Succulent Karoo is said to have a 'cyclonic' rainfall pattern with soft rain and moisture-laden fogs providing most of the precipitation. This is a lot less erosive than the thunderstorms that characterise the Nama Karoo's summer rainfalls. The Olifants and Doring Rivers are the main drainage systems in the region.

Here's a brief overview of the dominant plant types found in the Succulent Karoo:

	No. of species	*Characterised by*
Leaf succulents	1700	"Shallow rooted, compact shrubs with relatively small, succulent, evergreen leaves". Most common are the Mesembryanthemum family (known as *vygies* or 'mesembs', for short) which includes crassulas and haworthias. 700 of these species are considered compact or miniature forms, such as the many endemic Lithops or stone plants - the smallest perennial plants in the world.
Stem succulents	130	Succulents with thick stems, common to many desert areas. Includes euphorbias (over 30 species), pelargoniums, stapeliads and tylecodons (such as the Botterboom).
Geophytes (bulbs, tubers etc.)	630	Seasonal plants that store water in an underground 'organ', includes lachenalias, moraeas, romuleas and 'exquisite amaryllids'. Proportionately, a very high number of species when compared to other desert areas.
Annuals	390	Seasonal plants, such as daisies (part of the Astraceae family). Largely responsible for famous 'spring flower' displays. Proportionately, quite a low number of species when compared to other desert areas.
Trees	35	Low number of tree species, usually found along watercourses and in rocky landscapes where there is water runoff. Several species are remnants from the ancient summer rainfall regime.

Right, got all that? Good, because we're now going to zoom in some more. The Succulent Karoo can be split into four regions: Namaqualand, Tankwa Karoo, Little Karoo, and the Western Mountain or Hantam Karoo (around Nieuwoudtville). For the sake of brevity, let's skip the others and zoom in on Namaqualand for a quick overview of some its more exciting specifics:

Succulents	About 1000 species, which equates to around one third of the total flora and represents 10% of all known succulent species. There are 60 species of 'Stem succulents', including the iconic Halfmens and the various Aloe Tree species (also known as kokerbooms or quiver trees). There are at least 250 'compact' species, but these rare miniatures are hard to find (some only poke a couple of millimetres out of the ground). Needless to say, they drive botanists wild!
Geophytes	About 480 species (which is a lot) comprising roughly 16% of the total flora. Known informally as 'bulbs', these plants flower from March to September. Nieuwoudtville, on the south eastern edge of Namaqualand, is the self-proclaimed 'bulb capital of the world'.
Annuals	About 330 species. Most flower over a short period in spring, creating the 'carpets' of flowers that tourists want to see.
Shrubs	About 650 species, most of them evergreen. Includes several Fynbos shrubs, found mainly along the coast and on the high mountain slopes.
Grasses	About 200 species, some veld types can support extensive grazing.
Trees	About 35 species. Most are evergreen, with hard leaves.

To put that into perspective, Namaqualand supports around 3000 species distributed among 648 genera and 107 families, around four times the biodiversity of similar sized, winter-rainfall deserts elsewhere. And around half of Namaqualand's plants are found nowhere else in the world.

For example, according to the Critical Ecosystem Partnership Fund (CEPF), an average of 70 species can be identified within any 1000 square metre sample plot. As for the 'mesembs' or vygie family, there is such a high degree of speciation, including miniaturisation, up to 250 individual plants can be found within a single square metre - even though plant cover seldom exceeds 5% of the ground surface. Clearly, with its wealth of rare and narrowly endemic species, Namaqualand is a true paradise for those with a botanical bent.

We now have one more zoom-in to make, because Namaqualand can be split into five distinct geographical and environmental units, as follows:

	Description	*Location*
Knersvlakte	Flat plains with white, quartz gravel. Average rainfall: 150mm	Begins north of the Olifants River Valley at Vanrhynsdorp. The name comes from the gnashing *(kners)* of wagon wheels over the rough gravel flats *(vlakte)*. Bordered by the Matzikama mountains in the south and the Bokkeveld mountains in the east.
Hardeveld	Granite hills and mountains. Average rainfall: 200mm	Extending from Bitterfontein and Loeriesfontein to Springbok. Part of the Great Escarpment that extends around southern Africa.
Kamiesberg	Huge granite domes (up to 1700m high). Average rainfall: 400mm	Highest, wettest and coldest part of Namaqualand, located around the village of Kamieskroon.
Sandveld	Sandy coastal strip. Average rainfall: 150mm in south, 100mm in the north	Stretching from the Olifants River Mouth near Klawer to the Holgat River, north of Port Nolloth
Richtersveld	Transitional zone with several ecosystems. Average rainfall: 50mm on valley floors, 300mm on west-facing mountain slopes	From Steinkopf to Alexander Bay, with the Orange River as its northern boundary. Said to be 'starved' of sand by ridges that stop particles blowing in from the coast.

Flower Power

Much has been written about the annual wildflower spectacular that turns the dry plains of Namaqualand into a 'carpet' of colour every spring. In fact, the very sight of such prolific inflorescence tends to send most writers into paroxysms of poetic platitudes that border on the hysterical. I, however, am made of sterner stuff and will do my best to remain calm.

But, wow! Flower season in Namaqualand really is something to see! Hugely and profoundly impressive, this is a true natural wonder that everyone deserves to experience at least once. In other words, it's blooming marvellous (my apologies). But what causes this natural phenomenon and why is it over so quickly?

Well, it all goes back to survival. Every plant species in Namaqualand has developed a strategy to cope with the low rainfall. Succulents store water in their leaves or stems. Geophytes (bulbs) store water in underground organs. Others (such as trees and shrubs) grow deep roots or confine themselves to water courses. But the Annuals (which include the daisy family) have a different method.

After the winter rains, these cunning plants grow quickly: germinating, flowering, dropping their seeds and then dying all in a matter of weeks. The seeds then lie in the soil, waiting for the next good rainfall, whereupon the whole cycle begins again. Some seeds can survive for years underground, until there is enough rain to coax them into life once more.

And so, a few weeks after the winter rains, the stage is set for an eruption of yellow, white, orange and purple blooms that will pop the eyes and delight the soul. And the sheer volume of flowers on display is jaw dropping.

However, as Hendrik van Zijl (one of the flower gurus from Nieuwoudtville) points out, it's not just about the number of plants on display. It's the diversity of species that makes the floral spectacle so amazing. Consider this example: between the Goegap Nature Reserve near Springbok and the Skilpad Wildflower Garden in the Namaqua National Park, about 70kms apart, a total of 670 plant species can be found. Only 117 are common to both.

As such, all serious botanists will have made at least one Namaqualand pilgrimage armed with a wildflower guide, binoculars, sun hat and zoom lens. But even if you don't know your Iridaceae from your Asteraceae, a trip to Namaqualand during flower season is an outstanding experience that should be leapt at if you ever get the chance. The comprehensive Planning Guide included in the later pages of this book should help in this regard, especially the *When To Go* and *Flower Watching Tips* chapters under *Exploring Namaqualand.*

Now, before we continue, a reminder of my previous confession: I ain't no botanist but, in the pages that follow, I will be forced to relate lots of information about the formidable flora of Namaqualand and the Richtersveld. So, to make up for my shortcomings, I've relied on a range of books and sources that seem to know what they're talking about.

I've also kept things pretty general - both for the sake of necessity and because I didn't want to bog down the book with lists of Latin nomenclature. If you would like a more technical read on the diverse flora of this vast and varied region, there are plenty of excellent resources available. The South African National Biodiversity Institute's PlantZAfrica website is a good place to start (pza.sanbi.org). Whatever happens, don't make me go binomial on you!

Anyway, back to the Daisies...

The roughly simultaneous germination of annuals across the region means that millions of flowers are blowing in the breeze at the same time, desperate to get pollinated by the limited supply of suitable insects. This leads to fierce competition and every plant species has developed ingenious strategies to attract the right kind of pollinators.

Some rely on their corolla (petals), evolving showy displays of big, bright colours in seductive hues of yellow, white, red and orange. The petals of many *vygie* flowers, for example, are positively iridescent; luring in bugs with their shimmering purple power.

Some plants have even developed petals with spots, shapes and other markings that mimic specific insects, attracting either mates or predators to the pollen. Monkey beetles, for example, like to use the heads of certain daisies as a mating platform. The subsequent roll in the pollen covers the insects with what is in effect the plant's sperm, which they carry with them as they buzz off to other flowers. So, to encourage the attention of young insect lovers, several species of Gazania have developed markings that mimic female monkey beetles.

Similarly, the Bee Fly is attracted to shiny dots found around the flower head of the mis-named Beetle Daisy, which reflect light as if from the body of a fellow Bee Fly. Truly, nature is marvellous (and sneaky).

Other plant species have evolved in harmony with their pollinators, developing flower structures that are uniquely suited to the anatomy of their symbiotic partners. For example, some species of Pelargoniums and Irises have developed flowers with slender tubes that only fit the mouthparts of a single species of tangle-winged fly. Talk about hard to get.

And yet, despite the frenzy of floral procreation, you need to have realistic expectations of the Spring Wildflower experience. Don't expect a continuous sprawl of flowers running unbroken from Vanrhysdorp to Springbok. Namaqualand's floral displays vary greatly in size, ranging from random roadside clusters, to daisy-dappled fields, to densely packed pockets of petals, to grand swathes of colourful carpets.

The erratic distribution of the flowers is caused by several factors, including soil composition, the wind-blown dispersal of seeds, ambient temperatures, rainfall patterns, topography, and other geographical inscrutables.

Different parts of Namaqualand also bloom at different times. So, during flower season, you have to drive around quite a bit to find the best sites (either in terms of volume, diversity or rarity). This could mean long stretches between isolated stands of flowers growing in an otherwise scrubby landscape, or finding one farm field covered with inflorescence while the next doesn't appear to contain even a single bloom.

There are also no guarantees: some locations are reliably good year after year, some have a few good years and then peter out, others are ephemeral. This means that every tourist you encounter during those precious few weeks only has one question on their lips, 'Where's a good place to see the flowers?'. It's kinda like looking for lions in the Kruger Park, except that flowers have never eaten a tourist.

In other words, a trip to see the Daisies requires a combination of planning, luck and patience - the same triumvirate you would need for any kind of successful spotting (except maybe Train, which seems to mostly involve wearing anoraks in the rain).

One thing to be aware of is that the annual flower displays are actually an indication of degraded or damaged land that has been over-grazed or ploughed. As such, the daisies tend to grow on disturbed ground where the established vegetation has been removed or reduced. For example, on farmlands used for grazing animals or in disused fields that have been previously ploughed but not sown (sometimes called 'oldfields').

This is because the flowers are part of what is known as primary ground cover, i.e. the first plant species to start growing on freshly turned land. If the land is left alone too long, it will be colonised by bushes and shrubs (secondary ground cover) and flowers will not have space to grow once secondary plants become established. So, the best places for flower spotting are on fallow farmlands, grazing grounds and untended roadside verges.

As an example, consider the miraculously rich flower site at Matjiesfontein Farm, near Nieuwoudtville. The secret, they say, is as follows: after the flower die, sheep are let into the fields around end of September. They graze on the dried-up flowers and *'mis'* (crap all over the place). The animals are taken out in March to give the land a chance to rest and then, after the winter rains, new flowers grow again, in August or September. The Skilpad Wildflower Garden at the Namaqua National Park uses a similar method, but a good ploughing will also work.

Iconic Plants of the Richtersveld

Even within the context of Namaqualand, the Richtersveld is an environmental marvel with an array of unusual plants that attract succulent-spotters from around the world. When I was there, I met two amateur botanists from Germany who had been planning their Richtersveld trip for years. Needless to say, they were thoroughly prepared and positively brimming with excitement.

And I'm sure they weren't disappointed. In the Richtersveld, 360 flowering plant species have been counted in an area of 1 square kilometre. Mesembryanthemaceae, better known as Mesembs or *vygies,* are particularly well represented, with 50 out a total of 160 genera being present in the region. That's pretty good for a desert that averages only 68mm of rain a year.

One of the reasons for this incongruous biodiversity is that the Richtersveld is located in a transition zone between the winter rainfall zone of Namaqualand and the summer rainfall zone of the Nama-Karoo. In some places, this transitional zone is only 10 or 20km wide, which makes for some interesting intermingling of plant types.

Additionally, there are three main biomes present in the Richtersveld: the predominant Succulent Karoo biome, the smaller 'Desert' biome (in the north and east), and isolated bits of Fynbos biome (on the high mountain slopes). It's also worth noting that the mountain ranges, which tend to run in a north-south direction, stop the *malmokkies* and rain clouds from penetrating into the interior. So, seaward facing slopes get lots of precipitation while inland-facing slopes (especially in the eastern section) are drier and contain species more usually associated with the Nama-Karoo (such as euphorbias).

These conditions create dozens of micro-climates in the Richtersveld, and each valley or ridge has a subtly specific combination of rain, wind, soil, heat and exposure. Such isolated habitats encourage 'speciation' – the evolutionary process whereby a species adapts to its environmental conditions until it is biologically distinct from its parent population. In the Richtersveld, some of the endemic plant species have become so finely adapted to their specific environments, they are only found in a single valley or 'narrow' location.

Still, no matter how big or small, the theme common to all plants of the Richtersveld is survival. As described above, many store water (either in their leaves, stems or in underground organs) but the ingenuity of these determined lifeforms goes further than that. Some plants are almost entirely subterranean, with only a few tiny tendrils poking out of the sand. Others grow flat on the ground to avoid the wind, with broad leaves that trap moisture from the ground. Some grow fine hairs or spikes to catch the drops of dew. Some can close their pores to prevent evaporation. A few are psammophorous, a formidable word that means they exude a sticky substance which catches and secures a layer of sand to their surface, offering protection against sandstorms.

Although most plants in the Richtersveld are evergreen (which is unusual for a winter-rainfall desert) there are a few that drop their leaves in summer to reduce water loss. Others deflect the sun with tiny scales, or by growing a waxy bark, or by retaining old leaves. Some have become miniature, to reduce their need for scarce resources. Some only grow in the nooks and crannies of the rocks, keeping to the cool shadows. The plants of the Richtersveld are endlessly creative in their survival strategies.

All in all, the Richtersveld is said to contain over 2500 plant species, 40% of which are found nowhere else. Many of these plants have practical applications and are effectively utilised by the native people. 70 species are used for food (or *veldkos* - bush food), 40 have medicinal applications, and 54 have other functional purposes, such as ropemaking, soapmaking and firewood. There are also several hallucinogenic plants sometimes used for religious purposes. But don't go round licking the succulents - many of them are toxic!

Despite all the strange and rare species that haunt the fever dreams of ambitious botanists, the Richtersveld's most iconic plants are relatively common and easy to spot (but thrilling nonetheless).

The Halfmens

The amazing Halfmens *(Pachypodium namaquanum)* is a much-photographed pin-up plant that has come to symbolise the Richtersveld. A large 'stem succulent' or 'tree succulent', the enigmatic and endangered halfmens (meaning half human) is a cactus-like plant with a sprout of leaves on top of its 'head' and couple of curved appendages that bend out from the central stem. The head of the halfmens always leans towards the north and this inclination is explained by an ancient legend.

Many years ago, there was a warlike tribe who lived in the north. One day, during a battle, they were driven from their lands and chased over the Orange River, into the Richtersveld. Here, God turned them into strange creatures - half-human, half-plant. With their feet literally rooted to the spot, the tribe was stranded and to this day, they remain marooned in the mountains; forever gazing towards their former home.

It's a nice story, but the botanical reality is far more prosaic. The waxy rosette of leaves on the plant's 'head' is actually its energy source, absorbing water and the sun's energy. Thus, they incline towards the north to harness the sun more effectively.

Growing up to 5m tall, the halfmens develops mainly in the winter months, when it sprouts nectar-rich, trumpet-shaped flowers. In summer, it drops its leaves and relies on its thick, spiny covering as protection from the burning sun. The sharp spines also protect it from grazing animals and aid in collection of moisture from the *malmokkies.*

The halfmens is endemic to the Richtersveld and it's quite hard to find, although it's only listed as Near Threatened by the IUCN. I must confess that during my visit, I totally failed to spot one (but that says more about me). There are now about 25 species of *Pachypodium* (elephant's foot), with 20 occurring in Madagascar and 5 in southern Africa. New species, confined to a single valley or even a lone outcrop, may yet be discovered.

Kokerbooms

Aloe Trees are another staple of the Richtersveld landscape. Also called kokerbooms or quiver trees, these attractive stem succulents can live up to 400 years and come in a variety of shapes and sizes. They are fairly common and can be seen sticking out of rocky ridges and, occasionally, along the roadside. The name 'quiver tree' refers to the Bushman and Khoikhoi hunters, who carried their arrows in hollowed-out kokerboom branches.

Originally classified under the *Aloe* genus, phylogenetic studies in 2013 showed that the kokerbooms were genetically distinct and comprised an entirely separate clade. Accordingly, those fussy botanists split them off into a separate genus: *Aloidendron.*

There are 7 species of *Aloidendron;* 2 grow along the east coast of southern Africa, one in Somalia, one in Saudi Arabia and three in the Richtersveld.

The plain old Quiver Tree / Kokerboom *(Aloidendron dichotomum,* formerly known as *Aloe Dichotoma)* grows up to 9m high and is characterised by a large central stem with a broad spray of branches and leaves growing out of the upper reaches. It's found east of the Stinkfontein mountains and in the arid northern Richtersveld, where it tends to grow taller with simpler branch structures. The kokerboom forest (more correctly called a colony) in the Richtersveld National Park is a good place to place to check out these ancient aloes. Also known as *Choje* by the Khoi-San, it is listed as 'vulnerable' on the IUCN List of Threatened Species.

Pillan's Quiver Tree, also called the Bastard Quiver Tree or Basterkokerboom, *A. pillansii* grows up to 15m tall with a thick stem. It has a smaller crown of 'hair' with fewer, thicker branches and larger leaves than its *dichotomum* cousin. They kinda remind me of Sideshow Bob from The Simpsons, if that helps. You'll find them on mountain slopes close to the Orange River, from Baken to the Tatasberg, with a southern extension on the Dragon's Back mountain near Eksteenfontein. In the Richtersveld National Park, they can be seen in Helskloof and on Cornell's Kop. It is listed as 'critically endangered' on the IUCN List of Threatened Species.

The Maiden's Quiver Tree, or Nooienskokerboom *(A. ramosissimum)* resembles a shrub rather than a tree, growing quite low on the ground. It has many branches that spread out from low down on the central structure. It can grow up to several metres high and blooms with bright yellow flowers, usually in May. Found in the higher mountain slopes and occasionally in riverbeds. It is listed as 'endangered' on the IUCN List of Threatened Species.

Pearson's Aloe

Aloe pearsonii is rather rare shrub, endemic to Helskloof in the Richtersveld National Park and adjacent mountains across the Orange River in Namibia. It has many low branches with triangular leaves that grow in dense layers, with four leaves per layer. These layers curve downwards in an attractive geometric pattern. The colony at Helskloof is extensive and the plants literally cover the mountains of either side of the rocky road pass. The plant is named after Dr. HHW Pearson, first director of Kirstenbosch Botanical Gardens, who collected the plant in 1910. It is listed as 'endangered'.

Vygies / Mesembs

As mentioned above, there are many species of Mesembryanthemaceae in Namaqualand and the Richtersveld, contributing a great deal to the region's biodiversity. Despite their ubiquity, *vygies* only start to appear on the fossil record a relatively recent 12 000 years ago. However, this may be because desert environments are not conducive to the creation of plant fossils.

Vygies are succulents, with special bladder cells contained in their leaves. Their flowers are also very bright, even luminous, with lots of petals. This eye-catching inflorescence is designed to attract the attention of pollinating insects. Mesembs are sometimes called 'midday flowers' because they usually open their petals when the sun is at its brightest. Their leaves are not palatable and rarely eaten by grazing animals or insects. The Rosyntjieberg mountain in the Richtersveld National Park contains a high number of *vygie* species.

Hoodia Gordonii

Also known as Ghaap, Bushman's Hat or *//hoba*, hoodia has been used as an appetite suppressant by Bushmen and Khoikhoi people for thousands of years - an important medicinal plant that kept hunger at bay when food was unavailable. It's a rather unlovely-looking spiny succulent with flowers that smell like rotten meat, pollinated mainly by flies. But it's reputation as a potential weight loss product precedes it.

In 1977, the South African Council for Scientific and Industrial Research (CSIR) isolated the plant's active ingredient, known as P57, and had it patented in 1996. This was done without any recognition of the indigenous knowledge that lay behind the extract. Years of negotiations followed until, in 2003, the CSIR reached an agreement with the South African San Council to pay over a percentage of all hoodia-related revenue.

Over the years, however, hoodia has had its ups and downs. The license to P57 passed through several companies, including Pfizer and Unilever, with each spending substantial amounts on research and development. But, despite optimistic coverage in local and international media, hoodia has yet to gain traction in the multi-billion-dollar slimming and obesity management industry. This failure to launch seems due to a combination of factors.

Firstly, the plant's extract is hard to synthesise. Then, there appear to be certain components of the plant that can cause 'unwanted effects on the liver' and other negative side-effects. Most importantly, though, no high-quality scientific evidence has been published thus far to suggest that it even works as an appetite suppressant.

In 2008, Unilever stopped marketing their hoodia-branded diet supplements, saying they did "not meet our strict standards of safety and efficacy". But that hasn't stopped a whole raft of shady companies from jumping on the hoodia bandwagon, with a range of 'miracle weight-loss' supplements being hawked in health stores and spam emails.

The increase in demand for hoodia (no matter how spurious) has put the plant under pressure and it is now protected under CITES Appendix I - indicating that the species is threatened with extinction and cannot be exported without a permit. This is notwithstanding the fact that most of the dodgy Hoodia supplements out there don't actually contain any hoodia at all.

Botterboom

Tylecodon paniculatus is a cute, chubby dwarf succulent with a thick stem and fat leaves. Translated as 'butter tree', it is found in many parts of southern Africa including Namaqualand. Despite its yummy moniker, the plant is poisonous to stock (causing *krimpsiekte)* but it apparently makes a wonderful pot plant! There are also stories of kids using strips of botterboom skin as an impromptu sled, to slide down sand dunes. It can grow up to 2m high and is the largest of the tylecodons (not a dinosaur).

Bushman's Candle

Sarcocaulon patersonii is a spiny, fleshy shrublet with thick, waxy branches that protect it from sandstorms. The branches are flammable, even when wet, and can be used for kindling (albeit with a lot of smoke) giving the plant its common name.

Animals, Birds and Bugs

Namaqualand is not the place to go game spotting. Big 5 country this ain't. Yet, despite the arid climate, there is an impressive range of smaller mammals, reptiles, insects and bird life that will appeal to people with these acquired tastes. But before we look at the modern animals you can find, let's check out some of the creatures that used to live here.

The fossil record demonstrates that, in wetter times, the area contained prehistoric horses, elephants, giant shrews, enormous tortoises, short-snouted crocodiles, predatory 'bear-dogs', large proto-ostriches and other insane species. These are supplemented by fossilised footprints, burrows and impressions of trees (called dendrites) that indicate a fertile land covered with forests. The sea was also warmer in those days, and fossilised shark teeth and unusual oyster shells have been described by various explorers (dating back as far as William Paterson, in 1779).

More recently, Bushmen carved petroglyphs into the rocks of the region, creating petrified 'snapshots' of the lion, giraffe, rhino, hippos and even elephant that used to roam the plains. Today, however, large animals are rare and it's the smaller lifeforms that proliferate.

There is also verbal and written evidence that the plains of Namaqualand used to be heavily populated by large herds of springbok and other antelope species. In 1892, the magistrate based at Springbokfontein (now called simply Springbok) writes that he witnessed a migration of 'millions' of these graceful creatures, which had given the town its name.

Such flocks of game are, sadly, a thing of the past; hastened into local extinction through hunting, livestock disease (such as the Rinderpest epidemic of 1896) and human interference with the landscape. Nevertheless, you can still find gemsbok (oryx), klipspringer, duiker, vaalribbok and steenbok in the region, although they are more common in the restricted mining areas on the Namibian side of the border, where human activity is limited. The rare Hartmanns' Mountain Zebra is also present.

Mammalian predators include brown hyena, aardwolf, caracal and leopard (although these are very rare). You also get black-backed jackals, the Cape Fox, the bat-eared fox, the African wild cat, and striped polecats (also called the zorille or zorilla - derived from 'zorro', the Spanish word for fox).

Other mammals include meercats (suricates), small-spotted genets and several species of mongoose (or is that mongeese?). Primates are represented by chacma baboons and vervet monkeys (found mainly along the banks of the Orange River).

Bats, shrews, rats, mice, rabbits and gerbils are reasonably common, including the striped field mouse, karoo bush rat, Brant's whistling rat (!), round-eared elephant shrew, striped mouse, long-tailed pygmy mouse, Namaqua rock mouse, tree rats, Cape hare, Smith's red rock rabbit, ground squirrels, Namaqua dune mole rat, common mole rat, rock dassie (hyrax), dassie rat (which is not related to the dassie) and porcupines. Gerbils include the Namaqua short-tailed gerbil and the hairy-footed gerbil. There's also a high number of bat species.

In terms of reptiles (scaly) and amphibians (slimy), herpetologists will be delighted with the variety of species that slither and creep through Namaqualand. These include the world's smallest tortoise - the Namaqua or speckled padloper (adults measure around 100mm long) - the angulate or geometric tortoise, and the Namaqua tent tortoise. Lizards include the large Nile monitor (or waterlikkewaan), Karoo girdled lizard, armadillo girdled lizard, Smith's desert lizard and the rare Cape flat lizard.

Namaqualand is pretty dry, so amphibious species are relatively scarce. Some of the more interesting include the Karoo toad, the endangered Namaqua rain frog, the paradise toad and several new species of sand frog that keep getting discovered. In the Richtersveld, frogs may bury themselves in the sand and emerge only after good rains. The sudden eruption of frogs after a heavy rainfall has given rise to a local legend that they're brought by clouds drifting in from the sea.

In terms of chameleons and geckos, you get the unusual Namaqua chameleon (which prowls the gravel plains, instead of living in trees), Namib web-footed geckos, giant ground geckos, Smith's desert gecko, Austin's dune gecko, the recently discovered leaf-toed gecko, as well as a couple of skinks. For its size, this area represents one of the richest gecko faunas in the world.

Snakes are relatively rare but pretty potent, including the black spitting cobra and a variety of adders (including puff adder, horned adder, desert mountain adder and the Namaqua dwarf adder).

The handful of perennial rivers that flow from the escarpment towards the coast support a fairly traditional assortment of fresh-water fish species, including yellow fish, sharptooth catfish (barbel), banded bream and the endemic Namaqua barb. Cape clawless otters can be seen around river mouths, and big colonies of Cape fur seals are found along the coast.

The wide Orange River estuary is one of the most fertile places in the region. With mud flats, marshes, flood plains and islands, it supports an amazing diversity of birds - up to 10 000 of them at a time, representing over 60 species. These include flamingos (many hundreds of which can be seen perching precariously in the water), Cape cormorants, chestnut-banded plovers, Egyptian geese, Cape teal, great white pelican, South African shelduck and the African sacred ibis. About 14 resident species are listed in the IUCN Red List of Threatened Species, including the Damara tern, African purple swamphen, Barlow's lark and the Cape long-billed lark.

In light of this, the Orange River mouth has been declared a Ramsar Wetland of International Importance. Unfortunately, the site has been severely degraded by mining activity along both banks; its plight being barely noticed by environmental watchdogs because of its remote location within the formerly restricted diamond mining town of Alexander Bay. Various Namibian and South

African authorities are now trying to rehabilitate the wetland and restore it to its former glory.

Various bird species (197) have also been identified within the |Ai-|Ais-Richtersveld Transfrontier Conservation Area, found mainly on the banks of the Orange, along dry riverbeds and in the mountain ranges. They include the Lanner falcon, Black eagle, Southern pale chanting goshawk, spotted eagle owl, black-breasted snake-eagle, African fish eagle, Cape eagle-owl, jackal buzzard, rock kestrel, Cape spurfowl, bokmakierie, Namaqua sandgrouse, Cape bunting, Diderick cuckoo, red-chested cuckoo, African hoopoe, the Cape bulbul, red-eyed bulbul, tractrac chat, mountain chat, long-billed lark, dusky sunbird, swallow-tailed bee-eater, red-knobbed coot (sounds like a dirty old man), fiery-necked nightjar, pied kingfisher, various swifts, a couple of swallows and a bunch of incongruous ostriches (usually as part of agricultural breeding projects).

Finally, we come down to the insects. These little buggers play an important role in the Namaqualand ecosystem, contributing to the diet of larger species and pollinating the plants. As is usually the case, many have developed evolutionary strategies to thrive in the desert environment, such as waxy body coatings that retain water, special chemical processes that produce internal moisture, and ingenious forms of camouflage that blend into the rocks. Some termite species are known to burrow up to 20 meters down to find the water table. Several narrowly endemic species have also evolved hand-in-hand with specific plants and are now uniquely adapted to 'fit' those flowers.

Insects in Namaqualand can be grouped as primary feeders (who eat plants and/or nectar), secondary feeders (who eat the primary feeders), and detritus feeders (who chase after organic bits and pieces blown around by the wind). Pollination is done largely by bees (notably carpenter bees), bee flies and pollen wasps (the variety of pollen wasps in the western part of southern Africa is among the highest in the world).

Other insect species include: milkweed locusts, tortoise beetles, blister beetles, monkey beetles, mouldy beetles, crickets, ground grasshoppers, stone grasshoppers, praying mantids, millipedes, centipedes, cicadas, flies, and the like.

Several unique butterfly species include the Namaqua Arrowhead (a subspecies of the Boland Tholly), the Warrior silver-spotted copper, and the Roseate Emperor (actually a day-flying moth). And the Richtersveld is reportedly home to the world's largest diversity of Silverfish (also known as fish moths), with many endemic species.

Silverfish are interesting little critters: they are nocturnal, shed their skins, grow tiny scales, do not have a pupal or larval stage (emerging fully formed from their eggs) and they absorb moisture through glands in their anus - which is quite a good trick when you think about it. Incidentally, the common fish moth (the one that eats your clothes) is not indigenous to South Africa.

Arachnids, the eight-legged bogeymen of the insect world, are well represented. These include the trapdoor spider, buckspoor spider, Sicarus spiders, the very toxic black button spider, and sun spiders or romans (including 4 species endemic to the Richtersveld).

Several families of scorpion are present, including ground scorpions, rock scorpions and thick-tailed scorpions (some of which are among SA's most poisonous). So, if you're camping, don't forget to check your shoes in the morning!

The People of Namaqualand

The riches of Namaqualand include both the aforementioned botanical biodiversity as well as the complex tapestry of humanity that has settled across the region. In this section, we'll take a broad look at the early human history of Namaqualand before heading off into the stormy waters of the modern age, from the year 1500 onwards.

Later, we'll get to yet more desert riches as we uncover the mineral wealth (copper and diamonds) that drove development in Namaqualand over the last 150 years or so. But first, as per Julie Andrew's excellent advice, let's start at the very beginning...

Early Humans

The first evidence of human beings in Namaqualand is represented by crude stone tools, such as choppers and hand axes fashioned from a stone pebble or core. These Early Stone Age implements dating between 2.5 million and 250 000 years ago are associated with various *Australopithecus* and *Paranthropus* species (using what's known as Olduwan Technology) and early *Homo* species, such as *Homo habilis* and *Homo erectus* (using 'bi-facial' Acheulean Technology). Thus far, however, no human fossils have been found in this part of the world.

In southern Africa, the Middle Stone Age is said to range between 250 000 years and 40 000 years ago and is associated with the emergence of our species, *Homo sapiens* (translated as 'wise' or 'thinking' man, all evidence to the contrary). This era marks a transition from core-based tools to flake-based tools - a more sophisticated technology in which slivers of rocks are struck off a stone core to create scrapers, blades or points. Many examples of these smaller stone tools are found in Namaqualand, with several archaeological sites in the Richtersveld containing a large number of flakes and rock fragments, suggesting that they were tool 'factories'. The West Coast National Park, near Langebaan, also contains a remarkably tangible fossil footprint made by one of our *Homo sapiens* ancestors during this era.

The Later Stone Age, starting around 40 000 years ago, coincides with the development of punch-struck blades and other 'microlithic' tools that are more refined and task specific. These include blades, borers and points, many of which were attached to wooden shafts to form composite tools such as spears or knives. Bone and ivory were also used to create blades, needles and even fishing hooks.

The Neolithic (New Stone Age) is said to have begun around 7000 years ago as our ancestors slowly shifted away from a hunter-gatherer lifestyle towards a pastoral existence - i.e. keeping domesticated animals and planting crops. The

Iron Age in sub-Saharan Africa began around 4000 years ago when smelting techniques filtered down from the Middle East to West Africa via trade routes through the Sahara Desert (although there are academics who argue that Africa's Iron Age developed independently from Eurasia).

Several archaeological sites in the Richtersveld (dating back to over 3000 years ago) offer evidence of this kind of technology. Further testament to human habitation is also found in the form of processed animal bones, blackened hearths and a number of middens (prehistoric rubbish tips) containing human detritus, which are found along the coast.

So, according to the archaeological evidence, nomadic hunter-gatherers have been living in Namaqualand for well over 200 000 years. It could not have been an easy life. Water would have been scarce (there is evidence of ostrich eggshells being used as storage containers), the supply of wild plants for foraging would have fluctuated with the seasons, and there was always a risk of over-hunting the available animals. But, for once, humans seemed to understand that their survival depended on collaborating with the environment in a sustainable manner, and a delicate balance was maintained.

The Bushmen

It's hard to say when the Bushmen (or San) developed as a distinct cultural group - some say it was as long as 40 000 years ago, when a prolonged dry period separated people in the south-western part of the subcontinent from the more 'Negroid' tribes in the north. In any case, the Bushmen are the First People of southern Africa and one of the oldest identifiable cultures on Earth, utilising and refining the Later Stone Age technology described above.

The Bushmen also developed a social structure that revolved around their traditional hunter-gatherer lifestyles. As a rule, it was the men who did the hunting, while the women gathered bulbs, berries and other plants. Their tacit grasp of nature saw small family groups moving around the land in harmony with the game and the seasons.

In terms of religion, the bushmen enjoyed a sophisticated ideology that combined the natural world with the spiritual realm. This is expressed in the numerous rock paintings found across their realm, which often illustrate shamanistic trance dances and therianthropes (curious figures that are half-human and half-animal).

In Namaqualand, however, few cave paintings have been identified. Instead, we find petroglyphs - engravings made by cutting into the surface of rocks with a sharp stylus or rock hammer. These enigmatic and beautiful petroglyphs depict a variety of subjects, ranging from abstract geometric patterns to more realistic depictions of animals, such as zebra and eland. The study of these petroglyphs is still in its infancy and, sadly, many examples have been damaged by mining and/or careless visitors. Access to most of these sites is now restricted to prevent further damage.

Historically, the number of Bushman living in the Namaqualand interior would have been, of necessity, relatively low. This was, after all, a thirstland with few reliable water sources. The coast was a much better proposition, however, and there are several archaeological sites that demonstrate significant interaction between the Bushmen and marine resources, such as seals and shellfish. These coastal populations have been called 'strandlopers' (beach walkers) and evidence of their habitation has been found at various locations along the coastline of southern Africa - including Namaqualand.

Historically, the Bushmen's heartland was the fertile East Coast of South Africa, where they moved between the Drakensberg Mountains and the sea as the seasons dictated. Over the last couple of hundred years, however, these First People were persecuted by several waves of migrants, including the Bantu, the Dutch, the English and the Afrikaners, who effectively pushed the Bushmen into the undesirable desert regions of the subcontinent.

Today, Bushmen communities can be found in Botswana, Namibia, Angola, Zambia, Zimbabwe and South Africa with a total population numbering around 100 000 (although traces of their ancient genetics can be found in many modern South African tribes). Unfortunately, most of these modern settlements are terribly impoverished and the Bushmen continue to fight for better treatment and political representation. One particular Khoi-San group has been camping outside the Union Buildings in the Pretoria for over a year, waiting for a meeting with the president to discuss their demands.

Before we continue, a word about etymology. The term 'Bushmen' is problematic, carrying with it the taint of colonialism, racism and derision. The problem is that, as far as we can tell, the Bushmen never had a collective name for themselves. Instead, each tribe or clan was identified through their specific dialect or some other social characteristic. It was the Dutch settlers who lumped them all together under the dismissive term, *Boesman* (bush men).

In the 20th Century, in an attempt to address the issue, academics decided to resurrect an old Khoikhoi name for Bushmen: the San. But this term has its own problems. As we'll see in the following section, Khoe-speaking pastoralists had adopted agricultural technologies from the migrating Bantu and, thanks to their growing flocks of domesticated animals, thought very highly of themselves.

They thus named themselves the Khoikhoi (meaning 'men of men') and dismissed the lowly Bushmen as 'Sonqua' or 'San' (meaning 'foragers' or 'men with nothing'). For this reason, some modern Bushmen reject the exonymic term

'San' as an insult, which is why I stubbornly refer to them as 'Bushmen' throughout this book.

Incidentally, the term 'Khoi-San' is a portmanteau that refers to both the Bushman foragers and the Khoikhoi pastoralists.

The Khoikhoi

About 2000 years ago, a new group of people entered the picture. They were closely related to the Bushmen, with one major difference. They were pastoralists; nomadic farmers who shlepped around the countryside with herds of domesticated fat-tailed sheep. Later, they would also cultivate crops, keep cattle and, in colonial times, incorporate goats into their menageries. They still hunted wild game, preferring to keep their livestock for ceremonial purposes, but the arrival of the Khoikhoi nevertheless heralded the dawn of a new era.

The origin of the Khoikhoi is somewhat uncertain. Early colonial writers claimed that they came from Asia, moving south around the time of the great flood. Some even said they had Hamitic or Jewish origins. At the turn of the century, the historians Stow and Cooke hypothesised that they came from the great lakes district in central Africa before migrating down the west coast of the subcontinent. But modern historians, such as Richard Elphick, have made more reliable linguistic studies of the Khoikhoi and it is now accepted that they originated in the Zambezi Valley of northern Botswana.

Here, they made the transition from a hunter-gatherer society to a culture that kept domesticated animals and planted crops. This kind of farming 'technology' originated in the middle east about 10 000 years ago. It reached the northern Sahara around 7000 years ago and spread along trans-Sahara trade routes, where it was adopted by the Bantu-speaking tribes of West Africa. These people, in turn, carried the pastoral tradition with them when they began to migrate south, reaching East Africa around 4000 years ago and southern Africa sometime later (see 'African Diaspora' below).

It is thought that the Khoikhoi picked up the pastoralism habit from these Bantu tribes. However, there are some theorists who claim that the Khoikhoi developed a pastoral tradition all on their own, but this is still being debated.

In any case, once the Khoikhoi had embraced this new concept of 'farming' they took their sheep and migrated south, crossing the Orange River near its confluence with the Vaal between 2000 and 1600 years ago. From this point, they began spreading out into the eastern, southern and western Cape.

In time, the Khoikhoi would establish themselves as a number of distinct tribes, each with their own territories and dialects. These political units were organised around a hierarchical system, based on chieftains, headmen and family clans. So, for example, you had the Cochoqua and Guriqua in the south west, the

Chainoqua, Hessequa, Gouriqua, Attaqua and Houteniqua in the east and the Goringhaiqua, Gorachouqua and Goringhaikona around the Cape Peninsula.

At the mouth of the Orange River, the Khoikhoi spilt into two groups. The Great Namaqua settled north of the river in what became Namibia. Many years later, these Nama tribes along with the Bantu-speaking Herero people were persecuted by the colonists of 'German South West Africa', culminating in the tragic Herero and Nama Genocide that took place between 1904 and 1908. Around 10 000 Nama (led by Captain Henrik Witbooi) and between 24 000 and 100 000 Herero (led by Samuel Maherero) were exterminated - either through outright massacres or in concentration camps racked by disease and malnutrition. Only in the 21st century did the German government finally acknowledge this genocide (but ruled out paying reparations to descendants of the survivors).

The Little Namaqua, meanwhile, populated the area south of the Orange River, establishing five clans who lived between the river and present-day Vanrhynsdorp. These people gave the region its modern name and are the antecedents of present-day Nama people still resident in the area (most notably in the Richtersveld World Heritage Site).

Although the Khoikhoi and the Bushmen are related, both genetically and linguistically, there must have been a culture clash when the two groups first encountered each other. The Khoikhoi, for their part, held their herds in very high esteem, considering them a sign of status and wealth. The animals were also considered private property, so families with lots of animals were seen as 'rich' while those with few animals often had to take up positions as servants for more powerful clans. This was a significant move away from the more socialist structure of the Bushman groups, whom the Khoikhoi considered inferior.

So, the Khoikhoi and the Bushmen led different lifestyles based on divergent economic models, and this lead to inevitable conflicts over water, resources and territory. Furthermore, the Khoikhoi were still active hunters and competition over the limited stocks of wild game must have been reasonably intense. For the most part, however, the two groups seemed to find a way to get along and they co-existed as distinct cultural entities for about 1500 years - at least until the Europeans came along and irrevocably muddied the waters. There are even cases where Bushmen took jobs with Khoikhoi families: looking after their herds, supplying them with honey, or providing rain-making services in exchange for food.

In Namaqualand, however, the Bushmen seem to have dissipated soon after the arrival of the Khoikhoi (apart from a few Strandloper clans who continued to live along the coast). This may have been a result of migration from or integration with the Namaqua. After all, it is not a region that can support a large population.

Richard Elphick, on the other hand, has a theory that the division between herders and hunters was much more fluid, depending as much on luck as it did on economic systems. For Elphick, the Khoikhoi and the Bushmen were essentially the same people. Thus, a Khoikhoi tribe could easily lose their herds through drought, theft or disease, causing them to revert to the hunter-gatherer economy of the Bushmen. As this was considered an inferior way of life, the ambitious Khoikhoi clan would try to re-build its herds through theft, barter or service, and this created a cyclical model of pastoralism vs. hunting.

Based on archaeological evidence, however, it seems that there were indeed two distinct groups within the Khoi-San nation. But Elphick's model is still useful if applied to the colonial era, when Europeans put enormous pressure on the traditional lifestyles of indigenous people at the Cape.

Archaeological digs have also pointed out a connection between pastoralism and pottery. This is because farmers need to store surplus goods, whereas hunters tend to consume things on the spot. The presence of heavy pottery also implies that the Khoikhoi did not move around as much as the peripatetic Bushmen. This makes sense as their herds provided them with some food security, so they could afford to be more sedentary and were able to sustain higher population densities. Nevertheless, the Khoikhoi still practised a semi-nomadic lifestyle, moving with the seasons in search of good grazing land.

Each Khoikhoi clan, therefore, controlled a rather vaguely defined territory and members of the clan moved across their lands in a regular, seasonal pattern of transhumance. This led to the development of portable reed huts *(matjieshuise* or */haru oms)* that could be assembled at the various stock posts and watering holes which were inhabited periodically throughout the year. Occasionally, outsiders were allowed to use the clan's land in exchange for a tribute or payment to the chief. At no stage, however, was land allowed to be owned by any private individual. It is this ancient form of farming that is still practiced in the Richtersveld World Heritage Site.

|haru oms *and Matjieshuise*

The basic housing unit of the NamaKhoi was a dome shaped reed hut called a */haru oms* (or *matjiesbuis* - reed house - in Afrikaans). These dwellings are created by building a circular framework of green branches sunk into the ground, bent towards the centre and tied together with thin strips of leather. This secure matrix is then covered with handmade mats made of woven reeds. It was the man's job to build the frame, while the women made the reed mats.

The */haru oms* were eminently practical. The raw materials for construction were readily available across the region. In summer, the reed mats allowed air to circulate and offered shade from the hot sun. In winter, skins or extra mats were attached to the frame to keep the huts warm. Furthermore, when it rained, the reeds swelled up and kept water out of the huts and the round shape of the huts provided protection against strong winds. All in all, it was a rare example of form meeting function.

The */haru oms* were also portable. So, when it was time to move on, the mats were simply rolled up and carried to the next location. The frames were usually left behind to be re-used the following season. But not every member of the family was able to participate in the annual migrations. The very young and the elderly often stayed in permanent villages, which could include well over 100 people. These settlements also utilised */haru oms* as housing, although the huts were not taken down unless they were in disrepair. In fact, the */haru oms* were so suited to the environment that they were even adopted by the first white settlers who moved into the area and remained the most common form of housing in Namaqualand until well into the 1900s.

Today, the Richtersveld is the only place in the world where you still find the */haru oms* in regular use by nomadic stock farmers (although you can spot a couple in modern settlements, sitting incongruously in the yard next to neat brick homes). Admittedly, these modern examples are often supplemented by contemporary materials, such as plastic sheeting, but it is still testament to a continuous architectural tradition that stretches back a thousand years or more.

Sadly, the art of building the */haru oms* is in danger of being forgotten and only a handful of Nama people living in the Richtersveld Community Conservancy still retain the necessary skills. But this is a form of indigenous knowledge that must be conserved and there is an on-going effort to transfer the art to new generations. For example, a group of Nama from the Richtersveld recently went across the border into the *//Gamaseb* community in Namibia to re-teach their brethren how to build these traditional reed huts. Young people in the Richtersveld are also being encouraged to learn the technique, and it is hoped that the advent of tourism and the bestowal of World Heritage status (partly because of the */haru oms)* will give this programme extra impetus.

The African Diaspora

As mentioned above, starting around 7000 years ago, pastoral technologies from the Middle East were carried along trade routes through the Sahara Desert and adopted by several societies in West Africa. Among these early adopters were a group of 'Negroid' tribes living around the Niger Delta (in what is now the border region between Nigeria and Cameroon).

The people of the delta spoke a common language - Ntu. And it was the BaNtu (people who spoke Ntu) who embarked on a great diaspora, starting around 4000 years ago.

Also called the Bantu Expansion, it's unclear what triggered this great migration - drought, the spread of the Sahara desert, over-population, political upheaval, or plain old wanderlust may have all played a part - but whatever the trigger, the Bantu would continue spreading south and east in a series of migratory waves that saw them slowly populate the entire continent south of the Sahara. This is evidenced by the fact that most modern languages in the subcontinent are somehow related to the proto-Ntu tongue.

As each generation spread further down the continent, groups of Bantu would split off and settle down; forming themselves into the distinct cultural identities and language groups that we see today. The Bantu thus either displaced or absorbed the existing hunter-gatherer populations that they encountered along the way.

The first wave of Bantu migrants crossed the Limpopo River into South Africa between 2000 and 1500 years ago and slowly spread down the East Coast. Today, this Nguni-speaking stream has become the Swazi, Zulu, Xhosa and Ndebele nations.

A couple of hundred years later, a second wave of Bantu arrived and settled on the high plateau of the interior. They would evolve into the Sotho, Tswana and Pedi polities. And so, by the 16th century, the stage was set with Bushmen, Khoikhoi, Nguni and Sotho all jockeying for position across southern Africa. Then, from the sea came a new kind of settler, and things really started getting messy...

The Europeans Arrive

By the late 1400s, southern Africa was home to a number of indigenous people who can be roughly grouped into three cultural units. The Bushmen lived throughout the region, with large populations living in the Drakensberg mountains. The Khoikhoi were found mainly along the coastal plains, ranging from the Orange River to the eastern Cape. And Bantu tribes had settled up the East Coast and in the interior.

Although there were undoubtedly conflicts between these different groups, each with their own agendas and priorities, it seems that things were relatively stable in southern Africa. Then, like a spark to gunpowder, came the whiteys.

The first Europeans started sailing down the west coast of Africa in the mid-15th century, seeking a sea route to the riches of the East. At that time, valuable silks and spices such as cinnamon, pepper, cloves, nutmeg and turmeric were highly prized in Europe (the London Guild of Pepperers dates back to the 1150s). And the only way to transport these goods was along the slow and expensive Silk Road, which ran overland from Europe to Asia.

So, eager to skip the unreliable caravans and rampant banditry of the Silk Road, the Portuguese Prince Henry the Navigator sent out a series of naval expeditions in small caravels, to feel their way south along the unmapped African coastline. As such, each new voyage ventured a little bit further into the unknown before returning to Lisbon with their findings.

Years passed and sailors gradually learned the arcane secrets of trade winds to navigate ever further down the coast. And yet the African landmass continued to stretch endlessly into the south, with no eastward passage in sight. Prince Henry died in 1460, long before any of his sailors managed to identify the bottom edge of Africa, but he is nonetheless regarded as a primary initiator of the European Age of Discovery.

Then, in 1488, Bartolomeu Dias successfully rounded the Cape of Good Hope and opened the sea route to Asia - although, in truth, he accomplished this feat without actually realising it. Rather, Dias got caught up in a storm off the coast near Lambert's Bay and was blown far to the south. Once the storm had abated, he continued sailing south but couldn't spot any land, so he headed north and made landfall at what is now Mossel Bay, missing the Cape completely. He returned to Portugal shortly thereafter, for reasons we'll get to in a moment...

It took nearly 10 years for the next expedition to get under way, with Vasco da Gama finally setting off in 1497. After briefly docking at St. Helena Bay briefly, da Gama rounded the Cape (intentionally) and made his way up the east coast of Africa to eventually reach the shores of the Indian peninsula at Calicut in 1498.

The floodgates were now open and, from the 1500s onwards, a succession of merchant ships from Portugal, Spain, France, England, Holland and other European nations began sailing around the southern tip of Africa *en route* to the spice fields of Asia.

It was a long journey for ships under sail. Crews required fresh water, vegetables, fruit and meat to keep their health up, and this necessitated landing on the unknown shores of southern Africa to source supplies. At first, ships did not stop on the Namaqualand coast as the seas were rough and the anchorages poor. Instead they followed the lead of Dias and da Gama who had identified a freshwater spring close to the coast, near what is today Mossel Bay.

But getting water and food was not as simple as the Europeans would have liked. The Khoikhoi people (who would bear the brunt of dealing with the early white seafarers) believed that water sources belonged to the clan who controlled the area. As such, they did not take kindly to brazen Europeans simply helping themselves without asking permission or offering payment. And so, ominously, the very first meeting of white and black people in South Africa quickly degenerated into a fight.

This incident is recounted by the diarist of Vasco da Gama, who was writing about the previous voyage of Bartolomeu Dias: "One day, as he [Dias] was taking water from a very good watering-place that lies at the edge of the sea here, they defended this watering-place with stones thrown from the top of a hillock which is above it; and Bartolomeu Dias fired a crossbow at them, killing one of them."

Dias and his crew scurried back to their ship and sailed away, watching in consternation as the Khoikhoi knocked down the stone *padrao* (monument in the shape of a Christian cross) they had erected. This unpleasantness spooked Dias' crew and a near-mutiny forced the ambitious explorer to head back to Europe, denying him the honour of being the first European seafarer to reach Asian shores. Incidentally, on the way back, Dias sighted the Cape coast and named it *Cabo das Tormentas* (Cape of Storms). This fearsome appellation was later repackaged as *Cabo da Boa Esperança* (Cape of Good Hope) so as not to scare off subsequent expeditions.

Either way, things were clearly not off to a good start and, as the number of ships sailing around the Cape increased so too did tensions between the natives and the Europeans. Apart from disputes over water rights, the Khoikhoi were reluctant to trade away their cattle or sheep, as these animals were kept for ceremonial occasions. This infuriated the hungry Europeans, who developed a nasty habit of raiding Khoikhoi homesteads and stealing their livestock. Sometimes, the white men even kidnapped a couple of Khoikhoi to ensure favourable trading terms. This resulted in a series of skirmishes, including one memorable incident in 1510 where a Portuguese Viceroy and a bunch of high-ranking officers were trampled to death by the Khoikhoi's trained war-cattle!

The Legend of the Flying Dutchman

In 1500, a few years after Da Gama came back to Portugal dripping with glory, that old sea-dog Bartolomeu Dias set out on another fateful expedition. He was still determined to see the exotic East, but it was not to be. Once again, Dias sailed into a storm off the Namaqualand coast and this time his ship sank, killing everyone on board. The Cape of Storms had taken its revenge. Dias was dead.

But his spirit lived on, and soon sailors began to tell stories of a ghost ship that sailed, spectral, through the choppy waters off the Cape. If you got too close, they said, your vessel would sink and you'd join the undead crew, cursed to sail the seas forevermore. Other's said that, if hailed, the haunted vessel would try to send messages addressed to people long dead. Suffice it to say, spotting the Dutchman was a dire harbinger of stormy weather and impending doom.

Over the years, the nationality and location of the ghost ship changed from telling to telling but this macabre maritime tale has persevered, appearing in plays, novels, operas, songs and, more recently, video games, TV and films (Pirates of the Caribbean, anyone?).

One version specified that the ship was a Dutch vessel, captained by one Hendrik van der Decken, that was sailing back to Holland in 1641 when it sank. Another has the captain as Bernard Fokke, a sailor who made a deal with the devil in exchange for great speed on his journeys between Holland to Java (the main base of operations for the Dutch East India Company).

Other authors went on to elaborate on the Faustian sub-plot, where the Devil and the Ship's Captain strike a bargain in which the doomed man may escape his storm-tossed torment but only if he can find a faithful wife among the living. The irony of the story being that the devil knew it was a sucker's bet and the Captain is still sailing the Southern seas, looking for an honest woman. Hilarious, apparently.

In the 1840's, the story found its most canonical expression in Richard Wagner's opera 'The Flying Dutchman' and the legend was thus entrenched, with sightings being reported throughout the 19th and 20th centuries. Interestingly, in 2008, diamond boats prospecting the waters off the Namibian coast found the remains of a ship on the ocean floor, which seemed to match the description of Dias' vessel. But coins and artefacts found in the wreck have now been dated from a later period.

The Hated 'Hottentots'

Thanks to a series of fraught interactions between the sailors and the locals, contemporary European opinion was that the Khoikhoi were savage, primitive and treacherous heathen (who refused to hand over their property like good little natives). This perception of the Khoikhoi was repeated so many times over the years that it came to be considered as sociological fact. Meanwhile, a new name had been coined for them: 'Hottentots' - a pejorative term apparently derived in imitation of a popular chant the Khoikhoi liked to sing in their other-worldly language, filled with clicks. An alternate etymology is through the German *hotteren-totteren,* for 'stutter'.

Accordingly, contemporary European descriptions of the 'Hottentots' were scathing. One observer wrote that they were "entirely naked but for an ox-hide around them like a cloak... always stank greatly, since they besmeared themselves with fat and grease... begged for entrails, which they ate quite raw after scraping out most of the dung... they speak very clumsily". Another simply stated that they were the "most savage and beastly people as ever I thinke God created". A third account described the Cape coast as a "shore so evill that nothing could take land, and the land itselfe so full of tigers, and people that are savage and killers of all strangers".

Even the respected Swedish scientist, Carl Peter Thunberg, thought they were horrible, writing in 1775 that: "In a people so plunged in sloth, and so overwhelmed with filth, as the Hottentots actually are, one would not expect to find the least trace of vanity. It is however to be found even among these, the most wretched of the human race; for...amongst their ointments they mix the powder of a strong smelling herb which they called *bucku,* and which gives them so disagreeable, so fetid, and at the same time so rank an odour, that I sometimes could not bear the smell of the Hottentots that drove my waggon. The language, which frequently is almost the only thing that distinguishes the indolent Hottentots from the brute creation, is poor, unlike any other in the world, is pronounced with a clack of the tongue, and is never written. Idleness is so predominant amongst the greatest part of the Hottentots that few of the animals without souls surpass them in that vice. In arts and sciences they are as rude and uncultivated as they are in every other aspect."

Of course, that's an appalling piece of racist rhetoric and the idea that the Khoikhoi lived "without law or religion, like animals" is both insulting and inaccurate. They had a comprehensive system of political, economic and spiritual controls, but these were different from and thus invisible to the narrow-minded Europeans. For example, the fat and grease that they smeared over their bodies had both an aesthetic purpose (it made their skins glisten) and a practical function (it protected them from both the sun and various bugs and parasites).

Nevertheless, the disdain with which the Europeans beheld the Khoikhoi was perpetuated through the ages. And this was totally in line with contemporary understanding of racial hierarchies in which whites are superior, thus justifying the exploitation, enslavement and murder of local populations throughout the colonial era and beyond.

The Sad Story of the Hottentot Venus

Despite the abundant abhorrence for Hottentots and other base African tribespeople, back in Europe there was a perverse curiosity about these exotic 'primitives'. This led to a series of exhibitions and sideshow attractions that travelled the continent, featuring anthropological 'lectures' at which genteel audiences could openly ogle bold African warriors or poke Indonesian pygmies in the flesh.

Saartjie Baartman was one such attraction. A Khoikhoi woman, born in the Eastern Cape in 1789, Saartjie worked in Cape Town for several years before she caught the eye of a doctor named Dunlop by virtue of her unusually big bum (a condition known as steatopygia). Certain that the noble audiences of Europe would love the preposterous posterior of this particular freak, Dunlop convinced Saartjie's then-employer, Hendrik Cesars, to partner in a venture that saw all three decamp to England in 1810.

Although not technically a slave, Saartjie had little choice but to comply and found herself being exhibited as the 'Hottentot Venus'. Even back then, there was some consternation at this brazen exploitation and a group of abolitionists took Dunlop to court for forcing Saartjie to perform against her will. The case was dismissed when Dunlop produced a probably spurious legal contract indicating Saartjie's consent, and he continued touring with his Venus until his death in 1814.

Saartjie was then brought to Paris by a man named Henry Taylor before being 'sold' to an animal trainer, S. Reaux, who allowed giggling customers to touch her bum for an additional charge. During this time, Saartjie was examined by Georges Cuvier, founder and professor of comparative anatomy at the Museum of Natural History in Paris, who was looking for evidence of the 'missing link' between apes and man. Reaux may have also raped and impregnated Saartjie as an 'experiment'.

Saartjie died in poverty in Paris in 1815, aged 25 – just five years after arriving in Europe. Cuvier dissected her body and put her remains on display, first at the Muséum d'histoire naturelle d'Angers, then at the Musée de l'Homme in Paris. For 150 years, her brain, skeleton, genitalia and a plaster case of her body remained in their glass case, in full view of the passing public. In 1974, she was packed away into storage.

After years of appeals and negotiations, Saartjie's remains were finally returned home to South Africa in 2002. She has now been given a proper burial close to her birthplace in the Gamtoos Valley.

The tragic story of Saartjie Baartman and her dispassionate exploitation at the hands of European exhibitors has now become a complex symbol of South Africa's colonial past, inspiring many films, documentaries, books, theatre and dance pieces.

Jan Van Riebeeck and the VOC

After 150 years of rather unregulated seafaring, one European nation decided that the time had come to establish a permanent trading station at the Cape, aimed at selling supplies to the ships that were by now stopping regularly at Table Bay. This very much for-profit enterprise was spearheaded by the publicly traded Dutch East India Company (in Dutch the *Vereenigde Oostindische Compagnie* or VOC) operating by charter on behalf of the nation of Holland.

And so, in the fateful year of 1652, Jan van Riebeeck and a group of Company employees landed a flotilla of three ships at Table Bay with instructions to build a garrison and plant a vegetable garden. The new Commander was also responsible for establishing trading ties with the local Khoikhoi so that they may secure a reliable supply of cattle and sheep.

At first, it didn't go well. The Dutch struggled to grow their European plants in the strange African soil. And the Khoikhoi were very reluctant to barter with the pale-faced long-hairs, who were already building a suspiciously permanent-looking fort on the beach. It got to the point where the Company Men could barely feed themselves, never mind stock their 'refreshment station'.

Van Riebeeck also had trouble communicating with the Khoikhoi, having to rely on the services of a self-serving intermediary named Autshumao (called Herrie by the Dutch) and his unfortunate niece Krotoa (called Eva). Autshumao was an impoverished *strandloper* chief who had learned some 'European' when he was taken (willingly or not) on a voyage to England some years previously.

The stories of Van Riebeeck, Herrie, Eva and the other Peninsula Khoikhoi who bore this first onslaught of colonialism in southern Africa are poignant and fascinating, but they are too long to be narrated here. Suffice it to say that the Dutch settlement endured, while Herrie and Eva found themselves caught between two worlds only to be rejected by both.

In any event, as the new village of Cape Town grew, the Dutch and the Khoikhoi endured several stormy decades of conflict, including a couple of armed uprisings usually concerning land ownership and grazing rights. Ultimately, starting in 1713, a series of smallpox epidemics brought in by European ships wiped out large numbers of Khoikhoi across the country, effectively ending the independence of the Khoikhoi nation.

But all that lay in the future. What concerns us for now is the interaction between the Europeans and the Namaqua people who lived far to the north of Cape Town.

Initially, Van Riebeeck and the VOC had little interest in the country beyond the Cape Peninsula. They had their hands more than full in trying to deal with the intransigent Khoikhoi living in the vicinity of the Fort. However, the growing city at the Cape soon demanded more meat, and explorers were sent out to contact more distant (and hopefully more co-operative) tribes.

There was also another, more romantic reason for this exploratory urge. For many years, there had been rumours swirling around Europe; stories of a mythical city, located somewhere in the African interior, that was rich in ivory and gold. Some said it was called Vigiti Magna, located on the banks of the mighty Rio do Infanta. Others called it Cortado, Cammissa or Vallenta. Whatever its name, this was proclaimed to be the fabled Ophir of the bible (the place where King Solomon had his mines). It was even held that this city was ruled by an apocryphal white, Christian emperor named Prester John.

All in all, it was a crazy story concocted to explain the steady supply of gold that kept coming out of the African interior (after all, there was no way the savage natives were capable of such advanced technologies).

Then, in 1512, a Portuguese explorer named Antonio Fernandez set out from Delagoa Bay on the east coast and came across a grand stone city that he called Monomotapa (this settlement was one of the successors of Mapungubwe and Great Zimbabwe). Even though maps were very vague at this time, cartographers were quick to mark the city on their charts and Monomotapa became embroiled with the legend of Vigiti Magna.

So, by the later 1650s, Van Riebeeck had in his possession several tantalising (if hypothetical) maps that clearly showed the location of a great city filled with gold, which lay not too far from his new post at the Cape. He also heard local stories that told of the wealthy Namaqua people living in the north (who, like Prester John, were said to be Caucasian!). Clearly, he had to find out more...

Into the North

The first expedition to the north thus began as early as 1655, under the command of Jan Wintervogel, but the sandy plains, river valleys and high mountains soon forced these pathfinders to turn back, around the Malmesbury / Darling area. Then, in late 1660, Jan Dankaert set out with several men including two Khoikhoi interpreters and a certain Pieter van Meerhof (who was to participate in no less than six expeditions to the north). The going was tough but Dankaert persevered until he found himself at the foot of some mighty mountains about 150km north of Cape Town, at what became the town of Piketberg.

Luckily, Dankaert met up with some Bushmen who showed him a game path over the mountains and, from the summit, Dankaert looked north across a wide river valley. He descended the mountains near present-day Citrusdal and explored the banks of the fertile river, which he called 'Olifants' because he saw several hundred majestic pachyderms parading along the watercourse. This pass (later named Piekenierskloof) became an essential component of the route to the north, and is still part of the N7 highway from Cape Town to Springbok.

The next expedition left only ten days after Dankaert returned to the Fort, in early 1661. This one was led by Pieter Cruijthoff, with Van Meerhof acting as second in command. Once again, they travelled with a couple of Khoikhoi interpreters. As they journeyed, however, they met up with several groups of Bushmen who warned them against the Namaqua, saying that the travellers would be killed by this fearsome tribe. Undeterred, the plucky Europeans continued on their way, crossing the mountains and pushing north towards the Cederberg. Then, the party came across some deserted kraals that showed evidence of cattle and sheep herding.

According to Van Meerhof's journal, that evening they saw a fire burning in the hills, a short distance away. Eager to find out more, Van Meerhof and his two 'hottentoos' climbed a hill. "When halfway up Donckeman [one of the Khoikhoi interpreters] began to shout, 'Mr. Pieter, Namaqua,' and I saw above me some three-and-twenty figures standing on the rocks gazing towards us... my Hottentoos were so affrighted that they made to take the shoes from off their feet, the better to run back. They cried, 'Namaqua! Shields of ox-hide! Danger!'. I used my glass to see if it were so. I saw that they were armed with dry hides and had [prepared] skins hanging from their left arms, bow and arrows upon their shoulders, and in each hand a spear. On reaching the heights we could not perceive them [the Namaqua] whence they had disappeared amongst the boulders. I directed our Hottentoos to call out that if they would come to us we would give them tobacco and beads and copper, but they gave no reply. I waited an half-hour upon the mountain side, hoping they would return. Longer I durst not wait, for the night fell and it became very dark, ere I returned to our people. We hope they will return upon the morrow and come amongst us."

The next day, the fearless Van Meerhof waited and, sure enough, the Namaqua re-appeared, still keeping their distance. He instructed his 'Hottentoos' to call out to them, promising that they would come to no harm. Eventually, they approached the strange white-faced visitors and tobacco was passed around, even though most of the Namaqua didn't know how to smoke properly. With diplomatic channels thus opened, Van Meerhof asked which one was their 'king'. A suitably large chief, named Akembe, was duly pointed out and gifts were given over. The chief then invited the party to his home, a few hours away. Van Meerhof and his men stayed with the chief for three days before returning somewhat triumphantly to Cape Town.

The next mission, with Van Meerhof now in charge, left a few weeks later, in April 1661. Hoping to cement the relationship, they looked for Akembe's kraal, only to find that the clan had moved north in search of water. Nevertheless, they made some useful contacts with other Khoikhoi and Bushman tribes.

In November 1661, Van Meerhof was off again, this time under the command of Pieter Everaert. During this unhappy journey, one of the men was trampled to death by an elephant and the group ran out of water - a common problem, since most of these early expeditions set off during the dry season.

The indefatigable Van Meerhof (who was by this time married to Eva - Van Riebeeck's ill-fated Khoikhoi ward) made his next trip in October 1662, under the command of Pieter Cruythoff. This was the first expedition to include a wagon which, as it turned out, wasn't a very practical notion. After dragging the cumbersome vehicle over the soft sandflats, the wagon had to be unloaded at the foot of the steep mountains, dragged up the pass, reloaded to cross the mountain plateau and then unloaded again to make the trip down the other side.

As they proceeded, the thick vegetation in the Olifants River Valley made the wagon useless, so Cruythoff packed everything onto the backs of their six oxen and buried the wagon, intending to collect it on the return journey. As it turned out, the party met up with some hostile natives near Koekenaap and they didn't bother to reclaim the wagon as they rushed back to the Fort, leaving it to rot in the sand. It was on this journey that the Europeans first heard reports of a great river which lay in the north.

Another expedition in 1663, under Sergeant Jonas de la Guerre (and the last for Pieter van Meerhof) also brought a wagon and repeated the burial trick - only this time, when they returned after running out of water, they found the wagon had been unearthed by locals and burned, so as to collect the iron components. Wagons continued to be problematic in the mountainous regions of the Cape until 1682, when it was decreed that henceforth all wagons should be built in such a way that they could be easily taken apart and re-assembled. Even then, it took several hundred years before road builders finally tamed the peaks.

For his part, the Namaqualand stalwart Pieter van Meerhof met an untimely and unsympathetic end a few years later, when was killed while on a slaving expedition to Madagascar. Eva, his newly widowed wife, subsequently lost custody of her children, spent time imprisoned on Robben Island, and ended her days as an alcoholic on the streets of Cape Town.

Simon van der Stel and the Copper Mountain

Despite the best efforts of these early explorers, the fabled golden city of Vigiti Magna/Monomotapa and the great river on which it supposedly sat remained elusive. But there was clearly some kind of mineral wealth up in the north because the Namaqua people, first observed by Pieter van Meerhof in 1661, were dripping with copper.

As Van Meerhof wrote in his journal: "Their dress consists of all kinds of beautifully prepared skin...gorgeously ornamented with copper beads... Their locks they thread with copper beads, covering their heads all over. Around their necks they have chains, slung around them 15 or 16 times. On their arms they have chains of copper and iron beads which go round their bodies 30 or 40 times."

The Namaqua, clearly, were skilled iron workers capable of extracting and manipulating copper. This indigenous knowledge was once again demonstrated when a group of Namaqua visited Cape Town in 1681, bringing with them some specimens of rich copper ore. The Dutch governor of the time, Simon Van der Stel, was thus encouraged to send out a number of well-equipped expeditions to find the source of the Namaqua's wealth.

The first couple of journeys were under the command of Olof Bergh, who pioneered a route that avoided the Olifants River Valley by moving through the Sandveld along the coast. This avoided the barrier of dry, rocky plains north of the Olifants River that came to be known as the Knersvlakte (so named because of the sound the wagon wheels made when 'gnashing' over the pebbly quartzite). Bergh also became the first European to visit a cave north of Graafwater that became a regular pitstop on the road to the north, known as *Heerenlogement* (Gentlemen's Lodging). On his first trip, Bergh reached the Groen River near Garies and on his second try, he got even farther, reaching the vicinity of the Kamiesberg. However, on both occasions, he returned to the Cape empty handed.

In 1684, another party of Namaqua visited Cape Town. This time, Van der Stel sent a party under Sergeant Isaq Schrijver to travel back with the Namaqua. The precise route of Schrijver's group is not known, but he did penetrate far into Namaqualand (probably to Leliefontein) and, when he returned, he presented the governor with some samples of copper ore. These were melted down and the results were sent off to the Dutch East India Company's headquarters in Holland for investigation.

In the meantime, another expedition uncovered further information about the existence of a 'copper mountain' that was located not too far from the sea. This greatly excited Van der Stel who promptly put together a massive expedition, which he decided to lead himself. And so, in 1685, with the Company's blessing, the governor set off for the north with all due pomp and circumstance.

By all accounts, it was a very impressive procession. It included 57 whites, two Macassar prisoners (from Indonesia), three Malay slaves, a carriage with six horses for the governor, eight donkeys, 14 riding horses, two artillery pieces, eight carts, seven wagons (one of which contained a small boat) and 289 oxen. There were also over 50 Khoikhoi wagon drivers, interpreters and camp followers, as well as six additional wagons each drawn by eight oxen which belonged to freemen who accompanied the expedition as far as the Olifants River.

And that's not including all the provisions, muskets, gunpowder and barter goods that the massive party would need for their five-month journey. Scientifically speaking, one member of the group - Hendrik Claudius - was an artist who produced some of the first illustrations featuring the plants of Namaqualand, including the kokerboom.

Following the route established by Olof Bergh, Van der Stel pushed his team ever northwards. It was fortunate that the region was enjoying a particularly wet spring that year, so the barren wastes of the Sandveld and the mountainous Hardeveld beyond were unusually fertile. This helped sustain the unwieldy expedition and they made good progress.

After several weeks of travelling, Van der Stel and his gang reached the Kamiesberg. Here, they spent some time trying to recruit local Namaqua as guides. Eventually, a combination of tobacco, liquor, food and coercion secured the services of two young men who steered the party through the inhospitable hills to the north.

Eventually, on October 21st 1685, the party arrived at the 'Koper Bergen' located near the present-day town of Carolusberg, a short distance away from Springbok. They immediately went to work and sunk several exploratory shafts into the mountain side.

The results looked very promising, with the ore improving the deeper they went. They also sent out prospecting teams who explored the surrounding area, including O'okiep. Van Werlinckhof, the party's mineralogist, was particularly impressed and, after two weeks at the site, he declared that "I am entirely convinced of the favourable character of these mines; in the event of mining operations being continued, richer and richer, and better minerals will be found, for the hills concerned extend several miles in length and breadth, and hold minerals almost everywhere".

Van der Stel was understandably optimistic as he rode back into Cape Town. The expedition had been a great success. They had found the copper mountain and collected numerous ore samples, which were promptly dispatched to Holland for analysis. Moreover, the difficult journey had been completed without a single loss of human life. Even the six-horse carriage had made it back in one piece, apart from a dent inflicted by a charging rhinoceros.

Unfortunately, that's where the good news ended. The assay results from Holland were good but not outstanding (the ore contained between 7% and 11% copper). Furthermore, the country in which the copper was located was dry and remote. There was no suitable grazing land for animals and no practical overland supply route for human provisions. The sea was many miles away, cut off from the proposed mine by a range of jagged mountains, and investigations of the coast between the Groen River and the Buffels River had revealed no suitable anchorages. In short, Van der Stel's copper mine was impossible to exploit - at least for the time being - and no further mining activity would take place in Namaqualand for more than 150 years.

Today, a couple of Van der Stel's open test shafts can still be seen halfway up the side of the 'copper mountain'. You can also see various proprietary inscriptions he had carved on the rocks, identifying them as VOC property. The site is signposted from the N14 highway, just east of Springbok.

The Bastaards and the Trekboers

After Van der Stel's expedition to the Copper Mountain, the route to the far north was set. It wasn't a busy road, by any means, but over the next 200 years a stream of exotic people drifted into and around Namaqualand. These included hunters, explorers, botanists, European farmers (known as Trekboers), escaped slaves, and a number of so-called Basters or Bastaards (people with 'mixed' blood). With all these new arrivals competing for land and scarce resources, the number of conflicts in the region slowly escalated - especially during times of drought.

First, let's talk about those Bastaards - mixed-blood 'tribes' who the colonial powers classified as either 'Bastaards' (off-spring of Europeans and non-whites) or 'Bastaard-Hottentots' (children of Malay slaves and Khoikhoi). Although they were technically free subjects, most of these people did not qualify for citizenship within the VOC's colony because of their questionable lineage. As such, they spearheaded the movement of people into the north, where they sought a land for themselves.

Here, they intermingled with the indigenous NamaKhoi, often dominating the natives by virtue of their firearms, education and/or relative material wealth.

They also carried a modicum of political clout by virtue of their Christian religion, and a few even managed to claim farms or grazing rights from the colonial authorities, eventually growing quite prosperous.

The famous Adam Kok, founder of the Griqua nation, was one such individual. Kok moved from Cape Town to Piketberg, where he settled on the farm Stinkfontein, in 1751. Later, he and his family moved north to the Kamiesberg where they became active as middlemen in the trade between Europeans, the Namaqua and the southern Tswana people. Around 1780, some members of the family moved again to the Orange River, about 150km west of Kimberly. A mission station was established (Klaarwater) and a town emerged: Griekwastad.

A similar pattern played out across this wild and unclaimed region, with regular migrations and relocations due to drought, in-fighting, population growth and/or competition over resources. And the stiffest competition in that latter regard were the trekboers.

Who were the trekboers? Well, initially, all European farmers in the Cape were obliged to live within a short distance of the Fort, so that the ubiquitous VOC could keep an eye on them. By the early 1700s, however, the needs of the settlement had outstripped supply and additional lands were required to meet the demand for food and meat. The white farmers were thus allowed to ride out and claim new lands over the mountains (although the Company remained the only legal purchaser of any goods they produced).

This was the advent of the Trekboers (literally, travelling farmers) and these hardy Europeans proceeded to usurp territory up and down the Cape. Later, this land grab was formalised into a system of loan farms, which allowed farmers to claim huge chunks of territory in exchange for a low annual rent to the Company. Indigenous land rights were, of course, thoroughly ignored. Even the semi-respectable Bastaards were forced to give up their lands if confronted with a white farmer's claim.

And so, trekboers started spreading out from the peninsula. The first wave headed over the Hottentot's Holland mountains above Gordon's Bay and across the fertile Overberg in the east (where Swellendam was established). Then, they made their way into the land of Waveren and the Tulbach Valley around Ceres, which provided access to the Great Karoo.

Although Namaqualand with its arid climate was not initially affected by this white expansion, many Khoi-San and Bastaard groups subsequently moved into the region after being displaced from their original homes by the trekboers. This put additional pressure on the territorial and political integrity of the Namaqua people.

In time, the trekboers in collaboration with Dutch authorities at the Cape became involved in nominating and appointing Khoikhoi chiefs, even awarding them with a copper-headed 'staff of office' in exchange for their collaboration and support in trading ventures. This further undermined the Namaqua's traditional hierarchies. Then, in the 1750s, the trekboers started entering Namaqualand itself, where they summarily claimed vast farms.

In general, these European farmers were not very different from the indigenous nomadic farmers who had previously worked the land. In Namaqualand, for example, most of them adopted the traditional *matjieshuis* as their housing unit of choice. They also migrated with their animals, moving with the seasons to seek out the best grazing land. Obviously, this put them in direct competition with the Namaqua herders but guess who had the gunpowder?

More importantly, the European farmers had God and the government on their side and, with their Western concept of private land ownership firmly in place, the trekboers inexorably took over the countryside. Over the next 100 years, the Europeans slowly but effectively marginalised the native Namaqua from their ancient pasturage.

As Namaqua, Bushmen, Khoikhoi refugees and Bastaards were pushed further and further into the remote north, they found themselves competing with one another. The transhumance that had once defined their lives was being constrained and traditional migration patterns were shattered. Some capitulated and became servants of the trekboers, or took up work as labourers on their farms.

Others retreated to the relative safety of the mission stations or into remote places of refuge that came to be called 'native reserves', most notably around the Leliefontein mission in the Kamiesberg and in the Richtersveld (which, until 1847, was beyond the official borders of the Cape Colony).

Some groups even turned renegade and started raiding the kraals and villages of their neighbours. Indeed, the whole Orange River frontier (known as Transoranie) became something of a 'wild west' during this period, with dozens of robber bands of various racial compositions roaming the area, causing trouble.

One particularly unpleasant incident that lingers in the collective memory of Namaqualand took place in the mid-1800s, when a severe drought gripped the area. As a result, the people at the mission station of Steinkopf moved their families and herds to a small spring about 15km away. Then, one Sunday while the adults were at church, a group of marauding Bushmen invaded the camp, killing 32 Nama children. This site is marked by a stark tombstone and is known, simply, as Kinderlê (where the children lay).

Hunters, Explorers and Scientists

Not all the Europeans who entered Namaqualand were focussed on conquest. Many entered the region to explore, collect, trade and hunt. Johannes Rhenius, for example, went on two unsuccessful trading missions to Garies in 1721 and 1724. Co-incidentally, Rhenius was the son-in-law of Olof Bergh, who had pioneered the northern 'highway' in 1682.

The various hunters who prowled around the region are harder to identify. They didn't keep journals and often travelled secretly, without official permission. Nevertheless, members of these anonymous hunting parties are generally considered to be the first white people to have seen the Orange River. This 'discovery' may have occurred as early as 1728, when a group of farmers from Piketberg surreptitiously travelled to the north on an extended hunting trip. Here, they came across the wide river known to the locals as the *!Gariep* (Great River). It is said that they met another white man on the shores of the *!Gariep*, an elephant hunter named Pieter de Bruyn. But this account remains conjectural.

Another expedition, in 1739, did make it into the official records but for all the wrong reasons. A group of hunters crossed over the Orange into Great Namaqualand (Namibia) where they spent a month at the kraal of Chief Gal. When they left, they persuaded their servants to raid the kraal and steal the cattle, in exchange for a share of the profits. Then, as they rode south through Little Namaqualand, they continued raiding kraals as they went, stealing more than 1000 cattle in total and killing several women and children. All of this came to light after representatives from the aggrieved parties travelled to the Cape to protest. Even the servants who had done the raiding complained that they had not been given the cattle they were promised. In the face of popular support for the hunters, the Company decided to compromise by confiscating the stolen cattle and keeping it for themselves!

The first 'official' visit to the *!Gariep* is credited to Jacobus Jansz Coetse who undertook the journey in 1760. He was a farmer from Piketberg who went off to hunt elephants, leaving his wife to look after the family farm. Suitably unencumbered, Coetse travelled with two wagons and twelve Khoikhoi, traversing Namaqualand until he came to the banks of the *!Gariep*. He crossed the river at Ramansdrift near Gu-daos (the sheep path). This river crossing was often used by the Namaqua herders and it is now known by the corrupted name, 'Goodhouse'. In this unassuming manner, Coetse became the first white person to document his journey across the lower Orange River into the country of the Great Namaqua.

Following Coetse's journey, it was decided that a semi-official expedition should go out to explore the region north of the *!Gariep*. This was led by Hendrik Hop, who set off with fifteen wagons in 1761. Jacobus Coetse went along as a guide and Carel Brink acted as the chronicler. According to Brink, the Namaqua they met along the way were poor, had few cattle and were constantly being raided by 'Bosjesmans'. Hop's party crossed the river at Gu-daos and continued north to the Keetmanshoop area. Here, they were forced back by the hot and dry summer conditions.

While in the area, a member of the Hop expedition, Dr. Carel Rykvoet, took the opportunity to do some mineralogical investigations. He examined van der Stel's Copper Mountain and declared the deposits to be poor. He also ventured into the Richtersveld, west of Gu-daos, where he found deposits that were very rich - up to one third copper. However, he quickly realised that the rocks were too hard, the land too barren, and the distances too great for minerals to be exploited.

In the 1770s, a new group of explorer's entered Namaqualand. They were the scientists, ornithologists and botanists who were attracted by the region's bizarre plants and unusual fauna. This group included Francis Masson, a botanist from Kew Gardens who was sent by the king of England to collect seeds and live plants for the royal greenhouse. Masson spent many years travelling the globe, including two tours of South Africa in 1772-1774 and 1786-1795. He collected Stapeliads from the Kamieskroon district in 1774. Masson was often accompanied by another notable collector, Carl Thunberg, the 'father of Cape Botany'. Together, they visited the southern edge of Knersvlakte, near Vanrhynsdorp, also in 1774.

Gordon and the 'Orange' River

Two major contributors to the western canon of knowledge on Namaqualand were Robert Jacob Gordon and William Paterson.

Gordon, a Hollander with Scottish ancestry, was a prolific traveller who undertook several extensive journeys across South Africa. It was during one of these trips, in 1777, that he came across the 'Great' river near what is now Bethulie in the Free State. He named the impressive watercourse the 'Orange' in honour of the royal House of Orange, rulers of Holland. Gordon suspected that this river ran directly to the sea but couldn't prove it at that stage.

Two years later, Gordon teamed up with a regular travelling companion named William Paterson to try and find the mouth of the 'Orange'. Paterson was a young British botanist who had been sent to the Cape by his eccentric patron, Lady Strathmore. He enjoyed some controversy during his stay in South Africa and, at one time, was accused of being a British spy. Later, it was said that he had discovered gold on the banks of the Orange River but kept the secret to himself.

In any case, Paterson had already been to the banks of the Orange in 1778 while he was checking out the old copper mines around Carolusberg, which he found to be promising. So, he was familiar with the region when he and Gordon set off once more to the north.

A short distance out of Cape Town, they were fortunate enough to run into Hendrik Wikar, a clerk of the Dutch East India Company who had fled Cape Town in 1775 because of unpaid gambling debts. Wikar subsequently spent several years wandering along the Orange River in the company of some friendly locals and wrote an informal report on the region, which he sent to the Dutch Governor, Van Plettenberg. This report was deemed to be so useful that the governor pardoned Wikar, who was on his way back to Cape Town when he met up with Paterson and Gordon. No doubt, Wikar gave the two explorers valuable information about their upcoming journey.

Even so, the trip was arduous. The soft sand of the Sandveld had always been tough on travellers, but Gordon and Paterson were determined to keep to the coast instead of heading west to harder ground. They persevered and slowly pushed their way from the Buffels River (near present-day Kleinzee) to MacDougalls Bay (near present-day Port Nolloth), then through the Holgat River Gorge, until they reached the Orange River Mouth on 17 August 1779. This short stretch of about 120km took them nine days.

When they arrived, they unpacked a small boat they had brought with and, according to Paterson, "launched [the boat] and hoisted Dutch colours. Colonel Gordon proposed first to drink the State's health, and then that of the Prince of Orange; after which he gave the river the name of the Orange River in honour of that prince."

After naming the river for the second time (just in case it wasn't the same river he'd seen at Bethulie), they landed the boat on the north bank where they met some *strandlopers,* whom Gordon sketched. The next few days were spent exploring the large bend in the Orange that curves around the modern Richtersveld National Park. The explorers subsequently returned to the Buffels River where they parted ways; Paterson heading for Cape Town while Gordon returned to the Orange to follow the watercourse eastwards to the Prieska area (presumably to satisfy himself that this was indeed the same river he had first named in 1777).

There is a sad coda to this story.

Upon his return, Gordon became the commander of the Dutch Garrison at Cape Town. He continued to travel extensively through South Africa: taking notes, making illustrations and categorising the natural wonders that he encountered - a real renaissance man. The plant *Hoodia gordonii* is named after him. Then, in 1795, Napoleon started making trouble in Europe and overthrew the Dutch royal House of Orange. The British provided refuge to the exiled

Dutch king and took the opportunity to send a fleet of ships to the Cape, so that they may 'protect' the port from Napoleon.

Gordon's loyalties were thus torn between the dethroned royal family and his new Napoleonic masters in Holland, now known as the Batavian Republic. After the British defeated the similarly confused Dutch battalions at the Battle of Muizenberg, Gordon's indecision was roundly criticised. He was also suffering from ill health and other personal problems. And so, in 1795, shortly after the Dutch surrender, Robert Jacob Gordon took up his pistol and shot himself. Gordon's Bay, near Cape Town, is named in his honour.

Apart from a brief Batavian interregnum between 1803 and 1806, Britain was now in control of the Cape and, in the years that followed, several eminent scientist/explorers popped in to check out Namaqualand and the Richtersveld. These included the somewhat overblown ornithologist Francois le Vaillant (1783), Carl Ludwig Phillip Zeyher (1830) and Johann Franz Drège (1833/4). The latter is known as the 'father of SA phytogeography' (the distribution of plant species). This may not sound like the most impressive encomium but more than 100 plants have been named in Drège's honour, which isn't bad going.

In the 20th century, the scientific appeal of Namaqualand (and the Richtersveld in particular) continued to attract collectors intent on identifying new species. These include the brothers Rudolph and Max Schlechter, Dr. Louis Leipoldt and Selmar Schönland - a big lover of succulents, but then who isn't?

Typically, most of these researchers were from foreign countries and their collections were inevitably sent to institutions overseas. South African botanical studies really only got started after businessman and amateur botanist Harry Bolus established a chair in Botany at the South African College (now called the University of Cape Town) in 1902.

The first person to assume the Bolus Chair was Harold Pearson, who had an abiding interest in the plants of Namaqualand. He went on two trips to the region (in 1908-09 and 1909-10) and collected lots of new information and many specimens. Pearson went on to become the first director of Kirstenbosch Botanical Gardens in 1913 and helped create the National Botanical Institute (now called the National Biodiversity Institute). The rare *Aloe pearsonii* is named after him.

Then, there was Hans Herre of Stellenbosch University Gardens (who spent 22 years growing a captive specimen of the rare Welwitschia plant from Namibia), Gilbert Westacott Reynolds (who wrote the essential reference book, Aloes of South Africa), Neville Pillans (who gave his name to the Baster Kokerboom, *Aloe pillansii)*, amongst many others. Today, modern botanists are still drawn to the region and new species of plants are regularly identified, hidden away in the nooks and crannies of Namaqualand.

The Missionary's Position

As we've seen, the 'Hottentots' and Bushmen were written off by the Europeans as godless heathens and inveterate sinners. However, the same could be said for many of the white people who lived at the Cape. Van Riebeeck himself warned his colleagues that those who "absent themselves from daily prayer ... attending very little to their religion ... [are] warned henceforth to attend at the place appointed for the purpose, ... those remaining absent shall forfeit six days wine rations...".

In those days, the Company followed the Protestant Dutch Reformed Church of Holland (even though the first official minister, Johan van Arkel, only arrived at the Cape in 1665, more than 10 years after the settlement was established). Roman Catholics and German Lutherans were not permitted to practise, and even the ideologically similar French Huguenots were initially restricted in their worship.

Despite the promise of eternal salvation, over the next few decades, very few Khoikhoi or Bushmen were converted to the Christian cause. But this is not to say that the locals were without religion. They just weren't particularly interested in all that Heaven and Hell in the Hereafter malarkey. Instead, indigenous spiritual beliefs were usually organised around practical matters such as the need for rain, healing of sickness, fertility of crops, plenitude of animals, and general matters of day-to-day survival.

The Bushmen, for example, believed in a number of gods with the creator */Kaggen* being the supreme deity. The Khoikhoi, for their part, worshipped *Tsui//Goab* who was offset against */Guanab,* the god of evil. For both groups, the ancestors (spirits of deceased relatives) provided a link between the living and the divine. Shamanistic rituals, trance dances and hallucinogenic plants were a recurring feature of these religious practises.

So, the Khoikhoi and the Bushmen did not provide the church with many souls to save. But there was another group of 'infidels' at the Cape who were much more receptive: the slaves. At that time, the Dutch East India Company's policy did not allow for the enslavement of local Khoikhoi, so slaves were brought into the colony from farther afield: East Africa, Madagascar, Java (now Indonesia), Bali, Timor, Malaysia, China, India, etc. The first shipment arrived in 1658 and, over the next 160 years, about 63 000 hapless individuals were imported against their will to supply the Cape with labour.

A German Jesuit, Martinus Martiny, administered to the spiritual needs of the slave population at Cape Town, but the conversion of slaves to Christianity was hampered by a number of factors. Firstly, several regulations gave any professed Christians several civic liberties, and converted slaves were (technically) allowed to buy their freedom. The missionary movement was therefore not supported by the slave owners. Secondly, the religion of Islam had already taken root at the Cape with the arrival of Muslim slaves and political prisoners from the East Indies.

For many slaves, the Islamic religion was far more appealing than the rather restrictive faith of their masters, and this alternative ideology grew quickly among the disenfranchised. However, several half-caste groups (or Bastaards) tended to adopt Christianity, perhaps because it gave them a greater claim to social and political rights.

In any case, the Khoikhoi themselves were largely ignored until 1706, when two Danish missionaries were sent to work among the reviled Hottentots. As could be expected, the missionaries did not meet with great success and they complained that the Khoikhoi were "truly a wretched and miserable people [who] have no divine worship at all". They abandoned their efforts soon afterwards, presumably with a petulant sniff.

The Moravians

The next attempt at proselytising took place in 1738, when a missionary from the Moravian Church - one of the world's oldest Protestant denominations - arrived at the Cape. His name was George Schmidt and, with the blessing of the VOC's governing board (known as the *Heeren XVII)*, he established a mission station in the Riviersonderend Valley, in the Overberg.

Schmidt reported that the Khoikhoi in this region were on the edge of extinction and he quickly set about improving their lot. But his activities were heavily criticised by local Dutch Reformed ministers, who complained that he was un-ordained and therefore not qualified to baptise people into the church.

The authorities in Holland supported Schmidt and he stayed at his post until he was finally forced out in 1744. The following year, the explorer Anders Spaarman travelled through the region and heard the Khoikhoi complain about a preacher who had exploited their cattle and labour - this could only have referred to Schmidt.

Several decades passed before the Moravians sent another group of missionaries to the Cape. They travelled to Schmidt's old mission station in 1792 where they found the ruins of his house, a huge pear tree, and an old woman, Magdelena, whom Schmidt had baptised. Ever faithful, Magdelena had remained at the abandoned mission for nearly 50 years, where she taught her daughter to read from an old bible left to her by Schmidt.

Taking this as a sign, the old mission station was resurrected and renamed Genadendal (Valley of Peace). It is considered the oldest mission station in South Africa and, at one time, was the largest settlement in the colony after Cape Town. The Moravians went on to establish several mission stations in Namaqualand including Troe-Troe Zending in Vanrhynsdorp (1751) and Wupperthal in the Cederberg (1830). A few Moravian stations still exist today, virtually untouched, with their distinctive white-washed walls and thatched cottages neatly arranged in rows.

The London Missionary Society

The first systematic attempt to set up a network of mission stations among the indigenous people of South Africa was undertaken by the London Missionary Society (LMS), starting in 1799. Although these evangelical activities were initially focussed on the Eastern Cape frontier, where they contributed to the overall chaos in this region, several stations were set up in Namaqualand, often at the request of Christian 'Bastaards'.

Generally speaking, the LMS were concerned with improving the lot of the 'coloured races' by providing education and petitioning the government for more equitable treatment of these 'children of God'. Led by provocative luminaries such as Theodore van der Kemp, John Campbell, John Philip, James Read and David Livingstone (we presume), the LMS was also anti-slavery and therefore less than popular in many quarters due to its progressive stance on indigenous rights.

The first LMS exploratory trip through Namaqualand was made by Christian Albrecht in 1805. Later that same year, he and his brother Abraham established a mission among the Great Namaqua at Warmbad (in present-day Namibia), assisted by J. Seidenfaden. In 1811, however, Abraham died from tuberculosis and the mission was sacked by the boisterous chief Jager Afrikaner. The faithful fled south into the barren reaches between eastern Namaqualand and the western edge of what is now known as Bushmanland. Here, they determinedly opened a new mission at Cammas Fonteyn, near the modern village of Pofadder, which they renamed Pella after the biblical place of refuge on the Jordan River.

The LMS and other 'Lutherans' continued to make in-roads throughout Namaqualand. In 1813, the Rev. John Campbell called at Pella, and a German missionary, Christopher Sass, opened a mission at Silwerfontein. In 1815 the Rev J.H. Schmelen established the Bethanien mission in Namibia. In 1816, Rev Barnabas Shaw was invited to set up a Wesleyan mission at Leliefontein, on a farm which had been given to the indigenous people by Governor Ryk Tulbagh in the mid-1700s. This was done at the behest of Chief Haaimaap, otherwise known as Jantje Wildschut (Johnny Wildshot). In 1818, Rev. Schlemen travelled to Kookfontein (also known as Kokfontein or Besondermied) and established a mission station there, naming it Steinkopf in honour of his mentor and teacher in London. He also founded a mission at Komaggas.

Soon, the Rhenish Mission Society got in on the act and, in 1830, one of their inspectors, Dr. E Richter, visited the far north-west of Namaqualand to inspect this remote region. A mission station was subsequently established at Kuboes in the mid-1800s as a 'sub-station' of the Steinkopf mission. The population at Kuboes was a mixture of Nama and Bastaards, and the entire region came to be known as the Richtersveld in honour of the good doctor's visit. In 1852, the Rhenish Church (meaning from the Rhine River) also established the Concordia mission, very close to Springbok.

Strangely, the fate of the LMS's Station at Pella is unclear. Some say that it was raided by Bushmen, who killed the minister and his family, causing the inhabitants to flee. Certainly, in 1824, the traveller George Thompson reported that the place was deserted but he did find another mission station a few hours away at T'kams - the priest in charge explaining that the congregation moved around during the dry months to find water. Others say that the station endured intermittently (perhaps under the aegis of the Rhenish Church) before it was abandoned around 1870 because of an extreme drought that had blighted the region.

The Catholic Church

The Catholics established their first mission in Namaqualand at Springbok in 1869, but their timing wasn't good. Formerly a boom town, the copper rush was now over and the place was severely short of Catholics to whom they could preach. Undeterred, the plucky Father Gaudeul from France decided to take over the abandoned LMS rectory at Pella. As the Catholic-written history of the Pella mission station hyperbolically recalls, "when the Lutherans got wind of these activities, they wrote to the Cape and made strong objections, but their letters arrived when everything had been settled. There was weeping and gnashing of teeth, but the die was cast."

Alea iacta est indeed. By 1878, Pella boasted 100 inhabitants, 50 of whom were Catholic. In 1882, 23-year old Father Jean Marie Simon arrived at the humble mission station and, with no prior experience in construction, got the community to build a small cathedral and nunnery with only an architectural encyclopaedia to guide them. The church complex took several years to complete and still stands today. Father Simon would remain at Pella until his death in 1932, 50 years later. He became known as the 'Bishop for the Hottentots' and was an iconic figure in the area. From Pella, the Catholic Church went on to establish a number of missions across Namaqualand, Bushmanland and the Hantam Karoo.

These various mission stations, Protestant and Catholic alike, proved to be both a blessing and a curse. On the one hand, they contained clinics, schools and churches, and thus formed a social support network for the beleaguered Khoikhoi and Bastaards reeling under the onslaught of trekboers and other modern interlopers. On the other hand, the church was selling a very specific salvation narrative and indigenous belief systems were usually dismissed outright. More practically, the permanent villages that grew up around the stations encouraged a more sedentary settlement pattern, which contributed to the decline of traditional migratory lifestyles. In later years, when schooling became compulsory for all children in South Africa, the mission stations became essential components of the Khoikhoi's existence and thereby drove a final nail into the coffin of their transhumance.

The indigenous Khoikhoi languages also suffered due to the missionaries' model of education. Few Europeans could master the intricate tongue-clicks of the various local dialects and, although some material was translated into Khoikhoi, most of the communication between shepherd and flock was done in Dutch or English. As a result, only the Nama language (spoken in the remote Richtersveld and in southern Namibia) is still alive today - the sole survivor of a wider linguistic tradition that once covered much of southern Africa.

In conclusion, the missionaries can be said to have had a stabilising yet disruptive influence on Namaqualand. They provided a variety of important social services and gave the locals a small political voice. In many cases, the mission stations also fought for a 'ticket of occupation' that guaranteed permanent tenure for the indigenous people on the land around the station. This was particularly important in the face of encroachment by white farmers and, later, the mining companies.

But all this came at a cost and government often removed power from tribal chiefs and placed it with the heads of mission stations instead. The mission stations also gave the transient Nama herders little choice but to settle down and accept Jesus, fatally undermining their traditional way of life. The Lord giveth and the Lord taketh away, as they say.

The Copper Fields

We've seen that the copper deposits of northern Namaqualand were well-known but impossible to exploit, as they were simply too far from market. Sooner or later, though, someone was going to give it another try. After all, money is a powerful motivator.

The sequel to Simon van der Stel's expedition of 1685 thus began in 1837 with the arrival of Captain (eventually General Sir) James Edward Alexander, an avid explorer, prospector and hunter. While conducting a survey of Namaqualand and Damaraland for the Royal Geographical Society, the intrepid Alexander came across some particularly rich copper ore at Kodas (about 7km south of Sendelingsdrift). He collected samples and forwarded them to Sir John Herschel in Cape Town.

The results were very positive - 65% pure copper - and a certain Samuel Bennett approached the British governor, Napier, for a mining permit. Permission was granted and Bennett travelled to England to form a company that would exploit the deposits (although subsequent assaying at Hatton Gardens downgraded the ore to 27% copper). Alexander also returned to England and prepared a report on his findings, but it appears that nothing came of his venture.

There are reports that Alexander did indeed commence mining activities at Kodas and Numees; transporting the unprocessed rocks by ox-wagon to the Orange River and then sailing the ore down to the sea on a flat-bottomed boat. Modern researchers, however, can find no proof of this endeavour and credit the story to a later prospector, Fred Cornell, who wrote a romantic book about the 'Glamour of Prospecting' in the Richtersveld.

In the 1840s, a missionary named James Backhouse visited the copper deposits of Namaqualand and sagely observed that while "it might be collected advantageously by Hottentots and transmitted in their skin knapsacks to some place at the coast where they might exchange it for other commodities; but to smelt it in this country would be impractical [because of a lack of wood or coal]".

Undeterred by popular opinion, Bennett pushed ahead with his ambitious prospectus for a 'Cape of Good Hope West Coast Trading and Mining Company' that sought to set up trading posts, mission stations and mines across the region. This prospectus was issued in 1843 but no investors stepped forward to buy shares in the risky proposition (this was decades before the discovery of diamonds and gold made South Africa a mineralogical powerhouse).

A few years later, in 1845, another attempt was made to form the 'South African Mining Company'. Once again, a glowing picture of untapped mineral wealth was painted, but negative reports from a mining agent put a dampener on things.

Several contradictory letters from various stakeholders subsequently appeared in the papers. Thomas Fannin, the Honorary Secretary of the South African Mining Company, claimed that the mining agent was misled by members of a rival French faction who wanted to take over the mines for pittance. Opponents to the scheme pointed out that reports from the 1700s found the rock to be too hard to process, that the Orange was not navigable, that there was neither fuel nor grazing, that there was no suitable harbour on the coast, and so on.

Fannin argued against all the naysayers and, at the first meeting of the SA Mining Company in Cape Town, it was decided that a party be sent out to survey the site. Fannin was selected to lead the expedition and he headed off in a light ox-wagon, reaching the location of General Alexander's proposed mine on the banks of the seasonal Gannakouriep River, near O'okiep, at the end of 1845.

Ever the optimist, Fannin found that the mine was 'centrally situated' to four mission stations who would provide labour. He also declared that "no tribe or individual whatever has any claim, worth a straw, to any part of the district between the Kousie (Buffels) and the Orange River". Furthermore, he said, there was a safe harbour close to the mouth of the Orange, at Peacock Bay.

This bay was one of a series of coves along the coast already in use by small vessels, but it was dangerously exposed and unreliable. Other potential anchorages included Homewood Harbour and Alexander Bay - which, depending on who you ask, was named not after the aforementioned General but for a man named Alexander who ran a trading post at the location with his partner, Mr. Peacock, from 1839. Alexander was apparently killed by Peacock in a fight over a girl, but I digress.

Clearly, the partisan Fannin was overstating the case for mining in Namaqualand. The native Khoikhoi had little interest in becoming wage labourers, and the mission stations were far from the mine. The Orange River was riddled with rocks and sand banks, which would make navigation impossible in all but the wettest months (when the river often came down in flood). Furthermore, Fannin had never seen the harbour at Peacock Bay, so didn't know if it was suitable for larger boats.

Fannin was also wrong about the land rights issue. Technically, the district in question was outside the Cape Colony, which officially ended at the Kousie (now Buffels) River, south of Springbok. But there were obviously tribal authorities operating in the area, and several white farmers had already been granted loan farms in northern Namaqualand (even though the government at the Cape had no legal claim over the land).

This last point became moot when Sir Harry Smith, perhaps sensing that something was up, annexed the Richtersveld in 1847 - summarily moving the northern boundary of the colony to the Orange River.

Regardless, Fannin issued a prospectus for the SA Mining Company in 1846. Shares were sold for 10 shillings apiece, directors were appointed, and a mining team was equipped. They reached the mine later that same year and started digging. Samples were sent to Cape Town and the ore was found to contain 70% copper. But transportation continued to be a major obstacle.

There was a rough wagon trail to the coast, but heavy ore could not be profitably conveyed in this way. Sailing down the Orange, as originally intended, was no Sunday outing and ships still couldn't dock on the coast. Eventually, Fannin was reduced to transporting the ore overland to Cape Town.

In 1847, shareholders were asked to cough up an additional 10 shillings a share to keep the mine going. Fannin, for his part, sold his shares and bought a farm in Natal. By 1848, shares in the South African Mining Company were worthless and the whole enterprise petered out. Although ultimately a failure, this was the first commercial mining site in South Africa.

The Blue Mine

Sometime after the South African Mining Company wound up its affairs, a German named Von Schlicht went to Namaqualand and stopped at a farm called Springbokfontein (also known as Melkboschkuil or Koperberg). Here, he was amazed to see a rich vein of copper sticking out the mountainside, in plain view. He hurried back to Cape Town to try and raise money for a mining enterprise but, unsurprisingly, found no takers amongst the copper-weary investors.

Frustrated, von Schicht shared his sad story with a housemate - a man named Jencken - and then left the colony for several years. Jencken, in the meantime, began working for the trading house Phillips & King but got himself into financial trouble and wound up owing the company some money. He offered to repay his debts by relocating to Namaqualand and opening a trading store on behalf of his employers. To sweeten the deal, he told his bosses about von Schlicht's copper find and suggested that he check it out.

Once he arrived, Jencken's reports on the copper in Springbokfontein were euphoric and Phillips & King sent off an agent, John Wild, to investigate further. This was all done under a veil of secrecy because they didn't want to tip the hand of the government, or any other interested parties. Their clandestine approach was just as well because, at that time, the title to the farm Springbokfontein had not yet been granted to the Cloete Brothers, then resident on the land. And when the deed was granted in 1850, the government didn't think to retain the mineral rights.

Just then, the story goes, Von Schlicht returned to Cape Town. When he heard that his mate Jencken was in Namaqualand, Von Schlicht quickly assumed it had something to do with his copper find and raced up to Springbokfontein. At the farm, Von Shlicht found several sacks of copper ore all trussed up and ready to go, but there was no sign of Jack Wild or Jencken. So, he rushed to the farmhouse and began negotiating with the Cloetes. A long discussion ensued, and the deal was nearly finalised when they all went to bed for the evening.

Late that night, Wild returned to the farmhouse and immediately realised that something was most definitely up. He sprang into action, waking up the farmers and getting them to sign a deed of sale before the sun rose. And so, on March 15, 1850, Phillips & King purchased the relevant portion of the farm Springbokfontein for the princely sum of £50. This included mineral rights to the entire farm, the right to erect buildings for the purpose of mining, the right to graze such animals as might be needed, and the right of access to water. Phillips & King later purchased the remainder of the farm for more than £2000.

Within two years, the 'Blue Mine' at Springbokfontein began producing considerable quantities of copper ore, which were transported by ox-wagon over the mountains to Hondeklip Bay. The first shipment of 11 tons was despatched to Cape Town in 1852.

Von Schlicht was well and truly trumped, but he didn't give up. Instead, he began prospecting around the area to try and find another windfall. Within a few months, he did indeed identify several additional copper deposits but these were located on crown lands, not private farms. Reluctantly, he applied to the government for the mining rights, but the government wasn't about to be duped again. Rather, they made a public announcement (in 1853) that henceforth all mineral rights to various portions of crown land in Namaqualand would be leased to interested parties.

Of course, the city of Cape Town went bananas as news of the copper bonanza spread. In the Grand Parade, it was said that the copper mines of Namaqualand "extend, almost without interruption, over a surface of from 8000 to 9000 square miles, at all degrees of depth, and that the ore is found almost everywhere at the surface". Several prominent surveyors and geologists (including the redoubtable Andrew Geddes Bain) went to visit the area and sent back optimistic reports. Suddenly, everyone wanted to get in on the action. It was a copper rush!

Copper Boom!

Spurred on by stories of copper lying on the ground, just waiting to be collected, people scrambled to buy leases on 'centres' – defined as a piece of land no less than 10 and no more than 40 morgen to be leased at a rate of £1 per morgen per year, payable in advance. A diagram of the claim had to be lodged within 12 months, during which time the applicant had the opportunity to search within a radius of one mile from the central point described in the lease to identify the best spots for mining. Grazing rights were also included.

Unfortunately, Namaqualand is littered with superficial traces of copper that look good on the surface but aren't payable. There are also a number of worthless geological formations that look 'green' (i.e. copper-bearing). But the mania for speculation would brook no negativity and dozens of consortiums were quickly formed to take out leases on mining centres. In many cases, these sites were selected by people who had never set foot in Namaqualand. There was also a hot market for the re-selling of leases, and those who were quick off the mark were able turn a handsome profit by selling their centres to other companies, sight unseen.

As the copper boom increased in intensity, there were some cautionary voices who warned that the bubble was going to burst, just as it had done on the Australian and Californian gold fields just a few years before. And so it was.

Rumours spread of deep-pocketed British investors who were about to step in to buy out South African lease holders, but this proved without foundation. Transportation remained a problem and several 'mines' had large quantities of ore just lying about, with no way to convey it to market. Other companies sent up mine managers with no idea about geology, who dug up tons of ore that were found to contain not a trace of copper. To add to the confusion, native guides were hired at great cost to identify likely copper centres, which usually contained no mineral deposits whatsoever.

But it didn't matter. Copper Fever gripped the Cape. Even the defunct South African Mining Company was resurrected and proceeded to revive operations at its old Gannakouriep mine. This, perhaps, accounts for the story of Patrick Fletcher who is said to have been the first person to transport bags of ore down the Orange in a flat-bottomed boat called the Enterprise, in 1854. Apparently, this practice continued until 1857 and some say that the mine remained in sporadic service until the 1920s. Fletcher, incidentally, went on to have a long history in Namaqualand and his name crops up several times in the pages that follow.

Thanks to the limited success of these various mining ventures, very few companies managed to return any dividends to their shareholders and, after a few months, the boom started to lose steam. Then, someone announced that they'd discovered gold in Namaqualand and shares soared again, despite the totally bogus nature of the claim (although it is true that Namaqualand copper does contain traces of gold, silver and other valuable minerals).

By now, the sceptics were growing more vociferous. Newspaper editorials poked fun at the gullible public. Parody prospectuses were published for the 'Ladies Mining Company' (its solicitors were listed as 'Mesdames Fleece'em and

Do'em) and the 'Lunar Mining Company' (which promised to pull the moon down to Earth so that copper could be scraped off the surface).

But it was to no avail. More and more people headed north to dig in. Heavy mining machinery was lugged over the dry plains and hectares of land were taken over by the voracious mining companies. At the height of the madness, applications for over 2000 centres were made, although only 200 of these were paid for. And it is estimated that between £70 000 and £100 000 was tied up in shares at the peak of the boom, mostly from small-time investors.

Unlike most mining dilettantes, however, Von Schlicht knew what he was doing and his consortium, the Namaqua Mining Company, was quick off the mark to purchase a very promising site at Tweefontein (now Concordia). Ironically, the Namaqua Mining Company's cautious and realistic prospectus did not find favour with investors eager for a quick profit, and it struggled to get off the ground, eventually relying on a few private individuals for funding. Meanwhile, Phillips & King (which was also privately held) made several wise additions to their portfolio. The other companies, however, didn't have a clue and were soon facing bankruptcy.

By early 1855, it was clear that the situation was untenable. After two years, dozens of mining companies in Namaqualand had only exported 44 tons of ore (with two companies alone accounting for 33 of them). Hundreds of leases were forfeited through lack of payment and proposals were made to amalgamate all the copper mines into a single entity, to manage the process more effectively. Then, the government abruptly declared that it would grant no new leases. The boom had officially gone bust.

By 1857, just three companies remained in operation: Von Schlicht's Namaqua Mining Company, the Phillips & King group and the South African Mining Company, which closed soon afterwards. While a few unscrupulous businessmen had made a killing by pocketing the money from share offerings, most investors were ruined and limped into the taverns of Cape Town to lick their financial wounds.

Springbokfontein

After the copper boom ended, the two remaining mining companies got busy consolidating their claims and streamlining operations. As such, the Phillips & King group concentrated on their Blue Mine at Springbokfontein – the one that had kicked the whole thing off.

Before copper, Springbokfontein was a farmstead with one mud house and couple of reed-mat huts. Within a few years, it was a bona fide mining station with houses for officers (mainly Cornish miners) and workmen (from all over SA). There was also a mess room, storerooms, a wagon maker, a blacksmith, stables, a post office and a prison. Everything in town was built and owned by Phillips & King, and uninvited guests were not allowed to stay overnight in the private village. In several cases, thirsty travellers were denied food and water for their horses.

The mine manager (or Super) held supreme power over the inhabitants, often behaving like a dictator. Other officials could also throw their weight around and there is one instance of a resident jailer, Genricks, who terrorised the town before he was finally tried (along with his 'tame lunatic') for murder and indecent assault. Even when Springbokfontein got its first resident magistrate, in 1855, he relied entirely on the company for his accommodation and supplies - hardly conducive to an independent judiciary.

In addition to the Blue Mine at Springbokfontein, Phillips & King secured the leases to several other valuable properties including Spektakel, Nababeep and O'okiep. Collectively, they accounted for the bulk of the copper output from Namaqualand and the company became a dominant stakeholder in the region. Their only rival was the Namaqua Mining Company of Von Schlicht and his partners, who owned the nearby Concordia mine.

All in all, the copper mines made a huge contribution to the colony's balance sheet at the time. In 1860, copper was the second most important export from the Cape after wool (which was, admittedly, a much more substantial industry).

The wealth of Springbokfontein, however, was short lived. The mine was exhausted by 1861 and ceased operations. But the settlement managed to endure and, the following year, the government declared that it was to become a public village. A town was surveyed by Patrick Fletcher and residential plots were auctioned off. The first clergyman arrived in 1866 and the little mining town soon developed a social scene, with race meets and balls. That same year, diamonds were discovered at Kimberley, about 700kms to the east.

Also in 1866, a smelter was set up at the old mine to process ore from other Phillips & King mines (although this was later superseded by the reduction works at O'okiep) and the village gradually became something of an urban centre for the region. In 1911, the name was shortened to Springbok.

The company then dealt the town a heavy blow by relocating its headquarters to their more significant mine at O'okiep and, by 1877, Springbokfontein was nearly deserted. By 1881, transport costs had decreased to the point where the Blue Mine could profitably re-open for another 10 or 15 years, and the town revived itself somewhat. W.C. Scully, the new magistrate, took the opportunity to make civic improvements, often using prison labour.

By 1904, the town was once again on the skids and, by 1906, only 100 people lived there. A school was established in 1911 but, by 1913, the remote village still had only one hotel. Clothing and lodging remained very expensive in Springbok, and some civil servants asked for a transfer because they would've gone broke on their current salaries. Still, there was obviously some money hanging about the place and, when the first registration of cars in South Africa took place in 1914, there were 10 licensed drivers in Springbok (out of a total of 13 for the whole of Namaqualand).

Phillips & King

The Phillips & King mine at Spektakel was another precarious proposition. The lease was granted in 1853 and pits were sunk. By 1856, only one pit had proved worthy of exploitation but it was really rich, outstripping the mighty O'okiep mine by 1861. By 1863, Spektakel had grown into the largest village in Namaqualand. A school was established a few years later, but the mine was already petering out. Workers were transferred to other mines and the school closed down less than a year after it opened.

In 1867, production slowed to a meagre 49 tons of ore then failed completely. Production was re-started on a small scale the following year and smelting works were constructed to reduce the ore to more profitable grades (known as regulus).

With things now ticking over slowly, a mission school was established in 1869 and the grandly titled *Spektakel Examiner and Times and Namaqualand Advertiser* began circulating to a reported 600 eager readers. Two hot topics regularly discussed in the hand-written circular were the lack of a law officer and the on-going problem with stray dogs. In 1872, the mine failed again but continued to operate sporadically. The pattern was predictable: the town dwindled when the mine was dormant, only to recover a few years later when operations started up again.

In 1886, gold was discovered on the Witwatersrand but it was a particularly bad year for the mines of Namaqualand, with a global slump in the copper price causing many operations to close down. Prices rebounded two years later, thanks to the efforts of a London-based syndicate funded by the copper companies, and Spektakel was opened yet again. But, by 1890, there were reports that people in the nearby village of Komaggas were suffering because work had been suspended at Spektakel once more.

The mine was now valued at a meagre £100 pounds (£2000 if you included the value of buildings and equipment) but operations stumbled on until 1901, when it was finally put to rest as a result of the Anglo-Boer War. The last entry in the mine manager's journal reads "Mine abandoned due to marauding Boers". Today, Spektakel is a small village and a popular stop on the spring flower route.

Nababeep mine was a much more stable proposition. It began as a farm, Lelykepad (bad road) which was granted to Pieter van Zyl in 1850. In 1852 it was purchased by Phillips & King for £1000. For the next few decades, it was considered a very promising trial mine, slowly growing into a complex with several shafts, a smelting works, winding engines, stone breakers, etc. By 1902, it was the second most productive mine in the group. By 1908, the village had a population of more than 2000 people.

Nababeep closed during the copper slump of 1919, but reopened in 1937 and continued to operate, albeit under constant threat of closure, until the early 1980s. Today, there is a sleepy village at Nababeep with an interesting mining museum (including Clara, a steam locomotive that once plied the narrow-gauge rail route to Port Nolloth).

The big one, however, was O'okiep. The mine began its life in 1856 with one small shaft, and by 1860 it was the most important producer in the region. Ten years later, it was described as the richest copper mine in the world. Accordingly, O'okiep was a large settlement with stores, stables, workshops, machinery, steam engines, school, store, infirmary, residences and cottages. By 1870, the mine was 75- 90 metres deep with a population approaching 1500. A few years later, the mine was nearly 150 metres deep and it took 20 minutes to climb up the ladders that lead precariously to the surface.

Labour at O'okiep was divided into 'tut-work' (sinking shafts) and 'tribute work' (getting ore to the surface). Most of this was done by 'black' labourers under the watch of white supervisors. Salaries were relatively high, with qualified miners from Britain earning between £8 and £12 pounds a month. In stark contrast, workers of colour were paid 1s 6d per day (there are 20 shillings in a pound and 12 pennies per shilling, in case you'd forgotten).

Local women and children were employed to sort the ore by hand and do other 'menial' jobs. They were paid 4 pennies a day. At the time, this wage gap was considered entirely appropriate given the difference between "the skilled labour of civilisation and the unskilled labour of barbarism".

Despite the professed generosity of the company, O'okiep (and other mines in the area) often experienced a shortage of labourers, especially when the rains were good and locals returned to their farms. To compensate, workers were brought in from all over the world. By 1875, the population totalled 1752 people living in 73 houses and 367 huts and tents.

A contemporary traveller described the 'copper wonder' as follows: "There is a perpetual clatter which, to a stranger, is very fidgeting, but which is not noticed by those resident, unless there is a stoppage, when everyone looks up to see what is the matter. The people are called to work by a huge steam whistle, which can be heard for many a mile. Almost every nation finds its representatives there, English, French, German, Italian, Portuguese, the colonial Dutch and 'Africanders', and as for the numerous native races, I would scarcely like to say that African race is not there. Here you see men from the far interior, West and East Coast of Africa, Lascars, Indians, Kafirs, Fingoes, Hottentots, Bushmen and the various Damara nations, and all the wonderful crosses produced by marriage amongst such a mixed population."

And still the mine continued to grow. In 1882, it had a population of around 2000, eight stores, two churches, two schools, a hospital, a post office, a telephone service and a telegraph line. By this time, the mine was so successful it had even started polluting the environment, with reports of people dying from bad air and contaminated water.

But it was too good a proposition to slow down. In 1884, production was reported at 15 000 tons of 30% copper ore, the mine had over 900 employees, and the resident magistrate said that "I have never been in touch with a community where there is such a constant undercurrent of scandalous innuendo as there was at O'okiep". Apparently, moral decline is a sure sign of prosperity.

Four years later, the mine was directly employing 2000 workers with Damara labourers from Namibia camped on one side of the valley and Khoikhoi workers on the other. Popular prejudice against the Khoikhoi had not diminished over the years and it was declared that "The Damara is a steady, hardworking, reticent, thrifty native. The Hottentot on the other hand is thriftless, careless and happy-go-lucky. He is altogether a most disreputable character with one god - *dop* (booze)."

Nevertheless, O'okiep continued to produce ore until the mine finally ran dry in the early 21st Century. Today, Okiep (as it is now spelled) is a quaint place. The smokestack of the old reduction works is still standing alongside the steam-driven Cornish Pump - reputedly the only complete example of its kind in the southern hemisphere. The massive mine dumps are also intact, forming a dark ridge above the town; deep-green rubble glistering in the hot sun. The town currently has about 6500 inhabitants and a crippling unemployment rate.

The Namaqua Mining Company

The Namaqua Mining Company's property at Concordia was said to be more of a quarry than a mine. It began in 1853 and a neat compound was quickly laid out. It was never a particularly rich mine, but it was regular. In 1873, it had between 150 and 500 employees, depending on the season, and a reported output worth £15 000. A few years later, the population numbered 961 living in ten houses and 219 huts and tents. In 1875, mine activities were greatly reduced and things remained quiet until 1881 when reduced shipping costs made it feasible to resume operations. By 1886, things were looking better but a few years later it all went belly-up and the mine's land was valued at a mere £150 (with equipment and buildings, £10 000).

Still, you can't keep a good mine down and a smelting works was constructed in 1905. By 1908, the mine employed around 650 people but finally closed for good in 1931. Concordia was the plucky underdog of Namaqualand's copper mines, paying out a 400% dividend between 1888 and 1928. Today, it's a dusty village with little in the way of economic opportunities.

Despite solid results, fortune was fickle for the Namaqua Mining Company. In the 1860s, the original consortium was bought out by Von Schlicht and Henry Home Ley. Then, in 1869, Von Schlicht was bought out by Ley, but the mine went into liquidation shortly thereafter (partly as a consequence of Phillip & King's monopoly over the Port Nolloth railway line - see *Transport Problems* below).

In 1872, a group of Glasgow capitalists bought the company for £15 000 and it changed hands a couple more times before being re-incorporated as Concordia Copper Company in 1877. A few years later, the name changed to the Namaqua Copper Company, which then became the Namaqua United Company in 1886. This concern also went bang, only to be resurrected in 1888 as, once again, the Namaqua Copper Company - a name it retained until its ultimate demise in the 1930s.

The Siege of O'okiep

Although armed conflict between Britain and the Boer Republics broke out in 1899, it took until 1902 for the Second Anglo-Boer War (or South African War) to reach Namaqualand. By this time, the gruelling campaign was in its final stages, with the British having starved the Boers into near-submission through a brutal combination of 'Scorched Earth' tactics and concentration camps.

Unbowed, General Jan Smuts was leading his Boer commando on an expedition through the Cape Colony in 1902. And, since he was in the area, it was decided to launch a raid on the Copper Fields - perhaps in an attempt to draw British troops away from Cape Town. Concordia quickly surrendered to the Boers without a shot being fired. This was greatly resented by the other mines and the Boers proceeded to use Concordia as a base from which they captured Springbok in a spirited battle that saw 4 British dead and 6 wounded. Only O'okiep remained under the Union Jack.

By the 4th of April, Smuts had effectively surrounded the defiant settlement and, the following day, he sent a letter to Lieutenant-Colonel Shelton demanding surrender. Shelton was sanguine. He had built up substantial defences at O'okiep and commanded scattered garrisons including half a company of the 5th Warwickshire regiment, the locally raised Namaqualand Border Scouts and a Town Guard. His answer came forthwith, reportedly as follows: "In reply, I beg to inform you O'Okiep is a fortified town and that I am comfortably supplied with men, ammunition and provisions". Ouch!

On the 8th of April, Smuts launched an attack on the town. Private Carolus Johannes, a member of the Town Guard, was shot in the head, chest and stomach while reloading his rifle. The next day, a fresh sortie was launched but it too was repulsed - even though the Boers sent a carriage-load of dynamite down the tracks towards the mine (the makeshift bomb-train either derailed harmlessly or exploded before reaching the defensive walls, depending on who you ask).

On the 11th of April, Smuts sent another letter suggesting that the women and children inside O'okiep be moved to Springbok, for their own safety. This offer was politely rebuffed by Shelton and everyone hunkered down for a long siege.

Meanwhile, with about 900 people trapped at O'okiep, refugees from across the region hurried to Port Nolloth, hoping to meet the two British gunboats that were said to be on the way. Then, Smuts was called away to attend peace talks in Vereeniging, over 1000kms distant, and left his commando to held the fort, so to speak.

Finally, on the 4th of May 1902, a relief column under Colonel Cooper arrived from Port Nolloth and broke the siege, just as Shelton's supplies were about to run out. This was one of the last actions of the war, which ended with the signing of a peace treaty by the end of the month. Several medals for the defence of O'okiep were subsequently issued, as the Brits are wont to do. And the Boers, as the saying goes, lost the war but won the peace...

Copper Bottom

At the outbreak of World War I, all copper mining in Namaqualand was suspended. The government stopped the shipping of copper ore to Britain, preferring to keep the cargo space for products more central to the war effort. The Namaqua Copper Company never fully recovered. Major operations were stopped in 1918 and smelting stopped in 1930. By 1931, the company was defunct, retaining only the mineral rights to its lands.

The Phillips & King group, on the other hand, had all the good mines and enjoyed a more sustained corporate history. After commencing operations in 1853, the company did well until two partners in the firm died, in 1862. This necessitated the dissolution of the concern and the whole enterprise was taken over by the newly formed Cape of Good Hope Copper Mining Company Ltd. (commonly known as the Cape Copper Company). In the new company prospectus, it was announced that company-owned mines had already exported 19 000 tons of high-grade ore worth £500 000 pounds with a profit of £115 000.

For the next couple of decades, the Cape Copper Company continued to deliver solid results. But the outbreak of World War I put a serious dent in its finances. To make matters worse, 1918 was a bad year all round; falling ore grades, shortage of supplies, and lack of access to markets all exacerbated the situation. Then, in 1919, the Cape Copper Company suddenly suspended its operations with "a callousness and want of consideration and forethought [for their employees] which [was] nothing short of culpable".

In effect, on a single day, the company dismissed its entire staff - most with just a week's severance pay. The shareholders, however, had done very well making £217 for every initial share of £8.

A year later, the company started up again; mining on a small scale and selling off its accumulated stocks of ore. It was eventually bought by an American consortium, who paid $750 000 for the company's property. This new concern was named the South African Copper Company Limited, and it was involved mainly in exploratory work. In 1937, the O'okiep Copper Company was incorporated to buy out the South African Copper Company. Shares in the new enterprise were taken up by a variety of international mining companies, with the American based Newmont Mining Corporation as the largest shareholder. The O'okiep Copper Company's assets included 105 000 acres of land, mineral rights to another 50 000 acres, mining equipment, the railway to Port Nolloth and the jetty at Port Nolloth.

In 1939, the company bought the mineral leases held by the defunct Namaqua Copper Company for £2125 pounds. It now owned all the mines in Namaqualand. In 1940, it began milling and smelting operations and, in the following year it posted sales of £467 010 pounds, £109 125 of which were profit. These returns improved during World War 2, when the company secured contracts with the British and American defence departments.

After the war, East Okiep mine was opened and a pipeline to the Buffels River was constructed to supply water, which had always been in short supply. In 1951, another mine called Wheal Julia opened. Several others followed: Hoit's mine, Homeep, Nigramoep, Jan Coetzee (famous for its quartz crystal formations) and Carolusberg (the location of Van Der Stel's original excavations, in 1685).

By 1975, the O'okiep Copper Company employed exactly 1036 whites, 1996 coloureds and 2080 Africans. But the life span of their mines was limited and, by the 1990s, only Carolusberg and Nigramoep remained operational. In 1997, the company gave all the houses in Okiep, Carolusberg and Nababeep to their current occupants, irrespective of status.

At that time, the company was managed by Goldfields of South Africa, but it was bought by Metrorex in 1999. Nigramoep, the last active mine, closed in 2004 and surface explorations were abandoned the same year.

Processing of stockpiles continued until 2005, when it was announced that the equipment of the O'okiep Copper Company was to be transported 'Meccano-like' to a new copper mine in the Democratic Republic of Congo. Today, there are no active copper mines in Namaqualand. One of the region's defining industries had come to an end.

Or has it? New mining technologies have been developed that could make old payloads viable again. And a rise in demand for 'tech' minerals, such as zinc, nickel, lead, copper, and cobalt (used in the production of cell phones and renewable power systems), has drawn investors back to the Northern Cape. Vendata Resources, for example, has already sunk $400 million dollars into their Gamsberg mine at Aggeneys, east of Pofadder; eager to exploit 'one of the largest zinc ore bodies in the world'. Meanwhile, a new generation of mining entrepreneurs is scouting around Namaqualand, looking to revive old operations.

Who knows, maybe there's another boom around the corner?

Transport Problems

As we've seen, the biggest problem facing the copper mines of Namaqualand was the dearth of effective transport routes. The region had few roads, and those that did exist were in a terrible state. Heavy, bulky ore couldn't be profitably transported overland to Cape Town, and the Orange River wasn't an option. This meant the sacks full of rocks had to be carried by wagon to the coast (about 120km and a mountain range away) and shipped to Cape Town, from whence they could be sent to England for processing. But first, they needed to establish an accessible port on the hostile Atlantic coastline.

Accordingly, in 1854, Captain HJ Nolloth surveyed the entire Namaqualand coast up to the Orange River mouth. He declared that there were two potential anchorages, although neither was particularly good. Both had an outer anchorage about a mile from the shore and an inner anchorage (for smaller boats) with a pronounced sandbar. They were called Hondeklip (Dog Stone) Bay and Robbe Bay (Bay of Seals). The good captain's preference was for the latter, which was soon re-named Port Nolloth in his honour.

For the mines clustered around Springbok, it was a tough choice. The path to Hondeklip Bay was very mountainous, while the Port Nolloth route had a poor supply of water for the draught animals. Both routes had to traverse the western Hardeveld mountains and then cross a strip of soft, deep sand (which was a nightmare for the heavy wagons). The Port Nolloth route had fewer mountains but a wider expanse of Sandveld to negotiate. And so on.

Back in 1852, the first shipment of 11 tons of ore from the original Blue Mine in Springbokfontein had been sent by wagon over the rough path to Hondeklip Bay. Through sheer inertia, perhaps, this tortuous track became the preferred route to the sea and a new profession was born to take on the challenge - the era of the Copper Rider had begun.

Despite the best efforts of the copper riders, who were usually local farmers of various ethnic groups, the primitive road took a heavy toll. Sacks of ore burst open. Wagons were shaken to pieces. Water for the animals was scarce. Wheels got stuck in the sand. And it was slow going. Each journey to the coast took roughly 6 days, and another 4 days to get back.

Against the odds, however, a procession of heavily laden wagons weighing up to one and a half tons began bumping along the rough gravel path (although many wagons arrived at the coast much lighter as a result of ore falling off along the way). By 1866, there were about 300 wagons and 6000 draught animals plying the route.

Most of these wagons were hauled by sorry asses, arranged together in teams of up to 10 mules each. In times of good rain, oxen were used. The copper riders also tried using Scotch carts, but these light-weight buggies couldn't withstand the battering. The geologist-surveyor, Wyley, even suggested importing camels to use as draught animals during the dry summer months. While this is a ridiculous concept, it's not as bad as an earlier idea, expressed in 1802, that proposed using giraffes!

Transporting the copper was not only difficult, it was expensive. In 1855, the cost of getting ore to the shore equalled the cost of mining the stuff in the first place. The figures broke down like this, roughly per ton: copper riders were paid £7 10s to travel to the coast, and £3 for the return journey; shipping to Table Bay cost £1 10s; shipping to London cost between £2 and £3; transport from London to the smelting works at Swansea a mere 10 or 15s. This amounted to a total transport cost of £16 pounds per ton (£10 of which was for the short overland route of 120km).

These high prices meant that only the highest-grade ore could be profitably exported, while hundreds of tons of lower grade ore were stockpiled at the mines. The riding season was also limited to the wet winter months, when there was enough water, so transportation of ore was sporadic.

The mines made repeated calls for improved roads or, even better, a railway that would make transport of ore much more efficient. But the government didn't see why they should pay for the construction of proper roads when the mines were making a decent profit as things stood. The mine owners countered that their leases were too short to justify spending large amounts of money on infrastructure and, in any case, many operations were low on capital and high on speculation. It was a stalemate.

In an attempt to settle the issue, two Select Committees were set up in 1854 and 1855. Both committees considered the development of mining in Namaqualand to be of national importance, and both recommended the construction of railway line from Hondeklip Bay across the Sandveld, creating bulk transportation system that would unlock the value of lower-grade ores.

The government refused to budge, despite the sage advice of respected surveyors A.G. Bain and Charles Bell. There were some suggestions of floating a private consortium to construct the railway as a profit-making exercise. But this didn't materialise because, just at that moment, the copper boom went bust and no-one was prepared to invest.

Hondeklip Bay vs. Port Nolloth

The two remaining copper companies (Phillips & King and the Namaqua Mining Company) were left to their own devices. Phillips & King, the larger of the two, took it upon themselves to repair the track to Hondeklip Bay at their own expense after each riding season, but the route seemed to deteriorate year to year. Various government agents protested about the situation in support of the mines, who brought a lot of money into the colony, but nothing was done.

To compensate themselves, Phillips & King quietly bought up almost all the farms between Springbok and Hondeklip Bay. This left their rivals in a tenuous position, but the Namaqua Company managed to secure their own outspan on one of the plots along the way. The NMC also sent their wagons to Port Nolloth when the erratic water supply would allow.

Things proceeded in this manner until 1862, when another Select Committee was appointed to investigate the construction of a new road, which they duly recommended. The committee also considered an application from Phillips & King (by now called the Cape Copper Company) to construct the formerly proposed 16-mile railway line from Hondeklip Bay to Riethuis farm. This section of track would eliminate the difficult stretch across the Sandveld, and the committee agreed to the proposal on condition that public goods would also be transported, and that the line be sold back to the govt at cost after 10 years. As it turned out, no funds were forthcoming and the status quo remained as such.

By this time, Hondeklip Bay had developed from a single trading store (owned by a Mr. Grace) into ramshackle village with four trading stores, dozens of wooden shacks and a jetty. It was, by all accounts, a horrible place. There was no inn, tavern or canteen, and drinking water had to be shipped in from Cape Town. The only other potable liquid available was brandy, which was sold in 16-gallon casks. This led to widespread drunkenness and regular outbursts of violence among the copper riders. Worse, there was no jail and the lone peace officer certainly had his hands full dispensing rough justice.

The anchorage at Hondeklip Bay was similarly problematic. It was exposed to strong winds and rough seas, and there was a shortage of moorings in the inner harbour. Nevertheless, this was now the de facto shipping hub, and the Cape Copper Company set about constructing houses, storerooms and other utilitarian buildings. In 1862, Hondeklip was made a magisterial district and a customs officer was appointed. Within 10 years, exports from the port amounted to £800 000, with imports of £450 000 (mainly supplies destined for the mines at Springbok).

But the town was still a dump. A contemporary visitor described it thus: "The wood [of the houses] is covered with tar, which prevents decay, but does not improve its appearance. The ground on which it stands, and for miles around, is loose sand, which is blown about by the wind. The frequent sea fogs are very damp and unpleasant... It would be difficult to find a more disagreeable place."

By 1865, both routes to the coast were in a terrible state, and the situation was getting worse. The Divisional Council of Namaqualand (established in 1861) complained that it spent most of its revenue keeping the Hondeklip Bay road in so-called repair. The farmers living in the Hardeveld and at Kamiesberg were also unhappy about their rates going into a road that was of little use to them.

So, yet another Select Committee was established 'on Namaqualand Roads and Tramway'. This time, the government brought in a roads inspector, our friend Patrick Fletcher, to decide on whether the new, engineered road should be constructed to Hondeklip Bay or Port Nolloth. Meanwhile, the Cape Copper Company got in their own engineer, Thomas Hall.

Surprisingly, since the Cape Copper Company had a stranglehold on the Hondeklip Bay route, Hall advised that the Springbok to Port Nolloth road was preferable and proposed building a tramline from Port Nolloth across the Sandveld to the farm Muishondfontein. Fletcher, on the other hand, suggested improvements to the Hondeklip Bay road, even though it would be expensive to build and maintain. This latter recommendation was apparently based on the needs of copper riders already entrenched in the Hondeklip area.

It was subsequently decided that a new road to Hondeklip Bay should be constructed. The Cape Copper Company was also given permission to build a tramway from Hondeklip Bay across the Sandveld (although this never materialised).

The Mason's Road

And so, in 1867, construction on the long-awaited 'proper' road to Hondeklip Bay commenced under the supervision of Patrick Fletcher. It was called the Messelpad (Mason's Road) because steep mountain slopes required the construction of high, dry-stone retaining walls all along the route. Convicts were used to supply the labour, and accommodation and transport for these road gangs was supplied by the Cape Copper Company. Even so, by the time the road was complete, in 1871, it had cost a total of £10 000. The Messelpad still exists today and offers the modern motorist a wonderful gravel diversion. The ruins of the old convict compound can still be seen.

Unfortunately, the Messelpad came too late for Hondeklip Bay. In the late 1860s, the Cape Copper Company revamped its transport operations by putting the riders under contract. From then on, only 30 or 40 men were permitted to transport the company's ore. And they were paid at O'okiep, where supplies were bought from concession stores, thus depriving the Hondeklip traders of their most important clientele.

In 1869, the decision was somehow made, finally, to develop Port Nolloth as the major seaport in the region. The Cape Copper Company was granted permission to build a railway line across the soft Sandveld, from Port Nolloth to Muishondfontein. Thomas Hall was recalled and began construction. The first 46 miles of line was opened in 1870.

The new access road lead from O'okiep, down the Anenous Pass (meaning 'side of the mountain') and to the railhead at Muishond. It proved most popular. Ore exports doubled within the year, and copper riding over the nearly completed Messelpad decreased dramatically.

Within a few years, Hondeklip Bay was a shadow of its former, boisterous self. The copper riders had departed and all but one of the shop keepers left town. By 1877, Hondeklip Bay had ceased to be a separate magisterial district and was no longer regarded as a port. The town barely survived and only became viable again with the growth of the fishing industry. A cannery was built in 1925 but closed in the latter part of the twentieth century. It still smells, though.

Port Nolloth, meanwhile, boomed. In 1856, the town had only a couple of inhabitants, four or five wooden houses, and a single trading station run by F.W. Dreyer. By 1870, a few months after the tramway opened, it contained around 200 residents. Captain Nolloth himself, now retired, was appointed the first harbour master.

But it remained an unattractive place. Makeshift houses sprawled across the soft sand, interspersed with canteens and bars. There was no jail or magistrate, and living conditions were very rough. But it was, in many ways, a far superior port to Hondeklip with a safe inner anchorage protected from the elements.

In the Port's early days, sacks of ore from the mines were carried down to the beach and into the sea by 'coolies', who then heaved the bags into the bobbing boats. By 1874, a jetty had been constructed with a miniature railway running along its length, allowing ore to be dumped directly into waiting vessels. Moorings and navigational beacons were erected, and a fortnightly ship from Cape Town brought in much-needed supplies. In the same year, Port Nolloth became a magisterial district and a customs officer was appointed. Drinking water for the settlement was sourced from a spring about 5 miles away and transported to town in a 'rol-vaatjie' (basically a barrel fitted to an axle).

By 1882, the town had 2000 inhabitants and the *Namaqua*, a Union Castle steamer, regularly plied the Cape Town-Port Nolloth route. Unfortunately, there was no passenger landing area and, to get from a boat to the jetty, you either had to climb up a rocking ladder or get hoisted ashore in a basket dangling from a wire pulley.

The town continued to grow apace. 1886 saw the establishment of a newspaper and a cricket club. 1896 saw the installation of a sanitation system. A lighthouse was erected in 1909. But the fortunes of Port Nolloth took a tumble when the Cape Copper Company abruptly stopped production in 1919. Poverty overwhelmed what was essentially a mining town, and visitors in the 1930s reported seeing young children begging for a cup of fresh water. Fishing turned out to be the saving grace of Port Nolloth and it is now a lovely, quirky village with well-developed tourism facilities.

The Anenous Pass

Meanwhile, back in the nineteenth century, the Cape Copper Company applied for an extension of the narrow-gauge railway from Muishond to their mine at O'okiep. This was granted in 1871 and work began on the Anenous Pass section (which climbs an imperial 1330 feet in only seven and a half miles).

The railway finally reached O'okiep in 1876 at a total cost of £170 000, including the complementary jetty at Port Nolloth. This is a bargain when you consider that an estimated £500 000 of lower grade ore was stockpiled at the mines, just waiting for cost-effective access to markets.

At first, teams of mules were used to pull railroad trucks along the track (as was stipulated in the various government acts that authorised the construction of the line). However, Hall wanted to try a steam engine. Two of these locomotives arrived in 1871 and were put to use over a section of the line. But they required a lot of water (not good in a desert) and often broke down. So, the trusty mules were put back into service and continued to pull coaches along the track as follows: freight trucks were grouped into threes and pulled by six mules in single file, while passenger 'specials' were pulled by three mules. This was doubled for the uphill section of the Anenous Pass and mule teams were changed every 28 miles.

The only notable exception to this system was on the down run, when cars were tied together at the top of the pass and allowed to coast all the way down to Port Nolloth, with only a brakeman checking the speed. If that sounds hairy consider that when going up the pass, a man sat at the front of the train scooping sand onto the tracks to prevent the wheels from slipping. Contemporary passenger accounts are filled with wonder and terror in equal measures.

From 1878, the light rails were replaced by heavier tracks in anticipation of the re-introduction of steam locomotives. This took place in 1886, when special condenser-type engines were brought in. These didn't work too well in the high temperatures, however, and were soon replaced with Kitson 'mountain type' locomotives. This shortened travel time from two days (during which people would overnight at the Klipfontein Hotel, at the top of Anenous Pass) to a brisk eight-hour jaunt. By 1896, steam traction was used along the entire line, although mule teams were still maintained for times of drought.

All in all, the railway line was a huge success and Namaqualand's copper fields finally got the transport solution they were looking for. But it wasn't all sunshine and light. The line, as you'll remember, was owned by the Cape Copper Company and things were often made difficult for both their rivals at Concordia Mine and members of the public. Although they were legally obligated to act in the interests of developing the country, discriminatory tariffs were charged and numerous complaints were laid.

However, the government was reluctant to act against the mighty Cape Copper Company and, after 10 years of operation, they declined to exercise their option to purchase the Port Nolloth line at the cost price of construction, thus forfeiting the right entirely. The Cape Copper Company was now pretty much free to do as they pleased.

But progress is inevitable, even in the wilds of Namaqualand. And in 1927, the South African Railways mainline from Cape Town reached Bitterfontein (200kms south of Springbok). Now, the mines found it more effective to transport ore via flat roads to the new railhead, effectively ending the life of the Port Nolloth railway. It remained in the possession of the O'okiep Copper Company (successor to the Cape Copper Company) and continued to operate until 1942. The line was sold for scrap in 1944. Remnants of the railway can still be seen in the pylons that now carry power lines over the mountains.

The road pass endured, however, and in 1950 John Williamson and Graham Ross were sent to upgrade the route. The new road opened in 1953 and was tarred in 1978. Graham Ross passed away a few years ago, aged in his nineties, but he was a generous correspondent and supportive reader. So, I'm sure he won't mind me quoting this story from his unpublished research project, in which he describes the life of a *padmaker* (road maker) in Namaqualand in the 1950s.

"We set off with John's wife so that we arrived at the top of the old pass at sunrise. We studied the mountainside through our binoculars. We pranced along the rim like mountain goats and looked down from the north, then retraced our steps and looked down from the south. We drove down the pass and looked at the mountain from the bottom. The existing road was far too steep to be considered for reconstruction, but we thought there might just be two possible new lines. So we drove up the escarpment again and, while Mrs Williamson took the car down to the bottom and off on a sand track to a position at the bottom of the first line, John and I started traversing down the mountainside with abney levels and flags. Halfway down we found that the first route would not 'go', and so we climbed up again and tried the second route. This one we were able to take to the bottom all right, but it was the sort of route that would have gladdened the heart of anyone who had a monopoly on the sale of explosives: very tough, very hard, and very expensive.

"By now it was well after midday in the middle of summer, and we were rather tired and hot and thirsty (John did not believe in carrying water, and he was the senior man!). Mrs Williamson was dutifully sitting in the shade of the car where we had thought the first traverse would come down, but we were quite a few kilometres to the north of that position, so there was nothing for it but to walk along the floor of the mountain to where the car was. The sand was soft, and we were strung around with abney levels and binoculars and were carrying the spare flags, and it seemed an awful long way to the car!

"To expand our field of investigations we arranged for the loan of the local mine inspector's jeep. Some days later we found ourselves jeeping along the old narrow-gauge rail track. For some reason, all the culverts had been removed, leaving vertical sided ditches across the formation. Crossing these called for considerable ingenuity, and when we got to the steeper side-slope sections we loaded up some old sleepers and used these as rather precarious and creaking bridges. We finally worked our way around to the western face of the escarpment and to a point where we were able to see an attractive road route branching away from the rail track at a gradient steeper that permissible for trains. Success!

"We now had to get down from the mountain, and I assumed in my innocence that we would continue along the rail track, bridging the culverts as we went, however tedious that might be. But John looked at the mountainside, which I swear was steeper than the natural angle of repose of the material, grinned, did a series of nifty backing and filling manoeuvres which got the jeep facing downhill, and said 'Right! Let's go!' I held on to all the odd bits of jeep which I could get to with my hands and feet while we were off straight down that scree slope, accompanied by a cloud of dust, stones and rocks. It was a wonderful experience, but not one which I would willingly repeat. In hindsight we were probably lucky the jeep kept going straight, but John did it - and I must say it was nice not to have to walk back to the car through the soft sand when we got to the bottom.

"This pass route was developed and found to be so superior to the alternatives that it was used as a tie point and the road was relocated both to the east and the west to fit in with it. The pass was built to gravel standards at a cost of 62 000 pounds, and opened by the Minister of Transport in July 1953.

"The pass has now been surfaced, and today is a very pleasant drive. If you pause halfway down at the view point on the neck and look off to the south through your binoculars, and if the sun is in the right position, you may pick up the scar of the old Anenous Pass down the escarpment, and then you realise how really steep it was."

Diamonds in the Sand

The Namaqualand copper fields were already in decline when a new form of mineral wealth was discovered in the desolate north - diamonds! We've already seen (if you've been reading carefully) how millions of years ago, diamond-bearing Kimberlite pipes intruded from the Earth's mantle to the surface. From here, the diamondiferous gravel was washed away into the Orange River and carried all the way down, into the Atlantic Ocean. The northern Namaqualand coast and the southern Namibian shore are thus lined with several diamond-bearing terraces, located both above and below the current waterline.

Strangely, none of the early explorers and prospectors who roamed the region recorded any trace of these gems, and the secret wealth of Namaqualand lay hidden for hundreds of years. Until, in the late 1800s, a German named Franz Lüderitz set off from Angra Pequena (now Lüderitz Bay) on a prospecting mission.

Lüderitz was an interesting bloke. He was a merchant from Bremen who had grown bored of working in the family business. One day, he looked at a map of Africa and saw an empty space that no other colonial power had yet claimed. He decided that he would take it since "nothing better (was) left".

In 1882, he approached the German government and got their permission for his venture. Then, through an agent named Vogelsang, Lüderitz persuaded the local chief, Joseph Fredericks, to sell him a large chunk of land around Angra Pequena for 10 000 Reichsmarks and 260 rifles.

Within a few months, Vogelsang made several additional purchases and Lüderitz became the proud owner of a huge territory that stretched from the north bank of the Orange River to the Kunene River. Fearing that the British would annex his new possession, Lüderitz asked the Imperial German government to take control of the land as a protectorate. This was completed by 1885 and German South West Africa was born, with Lüderitz retaining several key concessions.

Somehow, a year later, Lüderitz was broke so he sold his concessions to a chartered company, the Deutsche Kolonialgesellschaft für Südwest Africa. And with that, he set off on a fateful journey to discover yet more valuable minerals in the sandy wastes of his newly created colony.

These explorations took him down to the north bank of the Orange River, where he unpacked a small boat from his wagon and proceeded to sail down to the river mouth (at modern-day Alexander Bay) before turning the vessel north, heading back along the coast to his eponymous bay.

Regrettably, Lüderitz disappeared *en route* and is presumed to have drowned in the dark, cold Atlantic waters off the aptly named Skeleton Coast. Later, rumours would hold that he had indeed discovered diamonds on this expedition but died before he could tell anyone.

The first official diamond find was made 22 years later, in 1908, when a railway worker named Zacharias Lewala picked up some shiny pebbles on a beach near Lüderitz Bay. Lewala showed the gems to his supervisor, August Stauch, who immediately applied for a mining permit. News of the find spread like wildfire, sparking a major diamond rush. It was said that the diamonds were so abundant, all you had to do was crawl along the beach and scoop them up. They were even supposedly visible in the moonlight!

But the German Colonial Government simply couldn't tolerate such disorderliness and, once they realised the diamond fields were no flash in the pan, stepped in to institute control. A central market was established in 1909 and, in 1911, a Sperrgebiet or 'Forbidden Zone' was declared. This vast single-concession area, cordoned off by a double-line of tall, barbed-wire fences, extended 360 km northwards from the Orange River mouth and 100 km inland from the coast.

The first mining town to be established in the area was at Kolmanskop, where 5 million carats were recovered in just 6 years of mining. The town grew so rich that, apocryphally, water was shipped in from Cape Town just to irrigate the rose gardens. Kolmanskop also got electricity at a time when most towns in Germany still had gas streetlights, and the first X-ray machine in southern Africa was installed at Kolmanskop hospital.

After the First World War, however, Germany lost control of South West Africa and South Africa took over. The diamonds of SWA were thus up for grabs and Sir Ernest Oppenheimer (who had just established the Anglo American Corporation) was quick off the mark. He swiftly formed Consolidated Diamond Mines of South West Africa (CDM) in 1920 and, in 1923, CDM signed the Halbscheid Agreement with the South West African Administration. This granted CDM exclusive mining rights for the Sperrgebiet.

In 1928, soon after Oppenheimer assumed effective control of the De Beers diamond cartel, vast diamond reserves were found around the Orange River mouth and operations moved away from Kolmanskop. The company-built town of Oranjemund was established by CDM in 1936, and Kolmanskop was abandoned in the 1950s. It is now a well-known and photogenic ghost town, slowly being devoured by the smothering desert sand.

CDM continued to operate out of Oranjemund and, after Namibian independence in 1990, the company became Namdeb – a partnership with De Beers and the new Namibian government, which retained all of CDM's old concessions. Today, Oranjemund is still the centre of Namdeb's operations and is reached by crossing the Oppenheimer Bridge over the Orange River, just outside Alexander Bay.

Once highly restricted, Oranjemund is now opening up for tourism and permits for visitors are no longer required. They have also tarred the road from Oranjemund to Namdeb's most important onshore mines at Rosh Pinah, Deberas and Sendelingsdrift. This fancy new thoroughfare can used as part of your journey through the |Ai-|Ais-Richtersveld Transfrontier Conservation Area (see *Richtersveld National Park* below).

The 26 000 square km Forbidden Territory remains inviolable, however, and special permission must be arranged for visitors. Even so, now that the onshore diamonds are finally running out, there are plans to create a Sperrgebiet National Park, which will grant the public access to this pristine stretch of the Skeleton Coast for the first time in a century.

Today, it is thought that Namibia has the richest diamond reserves in the world. More than 100 million carats have been recovered since 1908 (about 55% onshore and 45% from the sea floor) and there's still an estimated 1.5 billion carats waiting in reserve. All in all, diamonds currently make up about 45% of Namibia's GDP.

Diamonds in the Richtersveld

Over on the south side of the Orange River, the diamonds of Namaqualand lay similarly undisturbed until the early part of the 20th century when several prospectors began picking their way along the coastline. Fred Cornell was the best known of this generation of fortune-seekers. He spent 20 years in South Africa and his wanderings took him through most of Namaqualand, the Richtersveld and Namibia. As he went, he kept his eyes peeled for gold, copper and diamonds, but he didn't report any significant finds. Instead, he wrote a book called 'The Glamour of Prospecting', which was exceedingly popular.

Some say that Cornell did indeed find diamonds but kept it a secret. And it does seem hard to believe that he could spend so much time in the area and not stumble across a single gem (although many others had come before Cornell without finding anything gemological). In any event, Cornell served with honour in World War I and received an award from the Royal Geographical Society for his work. Sadly, while in London, he died in motorcycle accident, in 1921.

Then, there was Ernest Martin, from Aus in Namibia, who supposedly found diamonds at the Orange River mouth sometime in the early 1920s. The story goes that he put up beacons to mark the claim but didn't get round to working it - which seems rather daft - and nothing came of the discovery.

It was only with Jack Carstens' discovery of 1925 that the ball really got rolling. Carstens was from Port Nolloth, the son of a storekeeper who moonlighted as the local Reuters correspondent. One day, Jack was exploring the Oubeep farm, south of the port, when he picked up a shiny lump of rock. Once confirmed, news of the first diamond on the Namaqualand coast spread fast, thanks to Jack's dad's newspaper connections. The hunt was on and dozens of treasure hunters headed up to Port Nolloth, to see what they could uncover.

The next find was made soon afterwards by Robert Kennedy, an experienced prospector who was taking a swim in the cold water off 'The Cliffs', north of Port Nolloth. By chance, Kennedy looked up at spotted a chunk of diamond-bearing rock in the bluff. He would recover 14 diamonds from the site.

Then, amazingly, a teacher spotted a rough diamond embedded in the wall of a newly built school building on the farm Kleinzee, near the mouth of the Buffels River. Jack Carstens was called in and a syndicate was formed to buy the farm. Within a week, 500 carats had been recovered.

Meanwhile, another prospector named Solomon Rabinowitz was scratching around in the gravel beds near the mouth of the Orange. Hidden among the oyster shells, he found 334 diamonds. Clearly, there were rich pickings to be had and, by 1926, the mining rights to most of Alexander Bay had been snapped up. After some consolidation, the lower elevations were effectively claimed by the Luderitzbucht Syndicate, and the upper elevations by 'Caplan's Syndicate' (headed by a storekeeper from Port Nolloth).

That same year, the famous German geologist Hans Merensky bustled into Namaqualand. He had a theory that the diamonds were linked to fossilised oyster beds on old marine terraces. He quickly formed another syndicate with Dr Ernst Reuning, Dr IB Celliers and J.J Buschau to search for this 'oyster line'.

Things were now hotting up, with deals being brokered at a feverish pace. Accordingly, a police sergeant, Van Wyk, sold his claim to Caplan for £15 and Caplan then gave Merensky permission to inspect the upper levels of this claim, unaware of his 'oyster line' theory. While this was going on, Reuning offered to buy the claim from Caplan and a price of £17 500 was agreed on. Almost immediately thereafter, a 16.5 carat octahedron was found.

With Caplan kicking himself, Merensky scrambled to find the money to pay for the claim before the offer expired. A deal was subsequently made with HO Althauer and Julius Jeppe to form HM Associates, with Merensky getting 50% of the company and the other two backers getting 25% each. Merensky's previous partners were thus pushed out of the deal and Reuning only got a token £150 pounds per month, plus a bonus of £5000 pounds if the claim was successful.

With the stakes rising, Merensky optimistically applied to the Minister of Mines for a mineral lease over all public lands in the area, but this was refused. Instead, the government forbade prospecting on crown lands and transferred all mineral rights to the crown. The only exception to this was the private farm Kleinzee, which was offered to the government for £200. Inexplicably, the sale was turned down and Kleinzee was sold to the Cape Coast Exploration Company instead. This enterprise was later bought by De Beers, which continued to operate the Kleinzee mine until its recent closure.

In the face of a government clamp-down, Merensky's HM Associates fought to have their original claim recognised by the Department of Mines. This was eventually accomplished, along with a further 5 claims the company had purchased. The first shipment of diamonds from Merensky's workings totalled 12 253.5 carats, and Ernest Oppenheimer immediately bought a 74% interest in HM Associates.

Then, in 1927, a Precious Stone Bill was passed that empowered the government to establish a State Alluvial Diggings around Alexander Bay, leading to the creation of the company known today as Alexkor. The Bill also allowed for the state to monitor and control the output of all diamond producers. This was bad news for HM Associates who, by now, had recovered 461 393 carats. Fearing an oversupply, the government froze the sale of Merensky's diamonds.

In 1929, Merensky sold the remainder of his company to Oppenheimer for £3 million and HM Associates went into voluntary liquidation. In 1932, the Merensky diamonds were ceded to the Diamond Corporation, a newly established central-selling organisation that sought to control the sale of all South African diamonds; manipulating the release of gemstones to market in order to keep prices buoyant. Finally, in 1937, the Merensky diamonds were put on sale in London. Additional sales were held at the New York World Fair of 1939 and in Bermuda, a few years later.

In the decades that followed, Alexkor built a town at Alexander Bay which was, until recently, highly restricted. Meanwhile, De Beers expanded their operations from Kleinzee to include the Koingnaas Complex near Hondeklip Bay. And, in the 1960s, a newly formed company secured leases along the southern banks of the Orange River. This became the TransHex Corporation, which (until recently) mined at Sanddrift, Baaken and Reuning, close to the Richtersveld National Park.

Most of the Namaqualand diamond mines did exceedingly well. De Beers alone recovered 31 million carats in 75 years. And, at Reuning, a 43-metre-deep splash pool in the Orange River collected a glut of diamondiferous deposits containing as much as 41 carats per 100 tons of gravel. This so-called 'Glory Hole' has now yielded gems worth a modern equivalent of R4 billion.

Diamonds in the Sea!

But those glory days are in the past. Today, Namaqualand's onshore diamond fields are almost worked out and attention has shifted to marine deposits on the sea floor. The exploitation of underwater diamonds began with a Texan oilman, Sam Collins, who had a company that specialised in sub-marine pipelines. In the early 1960s, Collins heard a story about a farmer who was pumping up diamondiferous gravel off the Namibian coastline. He leapt into action, bought the farmer's concession, and started working out ways to profitably suck up sand from the seabed.

Obviously, De Beers kept a close eye on Collins' Marine Diamond Corporation and, as soon as they saw the scheme was payable, bought him out in 1965. Between 1961 and 1970, around 1.5 million carats were recovered from 20 meters below the ocean surface.

A slump in diamond prices caused De Beer's to abandon the sea-diamond enterprise in 1971, but prospecting continued. Then, in the early 1990s, sea-diamond mining resumed as the supply of onshore diamonds began drying up.

Today, Debmarine (a joint venture between De Beers and the Namibian government) delivers 70% of that country's diamond output. In 2018 alone, Debmarine produced 1.4 million carats and (as per their website) "our unique recovery technology has further ensured that the seabed is largely restored to its natural state after our operations move on".

So, clearly, sea diamonds are big business. In 2003, for example, a team near Alexander Bay found the Cirrus Diamond, a fabulous 111-carat gemstone. But it's also a risky proposition, and both Alexkor and De Beers have divided up their respective ocean areas, assigning several concessions to independent contractors.

These 'blocks' are now worked by small diamond boats, which slurp up gravel from the seabed through a big tube operated by a diver. Boats also use a technique whereby water is pushed down through a powerful jet, which shifts aside the thick sediment to reveal the coveted gems buried within.

Once on the boat, the gravel is packed into sacks and sent to onshore sorting facilities (security concerns usually forbid concessionaires from sorting on board). These semi-independent diamond boats have now become a valuable source of employment in an impoverished region, although rough seas and adverse weather conditions limit the number of days that boats can go out.

Diamonds Aren't Forever

Despite the on-going success of sea diamond operations, the output of onshore mines continues to dwindle. Many have already closed and the ones still operating have a life expectancy of just 5 to 10 years.

Accordingly, De Beers has drastically scaled back operations at their two South African mines, Kleinzee and Koingnaas. And the state-owned Alexkor is on the verge of bankruptcy due to dwindling yields (although mismanagement and corruption have certainly played a role too).

So, with the imminent shuttering of mines and unemployment in the region skyrocketing, there is a question of what to do next.

It is hoped that tourism could step in and at least partially fill the economic gap left by departing diamond mines. Alexander Bay opened its gates to visitors a few years back, and the private villages of Kleinzee and Koingnaas are currently transitioning into public towns. Furthermore, the extensive land holdings of the various mining operations have ensured that the coastline is in relatively pristine condition, and De Beers has already contracted large tracts of land for incorporation into the Namaqua National Park. One hopes that other compelling tourist facilities are developed in future, to help sustain the resident population.

Land Affairs

The indigenous people of Namaqualand always came second, especially with regards to land rights. This subjugation began with the arrival of white farmers and was continued by the mines. In the far north of the territory, however, the natives were getting restless.

As early as 1842, a memorandum was presented to the government by Steinkopf missionaries on behalf of the local people. This was occasioned by rumours that the Cape Colony was going to extend its northern border to the Orange River, thereby annexing the hitherto 'unclaimed' Richtersveld. The colonial government confidently replied that there were no plans to move the boundary, or "of interfering with the rights of those inhabiting the country beyond the boundary, by granting those lands to colonial farmers". These words rang a bit hollow since land beyond the frontier had already been granted to farmers (as early as 1776), and no formal 'ticket of occupation' was granted to the residents of Steinkopf.

In 1846, new rumours about the annexation of northern Namaqualand started bubbling up from the Cape. This time, there was some consultation with local chiefs about the plan, one of whom commented that "what the great chief or governor does, I cannot object to; but this only I say, that I will keep my ground, for me and my people, in order to lead a quiet and honest life".

In 1847, the freshly installed governor, Sir Harry Smith, unilaterally moved the borders of the colony north to the Orange River and east to the Keiskamma, roughly doubling the size of the territory. And he did this without explicit permission from London, nor did he consult with any Boer or Xhosa representatives.

It was a *fait accompli,* but no official government officers were installed in the Richtersveld so the missionaries and chiefs were left to go about their business in the usual way. Nevertheless, it was an uncertain time.

In 1851, Rev. Brecher of the Steinkopf mission again wrote to the government requesting clarity regarding the land rights of indigenous people in the area. He noted that "the chiefs and natives residing here wish to be placed under the protection of the British Government, and that the ground occupied by them may be reserved for their occupancy against the encroachments of farmers, traders, or any others wishing to settle on the same, as much unpleasantness has already arisen on this point".

In reply to this entreaty, the Colonial Secretary wrote back, saying the government would not "countenance any encroachments on the land occupied by the people of the institutions...nor has His Excellency any desire to disturb them in his occupancy". But the desired ticket of occupation was still not granted to the indigenous residents and tenure on their ancestral land wasn't guaranteed beyond these vague promises.

The matter came to a head in 1853, at the start of the copper boom, when the Namaqua Mining Company applied to the government for a lease on a promising mining centre at Tweefontein (later Concordia). This lease was happily granted but when the first miners arrived, they were greeted with a letter from Rev. Brecher pointing out that their new mine was actually located within the mission's grounds. Speaking on behalf of the local people, Brecher went on to say that the land was protected by the government's previous letter which had promised not to countenance any encroachment, etc.

Reluctant to start a ruckus, the Namaqua Mining Company signed a deal with the Steinkopf office bearers that granted the mine exclusive mineral rights over the ground in exchange for £100. The company then wrote to the government asking them about the legality of the whole situation, as they didn't want to pay twice. The reply was predictably self-serving. As far as the government was concerned, they had only guaranteed the people of Steinkopf would not be ejected from the land. Furthermore, said land was now the property of the crown by virtue of the same letter of 'protection' brandished by Brecher.

As such, the government retained all mineral rights to the land and held that any deal entered into between the company and the Steinkopf mission had nothing to do with them. The NMC had to negotiate a new deal and, by appealing for protection, the people of Steinkopf had inadvertently ceded their land to the government.

But the colonial authorities weren't heartless. They did graciously agree that the indigenous people should be compensated for the "use of land in respect of water and pasturage", and the NMC concluded an agreement with Steinkopf authorities for water and grazing rights (on condition that no alcohol be sold within mission lands).

The uncomfortable division between the occupational rights of indigenous people and the mineral rights to the land on which they lived was eventually clarified with the Mission Stations and Communal Reserves Act of 1909. This light-fingered piece of legislation explicitly "prohibited the 'natives' of the territory from any legal claims to mineral rights on the land which was reserved for them".

As a result, the locals were denied any direct benefit from the mining industries that had come to dominate the region. The only way they could make money from the boom was to take up employment on the mines, become domestic servants, or sell supplies to the mines.

Charles Bell, surveyor-general of the colony, believed that this was only fair and fitting. In an appalling and comprehensive display of contemporary racism, he wrote in the 1850s: "I asked [the indigenous people] if they were fit to open all the mines...or whether they could smelt and work up and use the copper themselves. The reply usually was 'no, no; take the copper, we can't raise it, and don't want it.'... You say you apprehend oppression; rest quiet...Are the present prices you receive for labour, for the carriage of ore, and for your crops, symptomatic of oppression? I think not, but your waste of these prices...in folly and vice, to the destruction of yourselves and your oxen, is an oppression from which no government can effectually shield you. And if, hereafter, your sons have difficulty in finding healthy and respectable wives of their own race, you will recollect, with bitterness, the drink, food, clothing, or indifference that induced you to shut your eyes while your daughters tempted the crowds of single men now landing on your coast."

Kuboes Mission Station

Meanwhile, up in the remote Richtersveld, the Kuboes mission station was being presided over by the good Reverend Hein of the Rhenish Church. The population was made up of NamaKhoi, some Bushmen and a couple of Baster families (formerly known as Bastaards).

A contemporary report states that "the inhabitants of Richtersfeld count only 47 families, comprising say 380 souls, nearly all of whom are Hottentots, with Paul Links, son of the late Captain Paul Links, as their headman; their live-stock consisting of about 50 horses, 560 horned cattle, and 3,200 sheep and goats. Most of them are very poor, and I fear they are in a retrogressive state."

The settlement was controlled by a *Groot Raad* (great council), which was made up of community-elected representatives and chaired by the head missionary. It oversaw the day-to-day affairs of the community including the "maintenance of order, settlement of disputes and granting of residence and grazing rights". The system was not without its critics but worked well enough until the above-mentioned Mission Stations and Communal Reserves Act forced the separation of civic and religious authorities, effectively replacing the missionaries with a secular Advisory or Management Board (made up of white outsiders).

To complicate matters, the precise boundaries of the Kuboes mission station (and, indeed, most mission stations in South Africa) were ill-defined. The people of the Richtersveld had been requesting clarity on the issue since the 1890s, as their land was being usurped constantly by various colonial and economic forces, but to no avail.

The community at Kuboes subsequently specified an area of nearly 700 000 morgen (600 000 hectares) as their traditional grazing land and requested an official ticket of occupation to guarantee their rights. But Mr S. Melvill, Second Assistant Surveyor-General, had other ideas.

In his report to Parliament 'in regard to lands occupied by natives on certain Missionary Institutions and other places in Namaqualand', Mevill stated that the claim was much too large. He suggested reducing the land to 450 000 morgen (385 600 hectares), conveniently excising most of the fertile land along the banks of the Orange as well as the coastal belt - in other words all the land that might be used for farming or fishing (diamonds had not yet been discovered).

As it happened, Melvill's expedient recommendations were ignored and no ticket of occupation was issued, as the locals were considered too primitive to look after themselves.

Despite the legal limbo, 5 farms on the coast were leased to white farmers in 1904. In 1919, a prominent farmer named Cloete even tried to claim the whole of the Richtersveld as his own, which provoked a bemused response from the Rev. Hein who said that "Richtersveld belongs to the Community, no individual can claim it". Then, when diamond fever struck in the 1920s, land around the Orange River mouth was leased to prospectors, even though this too was part of the Richtersveld community's original land claim.

Perhaps galvanised into action by the flurry of diamond mining, the South African government finally decided they'd better get around to settling the Richtersveld issue. Thus, between 1925 and 1926, a commission was set up to formulate recommendations. They decided that Melvill's proposed allocation was indeed incorrect - it was still too large. Another 143 000 morgen (122 500 hectares) was lopped off and the final size of the Richtersvelders' land amounted to just over 300 000 morgen, less than half their original claim.

This truncated territory was officially approved for the use of 'Hottentots and Bastards' under the authority of the Minister of Native Affairs, and a formal ticket of occupation (or reservation) was issued by the Minister of Lands in 1930 - although the land was still technically held in trust by the state.

A similar process played out at several other mission stations around the country and the resulting entities came to be known as 'coloured reserves' or 'coloured rural areas'. In Namaqualand, five of these were eventually established: Richtersveld, Steinkopf, Leliefontein, Komaggas and Concordia. Collectively, they were among the largest Coloured Reserves in the country, totalling over 1.5 million hectares.

The old management boards and councils were maintained as the de facto political authorities in these coloured areas. But, significantly, they now held the power to decide who qualified for 'citizenship' in the reserves and therefore who was entitled to housing, grazing land, voting rights in the council, etc.

Special concessions could also be granted to *bywoners* (literally sub-farmers or squatters who worked as herdsmen, sharecroppers or servants), as well as *vreemdelinge* (outsiders or strangers - including missionaries, traders, teachers and even some white farmers). These two groups could apply to the council for temporary housing and/or grazing land in exchange for gifts, tribute or service to the community.

The Bosluis Basters

By now, the various racial groups who lived in Namaqualand had intermingled and assimilated to a considerable extent. Although this resulted in a more peaceful co-existence between former rivals, the concept of a distinct Nama or Khoikhoi identity was severely undermined. This sense of 'nationhood' was further squelched by the apartheid-era population registration mania, which *sommer* classified the whole *bleddy* bunch of them as 'coloured'.

In effect, this meant that the former 'basters' came to assume a more prominent role in the political life of Namaqualand's coloured reserves. They were (relatively speaking) better off financially, numerically superior to the remnant Khoikhoi populations, and had the benefits of a more sustained education at the hands of the missionaries. In the Richtersveld, moreover, their presence was significantly bolstered by the arrival of the Bosluis Basters in 1949.

This new group of 'bastaards' had been forced to move from their home in the Pofadder district of Bushmanland by the Group Areas Act, an insidious piece of Apartheid legislation passed by the recently elected National Party in 1950. An extension of the old Land Act of 1913, this law stipulated that all racial groups had to be geographically segregated from one another - even within towns and cities - causing a string of forced removals that traumatised the country during the 1950s (including Sophiatown, District 6, South End, etc.).

And so, when the apartheid government of D.F. Malan cracked the whip, the Bosluis Basters (comprising about 68 families) had no choice but to pack their belongings into ox wagons and trek through the thirstlands in search of a new home. 300kms later, they arrived at their destination: the remote Richtersveld Coloured Reserve, long a dumping ground for unwanted and/or disreputable people.

It must have been a long and arduous journey, but they were assisted by the benevolent leadership of their pastor, Reverend Eksteen, who had been with the community since 1945. And so, after passing through Steinkopf and descending the Anenous Pass, they headed north for a bit and finally selected a site on the banks of a small spring called Stinkfontein, proper in the middle of nowhere. A church was soon built and the new settlement was named Eksteenfontein, in honour of their spiritual leader.

Incidentally, the Bosluis Basters get their name from their original home on the farm Bo-Sluis (above the sluice) and not from the Afrikaans word 'bosluis', which refers to a parasitic bush tick or louse. It's also worth noting that the equally unfortunate term 'baster', which is derived from the earlier form 'bastaard', is maintained with some degree of pride by several groups (including the Rehoboth Basters in Namibia). Several commentators have written that the fondness for this outdated appellation dates back to the 1800s, when their status as 'half-castes' distinguished them as being somewhat less inferior than 'hottentots' and other natives.

In any event, the arrival of the Bosluis Basters proved to be somewhat disconcerting to the local Khoikhoi. I was told that, at first, the two groups were rather wary of one another and, as recently as the 1980s, a marriage between a Nama and a Baster would raise eyebrows in Eksteenfontein. Today, however, the various demographics in the Richtersveld have become unified as a community and work together for the good of all (or as much as can be expected).

In closing off this section, allow me to mention that the Group Areas Act did cut both ways - occasionally. In the 1950s, about nine white farmers found themselves technically squatting on a coloured reserve and were removed from the Richtersveld. These included: the Avenant family who farmed at De Hoop in the present-day Richtersveld National Park (the graves of several Avenant children can still be seen if you know where to look), the Van Rensburgs who had a homestead at Grasdrif, the Graaff family at Gelykwerf, the de Vries brothers who farmed on the summit of the Vandersterrberg and at Koeskop, and the Bosman family who resided at Stinkfontein.

The Rebirth of a Community

In 1957, the 'coloured reserve' of the Richtersveld was given a tangible boundary with the erection of a fence that ran between communal lands and the privately owned 'corridor' farms along the river and coast. This physically curtailed the movements of the nomadic Nama herders and dealt a heavy blow to their old patterns of transhumance.

Even worse, the remaining communal land was now getting overgrazed and the subsistence lifestyle of stock farmers became unsustainable. Many people decamped from their villages to the mines, farms, fishing boats, towns and faraway cities in search of wage labour. The community of the Richtersveld was in what appeared to be terminal decline.

Today, less than 10% of NamaKhoi consider themselves farmers and most of these are elderly. The old stock posts are still inhabited to a degree but, again, it's the old folk who remain, with children only visiting on weekends and holidays. After all, it's a tough life out in the wilds with no mod-cons, a harsh climate and very little water, which is often brackish with high levels of fluoride and other unpalatable minerals. This causes white flecking and dark brown staining of the teeth, which is sometimes called the trademark of Namaqualand.

Meanwhile, the diamond mining industry on the coast was flourishing. In 1989, the Alexander Bay Development Corporation was established by the government to take over all 'assets, liabilities, rights and obligations of the... State Alluvial Diggings'. This generous deal included formal ownership of the land around the Orange River Mouth and all the lovely diamonds therein. Three years later, the entity was converted by an act of parliament into a company named Alexkor Limited, with the government as the sole shareholder. Title deeds to the land and all associated mineral rights were transferred to Alexkor by 1995.

But change was in the air. The democratic elections of 1994 ushered in a new era for South Africa, including a policy of land restitution in the form of compensation or reclamation. Accordingly, a new law was passed - the Restitution of Land Rights Act of 1994.

This landmark act (pardon the pun) made it possible for communities or individuals who had been unjustly removed from their land to lodge a claim, so as to "provide for the restitution of rights in land to persons or communities dispossessed of such rights after 19 June 1913 as a result of past racially discriminatory laws or practices". 69 000 land claims were subsequently lodged across the country.

In the Richtersveld, the *Sida !hub* Communal Property Association (CPA) was formed to make a land claim on Alexkor's properties, which extended for 85 000 hectares along the coast between Port Nolloth and Alexander Bay. This was duly lodged before the specified date of 31 December 1998 and heard by the Land Claims Court in 2000.

The plaintiffs in the case comprised various local communities and stakeholders, namely the people of Kuboes, Sanddrift, Lekkersing and Eksteenfontein. Due to the valuable nature of the claim, it was fiercely contested by both Alexkor Limited and the new, democratically elected government of the Republic of South Africa.

The defendants (Alexkor and the government) threw everything they had at the Richtersvelders. It was said they weren't a real community; that they didn't 'beneficially' inhabit the land because they were nomadic; that they had been deprived of the land by virtue of the 1847 annexation of Namaqualand, which fell outside the mandated 1913 cut-off date. And so on.

Although most of these tactics failed to win support from the judges, the 2001 judgement did rule that the claim was invalid. This was primarily because the court found that the community had not been removed from the land as a result of any 'racially discriminatory laws' since white farmers and prospectors had also been removed by the same process.

The community appealed the finding and the Supreme Court of Appeal overturned the Land Court's decision, stating that "their dispossession resulted from a racially discriminatory practice in that it was based upon and proceeded from the premise that due to their lack of civilisation, to which their race was inextricably linked, the Richtersveld people had no rights in the subject land". Round 2 to the Richtersvelders.

But Alexkor and the government appealed the appeal and took the case all the way to the Constitutional Court. The ConCourt also found in favour of the community and the land was finally and unequivocally granted to the people of the Richtersveld in 2003. Several years of negotiation followed until, in April 2007, an agreement was reached between Alexkor and the Richtersveld community.

Then, just weeks before the whole deal went before the Land Claims Court for final ratification, a dissident group of Richtersvelders lodged a complaint against the already-signed contract. Apparently, there were some problematic clauses and it was claimed that the wider community had not been consulted about finer details of the deal.

For a few nerve-wracking weeks, it looked like it could all go pear-shaped. But last-minute negotiations successfully resolved the crisis and on the 9th of October 2007, Land Claims Court Judge Antonie Gildenhuys confirmed the revised settlement. The legal battle had taken almost 10 years and cost the government over R50 million, but the people of the Richtersveld had triumphed.

Diamonds on the Soles of their Shoes

On the 1st of December 2007, Public Enterprises Minister Alec Erwin (the man responsible for contesting the claim) and Land Affairs Minister Lulu Xingwana formally handed over the title deeds of Alexkor's land to the Richtersveld leaders. Willem Diergaardt was quoted in the press as saying "I am overwhelmed with joy. I can't hold back my tears". He went on to say that there was going to be a celebration in the Richtersveld "and I can promise you it will not be a little celebration. It will be a celebration like South Africa has never seen before". Minister Erwin wryly commented that it was a "great occasion after an amazing legal battle".

The final settlement was intended to provide the community with some form of reparation for all the diamonds previously extracted from their land. It also looked to the future by establishing a financial foundation for ongoing development. More significantly, perhaps, it properly acknowledged the land rights of the Richtersvelders for the first time. In this sense, the legal battle was about more than money. It was about validating the cultural identity of a people after hundreds of years of mistreatment.

Briefly, the main terms of the Alexkor deal were as follows: The state handed over 194 600ha of land including the crucial 84 000ha of diamond territory along the coast and a strip of fertile land along the Orange River, which supports citrus, oyster and ostrich farms. It also granted the community an 'extraordinary reparation payment' of R190 million, a development grant of R50 million, and R45 million for property development.

Going forward, Alexkor wanted to continue mining but the government couldn't afford to buy the land back. So, a new mining company was established with the Richtersveld community holding 49% to Alexkor's 51%. This Alexkor/RMC JV (Richtersveld Mining Company Joint Venture) was granted all land mineral rights over the settlement area but, crucially, Alexkor maintained sole control of the marine rights.

With the stability of a signed settlement in place, numerous development plans were floated and predictions of prosperity for the impoverished region poured forth. The state was talking about a much-needed re-capitalisation programme and the Alexkor-owned town of Alexander Bay was transferred to the community. Plus, thanks to the efforts of those 'dissident' community members, all of Alexkor's obligations were underwritten by the state, particularly with regard to the rehabilitation of the landscape after decades of mining. Several 'good governance' clauses were also included to control the behaviour of the various community trusts and companies that would need to be established in the wake of the historic settlement.

So far, so good. But who exactly is this 'community' that would reap all the rewards? Well, the ownership of the land first had to be determined in terms of the Transformation of Certain Rural Areas Act of 1998. Under this legislation, communities could decide whether the ownership of former 'coloured reserve' land should be lodged with a Communal Property Association (CPA), given over to a local municipality, or split up and granted to individual owners.

In 2002, the various communities within the Richtersveld voted to transfer ownership of the land to a CPA which would own and administer the land on behalf of the people. This entity had already been established the previous year as the *Sida !Hub* CPA. It includes every adult member of the four Richtersveld towns (Eksteenfontein, Kuboes, Lekkersing and Sanddrift) where adult members are those over the age of 18 who have lived in any of the towns for five years or more.

The aims of the CPA include "improvement of the infrastructure, development of agriculture, tourism, and economic opportunities to support job creation, and capacity building of committee members so that they can make the right decisions on behalf of the community". Each division of the CPA has community directors, one from each town, as well as independent directors who are appointed either by the CPA or its trustees. The Richtersveld Community Conservancy (RCC) was also established to oversee the tourism and environmental activities of the CPA.

To accomplish all this, the CPA set up a number of commercial companies to run their now considerable interests. There was an agricultural company to develop the farms along the Orange River, an environmental rehabilitation company to reverse the damage done by years of mining, a property holding company responsible for renting out the houses in Alexander Bay, and a mining company to administer the community's 49% holding in Alexkor/RCM JV.

So, the future was looking bright for the Richtersvelders. They had their land. They had a substantial amount of money for development. And they had a large share in a major diamond mining company. Not bad for a bunch of Hottentots, Bushmen and Bastaards.

Land Claim Blues

Unfortunately, that's where the good news ends (at least for now). And since signing the settlement in 2007, very little has been accomplished. Instead, the CPA quickly split into factions that began suing each other in a hailstorm of accusations and counter accusations. R50 million went missing. Community in-fighting meant that the network of operating companies became dysfunctional. And so on.

Meanwhile, Alexkor (through a combination of corruption, theft, mismanagement, and dwindling diamond yields) is currently on the verge of bankruptcy. Plans to partner with De Beers and Transhex (the two other diamond miners in the region) to establish a joint diamond cutting and processing plant in Alexander Bay have come to naught. And ambitious dreams of improved infrastructure, better public services, entrepreneurial loans for small businesspeople, and an agricultural school remain firmly in the pipe.

Frustration at the stalemate has been expressed across the board. A progress report from the Department of Public Enterprises dated February 2018 seems exasperated at the "ever-present conflict" between members of the Communal Property Association, and stresses that a long-overdue payment of R45 million cannot be made to the beneficiaries because "no department between the Department of Public Enterprises and Department of Rural Development and Land Reform - is known to be leading the process. Each department is seen to be dilly-dallying and procrastinating on work to be done."

Alexkor, for its part, is ominously warning that the onshore diamonds are rapidly running out (they give it 10 years max) and stresses that plans for the long-term sustainability of these isolated communities need to be put in place ASAP. Meanwhile, tension in the Richtersveld mounts as small-town rivalries grow vicious in the face of real money, and the continued lack of development drives people deeper into perpetual poverty.

So, not great. But there is something you can do to help. Tourism is one potential lifeline for the region. After all, the landscape is utterly humbling, the botanical diversity is astounding and (although it's far away) a trip to the Richtersveld is truly unforgettable. In the *Planning Guide* below, you'll find all the info you need to visit for yourself.

Saving the Landscape

The landscape of Namaqualand is unique and unforgettable. Its barren beauty may not be as eager to please as the more obsequious vistas of the western Cape or the Garden Route, but its unmistakable majesty is imprinted on the mind of every visitor. Thankfully, this precious and precarious ecosystem is now being preserved in a number of conservation areas.

The glorious Namaqua National Park, located near the village of Kamieskroon, is one such reserve. It was originally established as the Skilpad Wildflower Garden by the World Wildlife Fund for Nature in 1988, with SA National Parks (SANParks) taking over in 1998. The NNP was formally declared in 2002. Since then, it has grown in leaps and bounds - from a small landlocked pocket into a large conservation area covering 140 000ha. This rapid expansion was facilitated thanks to the co-operation of local farmers and the De Beers mining company, who contractually handed over a 50km stretch of untouched coastline to SANParks in 2008.

Meanwhile, the first attempt to formally protect the dramatic mountain desert of the Richtersveld began in 1975, when the then-National Parks Board agreed to investigate the establishment of a new reserve in the far north. However, this was communal land that couldn't be bought, transferred or otherwise appropriated. It took nearly 20 years of negotiations with the local council to reach a deal.

Finally, by 1989, a contract had been drawn up. Then, just as the park was about to be proclaimed, a group from a 'Community Committee' lodged an injunction against the whole process. According to them, the council was 'unrepresentative and autocratic' and the community had not been given an opportunity to provide their input.

In truth, the terms of the original contract were extremely prejudicial against the local people. The 99-year lease stipulated that all livestock had to be removed from the park, no resources (plants or water) could be utilised, and there were no employment guarantees for community members. In other words, the establishment of the park would have entirely excluded the local people from land they had lived on for over 2000 years. It seemed as if the Parks Board wanted to save the land from the locals instead of for the locals.

The signing ceremony was postponed, and a series of meetings was held with all parties concerned. During these consultations, the Parks Board came to a realisation that local populations were, in general, an important component of any conservation initiative (both in terms of environmental management, ownership and as visitors). Furthermore, in the case of the Richtersveld, the indigenous people were actually an integral part of the eco-system with a traditional lifestyle that was just as endangered as any rare succulent.

A new contract was subsequently drawn up with much more equitable terms. The lease was reduced to 30 years, the grazing rights of local people were acknowledged (subject to a limitation of 6600 small stock units), access to natural resources within the park was similarly allowed, and a certain number of jobs were reserved for local people.

With this agreement in place, a joint management committee was established to run the park and the contract was signed in July 1991. This was the first contractual national park in South Africa (independently owned land, jointly managed by the Parks Board and the local community). Later, this model would be used to help solve the thorny issue of land claims in other conservation areas, such as the Makuleke concession area within the Kruger National Park.

In any case, the newly established 162 000-hectare Richtersveld National Park (RNP) was born and it was a very rugged baby indeed. Roads were virtually non-existent, campsites were super-basic, and the wilderness reigned supreme. Nevertheless, for the adventurer who really wanted to get away from it all, this was heaven.

Unfortunately, for a place so disconnected from the modern world, there were some very contemporary complaints from the local community. This mainly revolved around the stipulated registration of herders (only 28 families were allowed into the park at its inception) and the selective appointment of staff members.

Today, however, things are much more settled. The community has come to accept the park on its doorstep. Campsites boast attractive ablution facilities that complement the landscape. The roads are much improved (although a 4x4 is still required). And there are even several well-appointed chalets and hutted camps available. This is a cause of distress for old-timers who miss the untamed wildness of the original park, but most visitors will be thrilled by the current combination of untrammelled nature and moderate creature comforts.

Meanwhile, up in Namibia, the Ai-Ais Hot Springs Game Park had been declared between 1968 and 1988, a conservation area that included the mighty Fish River Canyon. In 2002, the formidable Huns and Chum mountains were also incorporated to form a vast 440 600-hectare reserve that stretched all the way down to the Orange River, adjacent to the RNP.

This paved the way for the formation of a Trans-Frontier Conservation Area (TFCA), defined as "the area or component of a large ecological region that straddles the boundaries of two or more countries, encompassing one or more protected areas as well as multiple resource use areas". The hugely important

TFCA process is spearheaded by the Peace Parks Foundation and there are many TFCAs in various stages of development across southern Africa.

In terms of the |Ai-|Ais-Richtersveld TFCA, discussions began between Namibia and South Africa in 2000 and a memorandum of understanding was signed between the two state parties in 2001. Consultations were held with local stakeholders, and management plans were drawn up and signed in 2002. Finally, in 2003, the official treaty was signed by Presidents Thabo Mbeki of South Africa and Sam Nujoma of Namibia.

The |Ai-|Ais-Richtersveld TFCA currently measures around 6 000 square kms, but this is just the beginning. There are already plans in place to enlarge the protected area into an enormous Greater *!Gariep* TFCA. This ambitious project would incorporate several additional land units to create a truly mammoth Transfrontier Park that stretches from the Richtersveld to the sea and far into the north, incorporating the Namib-Naukluft Park, the *//Gamaseb* and Brukkaros Community Conservancies, the Orange River mouth, and the vast Sperrgebiet or Forbidden Territory along the Namibian coast (already declared a national park, but not yet developed). There is even a possibility that World Heritage status may be expanded to cover this entire area, but only once mining has ceased and the land has been rehabilitated.

And even that's not the full picture. Some environmental visionaries have formulated plans to create the Three Nations Namib Desert TFCA. This mega-park would stretch from the Richtersveld all the way to the Iona National Park in Angola. Although still in its early stages, this initiative seeks to "involve rural communities productively in conservation through sustainable use of natural resources and in local economic development". The possibilities are endless.

At the moment, however, all eyes are on the |Ai-|Ais-Richtersveld TFCA. And things are looking good. Visitor numbers are up and the TFCA process has already stimulated investment in the area. On the South African side, poverty alleviation funds have been used to upgrade roads, interpretation centres, entrance gates and rest camps in the RNP. A new border post has been opened at the Sendelingsdrift gate (where a pontoon ferries pedestrians and vehicles across the Orange River). And the entire region is hoping that tourism will provide some much-needed economic stimulation.

The other major conservation area in the Richtersveld is the Richtersveld Community Conservancy (RCC). This entity began life as a concept paper in 1998 and evolved hand in hand with the World Heritage application process. It was supported by various international and local heritage agencies (such as NORAD - the Norwegian Agency for Development Cooperation, the Northern Cape Department of Arts and Culture, and Eco-Africa environmental consultants).

Through extensive workshops and consultations, the conservancy concept firmed up as part of a wider Integrated Development Planning process for the region. The community thus got behind the idea of creating a heritage area where natural and cultural resources would be protected under a policy of sustainable development. Various management plans were drawn up and, in 2004, a management committee was elected with a full-time conservancy manager and administrative officer. The headquarters of the RCC are in Eksteenfontein.

In 2005, the Department of Environmental Affairs and Tourism (DEAT) coughed up R6 million to help the conservancy develop infrastructure and accommodation. The Northern Cape provincial administration also started negotiations to incorporate the adjacent (and wholly undeveloped) Helskloof/Nababeep Nature Reserve to the conservancy.

Today, the RCC is a remarkable place dedicated to biodiversity conservation, and plans have been mooted to establish a scientific research station. But it is also a cultural reserve where ancient human traditions of transhumance are protected and supported, so that they may resume their previous vitality.

Unfortunately, tourism is a double-edged sword because tourists are, by their very nature, destructive beasts. Their feet trample delicate plants, their cars (if driven irresponsibly) can scar the landscape, and their mere presence in a remote village can corrupt the very traditions that attracted them in the first place. And, with the fragile ecosystems of the RCC and RNP already under threat from overgrazing and other environmental factors, uncontrolled tourism could make matters worse.

So, all new tourism initiatives in the Richtersveld are carefully planned and monitored so that the tourist cash cow doesn't kill the ecological golden goose. In other words, all stakeholders in the region are working together to make sure that tourism and development strategies are being implemented in a responsible and sustainable manner that upholds the integrity of the site.

Luckily, thanks to its distant location and limited infrastructure, tourist numbers are unlikely to become overwhelming and the region remains relatively pristine. Less happily, developments in the Community Conservancy appear to have been paralysed by intractable in-fighting and little seems to have been accomplished in the decade since I visited. The RCC websites haven't been updated in many years and contact numbers go unanswered (although that may be a result of the coronavirus-related lockdown that is in effect at time of writing).

One can only hope that the RCC will emerge from this dark period of factionalism and re-gain its momentum. Because this is a truly special part of the world that deserves to be explored and developed in a suitable manner.

Exploring the Richtersveld

OK, faithful reader. We now know all about the history of Namaqualand and the Richtersveld. But how do you get there, where can you stay, when should you go, and what is there to do? The answers to all these questions and more can be found in the pages of the Planning Guide that follows.

In this section, we'll take at a closer look at the Richtersveld in the north of Namaqualand (including the World Heritage site and the |Ai-|Ais-Richtersveld Transfrontier Conservation Area). In the succeeding sections, we'll continue our journey southwards through Namaqualand and the Hantam Karoo, ending a short distance from Cape Town. Let's hit the road...

Getting There

The jumping-off point for a Richtersveld adventure is the town of Springbok. There are no regular flights into Springbok - the nearest commercial airport is at Upington, 380kms to the east. There's no rail link either, as the tracks end at the town of Bitterfontein, about 200km to the south. That means you either have to organise a guided excursion through a tour operator, fly into Upington or Cape Town and rent a car, charter a plane, or drive yourself.

Personally, I'm a big fan of self-drive road trips and, despite the remote location, it's relatively easy to explore the Richtersveld on your own (although a sturdy SUV or 4x4 is recommended). So, assuming you have a set of suitable set of wheels, here's how to get there.

From Joburg or Pretoria: get on the N14 and drive west, all the way to Springbok. This is a long haul, about 1200km, so I would suggest breaking the journey in two by spending a night at either Kuruman (530km), Upington (800km) or the wonderful Augrabies Falls National Park (a substantial 910km from Joburg).

To be honest, it's a pretty uneventful drive through the thirstlands of the Northern Cape, featuring a largely flat and scrubby landscape dotted with the isolated hills and ridges (called Inselbergs, or Island Mountains) so typical of the Nama Karoo. I do recall, however, driving through the heart of a memorably apocalyptic thunderstorm that squatted squarely over the road like a mushroom cloud, visible for miles in advance.

Every now and then, a non-descript town will flash by, offering the promise of fuel or supplies. You know the type: bottle store, butchery, general dealer, grain silos and an NG Kerk. But, despite my faint praise for the route, there is always something to see if you look hard enough, so here are some potential roadside attractions, with distances from Joburg in brackets:

- Bird watchers might want to stop off at the Barberspan Bird Sanctuary (290km).
- As you transition from the Grassland biome of the Highveld to the arid Nama Karoo biome, the scenery starts to desiccate. Nevertheless, Kuruman (530kms) is a rather nice little town with parks and trees. A perennial spring called 'Die Oog' (The Eye) forms a pretty pond in the middle of town. A 'Kalahari Raptor Route' is also being developed.
- Kathu (590km) is the location of the Sishen iron ore mine and you'll see the colossal mine dumps looming up on your right, long before you reach the settlement. This is the starting point of an industrial railway line that runs all the way down to Saldanha Bay on the lower West Coast.
- Upington (800km) is quite a big town with the Desert Palace casino glittering avariciously in the savannah. This is the heart of the so-called 'Green Kalahari', which produces wine and table grapes along with raisins, currants and other dried fruits.
- The long road up to the vast Kalahari Gemsbok National Park can be accessed from Upington. This reserve is now part of the Kgalagadi Transfrontier Conservation Area, Africa's first Peace Park, established in May 2000. www.sanparks.org/parks/kgalagadi
- The roads between Upington and Kakamas are incongruously marketed as the Orange River Wine Route, which might appeal to adventurous winos.
- At Kakamas (880km), you can access the Augrabies Falls National Park (translated from Khoi as 'place of great noise'). If you have the time, it's really worth spending a few nights in this fantastic reserve where you can enjoy a range of activities including hiking, kayaking down the Orange River, mountain biking, or just hanging around and enjoying the view of the 56m-high waterfall as it tumbles through a series of granite cataracts. www.sanparks.org/parks/augrabies
- The landscape really starts drying up after Kakamas and by the time you reach the punchline *dorp* of Pofadder (1040km) it's positively dehydrated. This is the heart of the Bushmanland region. You'll finally reach Springbok about 160km later.

From Cape Town: take the N7 and drive north for a relatively moderate 560km to Springbok. This route is discussed in greater detail in the *Exploring Namaqualand* section below.

From Springbok: once you arrive in Springbok, which has plenty of nice places to stay over, drive about 50km north on the N7 to reach Steinkopf – the gateway to the Richtersveld. From here, take the tarred R382 down the Anenous Pass until you reach the turn-off to Eksteenfontein. You can now enter the Richtersveld Community Conservancy by turning right onto the gravel road to Eksteenfontein, or you can continue on tar to Port Nolloth and Alexander Bay. From Alexander Bay, a long gravel road leads along the banks of the Orange to Kuboes and the gates of the Richtersveld National Park.

Suggested Itineraries

The question here is, always, how much time do you have? But in the case of the Richtersveld, you definitely need more than a couple of days. After all, you wouldn't schlep out all this way for a quick weekend getaway (unless you're already in Springbok to see the spring flowers). Furthermore, it seems a waste to visit the Richtersveld National Park (RNP) without visiting the Richtersveld Community Conservancy (RCC), and vice versa.

So, here are a couple of suggested itineraries, starting from Springbok. Please note that all roads in the RCC are untarred but in good condition and accessible for most vehicles. The roads in the RNP are much rougher and some soft-sand driving is necessary, so a 4x4 or a strong SUV with good ground clearance is essential - check with reception before you go, if you're not sure. Whatever the vehicle, take along spare tyres, a toolkit and extra fuel cans.

If you have less than 5 days - RCC: Definitely spend a night at Rooiberg Guest House, then stay over in Eksteenfontein, Kuboes and/or Port Nolloth before returning to Springbok. Adventurous campers will want to check out the wilderness campsites tucked away in secret corners of the conservancy.

If you have less than 5 days - RNP: You're probably going to arrive quite late, so spend your first night at either Sendelingsdrift or the nearby campsite at Potjiespram. Then, if I had to pick, head for De Hoop and/or the spectacular Kokerboomkloof (although all RNP campsites have something special about them). If camping's not your thing, comfortable self-catering units are available at Sendelingsdrift Rest Camp, Tatasberg and Ganakouriep. Leave the RNP via Helskloof Pass and drive to Port Nolloth for your last night before returning to Springbok.

If you have a week: Split your time between the RCC and the RNP. Allow for a final evening in quirky Port Nolloth before returning to Springbok.

If you have more than a week: From Sendelingsdrift gate, cross the border into Namibia using the pontoon. You can now drive into the Namibian part of the |Ai-

|Ais-Richtersveld Transfrontier Park to visit the Ai-Ais hot springs and the Fish River Canyon. When you're done, return to Springbok via the Vioolsdrift border post on the N7 highway. It's a trip you won't forget in a hurry. Take your passport.

When To Go

The Richtersveld is, essentially, a desert so the usual rules apply. The summer months (mid-October to mid-February) are very hot and dry, with temperatures peaking at nearly 50 degrees. The winter months (May to July) can be cold and soggy, especially in the evenings and early mornings. So, shoulder seasons are your best bet.

Ideally, try to visit the Richtersveld during flower season in early spring (end July to mid-September). The temperatures are comfortable and the weather is usually clear. More to the point, however, this is the time when Namaqualand's wildflowers burst into bloom, dribbling the barren landscape with splotches of colour like a Jackson Pollock painting.

Do note, though, there are no guarantees when it comes to weather. I was at Eksteenfontein in late August when the rain set in for a solid 24 hours, with a freezing wind blowing in from the coast. We even had to make space at the guest house for an impromptu party of five very wet bikers who were forced to seek shelter from the miserable conditions.

In case you're interested, these bikers were all mates from Pretoria who went on annual motorbike expeditions across the country. This time, they had sent their bikes to Cape Town and were busy scrambling up the west coast to Alexander Bay, sticking mainly to the sandy byways that run close to the ocean. They carried all their camping gear and food with them, and Eksteenfontein was one of the few places where they spent the night under a roof. Sounds a bit nuts to me, but then they are from Pretoria. In any case, it was good to have the extra company and, that night, we all sat around the TV watching 'Survivor'.

The Richtersveld Community Conservancy

Getting Around

From Springbok, follow the N7 north to Steinkopf (about 50km) and take the R382 towards Port Nolloth. After about 10km, you'll start to descend the Anenous Pass, which offers great views out over the Sandveld. The pass follows the route of the old Port Nolloth-O'okiep railway, so take a moment to imagine navigating the pass in a narrow train carriage pulled by mules!

After about 36km, you'll come to a turn-off marked for Grasvlakte / Eksteenfontein. Take this untarred road and drive for about 50km. You are now in the Richtersveld Community Conservancy (RCC) with the turn off for Rooiberg Guest house on your right and Eksteenfontein about 6km straight ahead.

If you are feeling adventurous, you can also enter (or leave) the RCC via the Nababeep/Helskloof Nature Reserve. This small conservation area can be accessed by following the N7 north from Steinkopf to Vioolsdrift (70km). Then, before you cross the border into Namibia, turn left and follow the gravel road along the south bank of the Orange River, past the Peace of Paradise campsite, until you enter the wholly undeveloped reserve.

The condition of the Helskloof road (not to be confused with Helskloof Pass in the RNP) is variable, especially after wet weather, so the route might take a while and it's only suited for 4x4 vehicles. But, apparently, the views are amazing. I've also heard that the road is being rehabilitated, so it may not be as rough as legend has it. The Helskloof track will bring you out on the main road to Eksteenfontein, just below the turn-off to Rooiberg Guest House.

From Eksteenfontein, it is suggested that you follow what has been dubbed the 'Richtersveld Circle Route'. This tour takes in the other RCC towns of Lekkersing, Kuboes and Sanddrift. From the latter, you can choose to either enter the Richtersveld National Park or return to Steinkopf via Alexander Bay and Port Nolloth.

Please note that all roads in the RCC are untarred, except for the R382 that runs between Steinkopf, Port Nolloth and Alexander Bay. Most of these tracks are in pretty good condition and can be negotiated by ordinary cars (unless there's been heavy rainfall - check before you go).

Contacts

For some reason, perhaps related to issues discussed in the *Land Claim Blues* chapter above, tourism development in the RCC seems to have stalled since I was there in 2007. The websites listed below are the official online portals for the RCC but they don't appear to have been updated for several years. Other contact details may also be obsolete (I did try to check but the nation is currently in lockdown due to the latest coronavirus pandemic, and my calls went unanswered). So, please consider all details in the section that follows as tentative. Confirm everything for yourself before you go!

- www.richtersveld-conservancy.org
- www.richtersveldguesthouses.co.za
- www.south-north.co.za
- Richtersveld Municipality (Port Nolloth): www.richtersveld.gov.za / 027 851 1111
- Tourism Information Centre at Eksteenfontein: 027 851 7108

Rooiberg Guest House

This is a very special spot and a great place to experience the wild open spaces of the RCC. Originally built as a mining office, the Rooiberg compound now consists of a couple of cosy houses nestled at the foot of a huge, eponymous red mountain.

Apparently, they once tried to mine ore from the top of this mountain, flying the rocks down to the house by helicopter. The ore was then transported by car for analysis and processing. They found traces of copper, gold and lead on the summit, but the amounts were too small to be payable and the operation was abandoned. The community has since improved the buildings and converted it into a guest house.

The main house has a fully equipped kitchen, a large open-plan lounge and dining room, and an expansive stoep for enjoying the long, soft sunsets. There are several bedrooms with single and double beds (sleeps 12 in total) and two functional bathrooms with hot water. There's also a small 'honeymoon' suite separate from the main house and, in summer, you can choose to sleep in a genuine reed *matjieshuis* built at the back of the property. Campers are also welcome. It's all very basic, but very comfortable.

There's no electricity at Rooiberg, but there is a gas freezer, gas stove and outdoor braai area. A gas fridge was on the cards when I was last there, as were solar panels for lights, but I'm not sure if these have been installed.

Maybe it's for the best. At night, the gentle light from the supplied paraffin lamps and candles is perfect. And, with no other human activity for miles around, the dark sky is immaculate, offering stargazing that's simply overwhelming.

The compound is surrounded by a tall wire fence, which is rather unattractive, but I was assured that the barrier is necessary to keep animals away from both the water tanks and the delectable reeds of the *matjieshuise.* When the wind blew, however, holes in the steel fence poles emitted a series of high-pitched whistling tones, like an off-key choir. This strange song swirled around the isolated house, mixing with the low roar of the wind to create an eerie polyphony that was disquieting and beautiful at the same time.

The guest house used to be run communally, but this system had changed by the time I visited. As far as I could make out, at that stage it was being run as a private concern by people from the community who paid a commission to the RCC trust for each guest. I am not sure how it's being run at the moment (nor can I say whether it's still as charming as I remember it).

Be that as it may, I had a wonderful stay at Rooiberg. The small staff who looked after the place welcomed me with open arms, and it was comforting to know that they lived a short distance away, in case I got lonely.

Staff were rotated regularly but my hosts were the marvellously photogenic Hendrina, known as Tant (auntie) Kniekie, her son, and an *Oom* whose name I sadly didn't catch. They didn't speak English but, even though my Afrikaans is *vreeslik*, we managed to communicate well enough when they came over to chat with me on the stoep. They also had a very friendly dog, Fooitjies, which is always a big plus in my book.

If you're feeling active, you can hike up the Rooiberg (a steep walk of about 3 hours each way, with panoramic views from the summit); tramp over to the Kannikaip campsite on the Orange River (a moderate but long walk of 17 km that takes 5-6 hours, with beautiful scenery and a swim in the river waiting for you at journey's end); or simply wander through the jagged foothills.

There are also several 4x4 routes leading through the mountains. One track connects to the Kannikaip camp site on the banks of the Orange River. Another takes you to the forbidding Black Face Mountain and on to Eksteenfontein via a back road.

Rooiberg is entirely self-catering, so bring all your own food and drink. The nearest shop is in Eksteenfontein and it has limited supplies, so get your groceries in Springbok. It may be possible to organise limited catering at the guesthouse if you book and pay in advance. There is no petrol available.

Quoted rates are from R100 per person per night. Entrance to the Conservancy is around R30 per person per day. Enquiries can be made through the Tourism Information Centre at Eksteenfontein: 027 851 7108.

Eksteenfontein

This friendly village is the 'capital' of the RCC. The Conservancy administration offices are located here, along with a tourist info centre and a museum (which is a work in progress). So, it's a good place to get all the latest info.

The town is built along the banks of a small stream called the Stinkfontein. This rather unappetising name dates back to a time when the local Khoikhoi and

Bushmen were engaged in a bitter rivalry. The story goes that after one particularly fierce battle, several bodies were left to rot in the river and it started to smell. Ugh!

Despite its grisly etymology, the Stinkfontein is a lifeline for this attractive settlement set against grassy hills, with dark mountains looming in the distance. Goats roam through the village, bells tinkling casually as they trot between the colourful houses. It's a good town through which to stroll.

There's a humble church, built by Reverend Eksteen and his congregation of Bosluis Basters who established the town in 1949. And the primary school is full of romping children (there is no high school). It even has the name of the town spelled out in white stones on a prominent ridge (a classic feature of small *dorpies* in South Africa). All in all, it struck me as a humble place with a growing sense of pride.

When I was there, the school had recently appointed a teacher from Riemsvasmaak to teach students the Nama language, and the museum staff was busy collecting oral histories from people in the village. A large community centre on the banks of the stream housed the Conservancy offices, a library, a community hall, a crèche, a postal agency and a workshop for textile printing and needlework, which made T-shirts and other interesting souvenirs.

The famously nomadic NamaKhoi farmers who still live in their traditional *matjieshuise* are usually found in the vicinity of the town, and visits can sometimes be arranged. However, these herders are real people and not tourist attractions, so visits are at their discretion. Make arrangements well ahead of time if you want to meet these living recipients of World Heritage status.

Visitors may be disappointed to find they won't see many wrinkled old ladies wearing the traditional frilly *kappie* (bonnet), featured so prominently in photographic portraits by people such as the estimable Obie Oberholzer. In days gone by, these brightly coloured head coverings were worn for protection against the sun. Now, they are worn mainly for ceremonial occasions and at cultural events.

Back in 2007, Eksteenfontein had a population of around 800 with most of the men employed by the mines, either at Transhex, Alexander Bay or Kleinzee. The mine shifts were arranged so that workers worked 7 days on and 7 days off. This allowed them to return to the village regularly, to maintain contact with their families. A shuttle service from the mines kept this system functioning smoothly. Now that most of the mines are closed or closing, one wonders how the people of Eksteenfontein are going to generate an income.

Tourist accommodation is at the 'Kom Rus 'n Bietjie' (come rest a while) Guesthouse. The main house has several bedrooms and bathrooms, a large kitchen with all the necessary equipment and a TV room with couches. There are also a couple of stand-alone chalets that sleep 2, with an en-suite bathroom.

Quoted rates are from R100 per person per night. A daily conservancy fee will cost an additional R30 per person per day.

There are several remote campsites tucked away in the surrounding mountains, which sound totally wild.

There is no petrol in Eksteenfontein, so fill up at Steinkopf or Port Nolloth. There is a small general store that sells meat and a few other basic supplies, but it's a good idea to stock up beforehand. There was no restaurant in town when I visited, but meals could be arranged if you booked in advance (home-cooked repasts, prepared by members of the community, and brought to you on their very own plates, covered with lace doyleys). It's a homely arrangement that seeks to spread the economic benefits of tourism across the village.

There are no banks or ATM facilities in town, so make sure you bring enough cash with you. And don't rely on credit cards. There is (probably) cell phone reception and internet available.

The range of activities available in Eksteenfontein include informative guided town tours and donkey cart rides (try taking a cart from Eksteenfontein to the Rooiberg Guest House, about 15kms away).

If you have a 4x4, rough roads lead to the campsites at Fluorspar Valley, Sun Valley (both old mining sites) and Rosynebos. The multi-day Namakwa 4x4 Trail is more ambitious overlanding expedition that runs from Pella to Alexander Bay, including stops at all the RCC towns. For more information: www.namakwa4x4.com

Hikers can choose between several intriguing trails, including an easy hike from Eksteenfontein to the Rooiberg Guest house that meanders between old stock posts and tall kokerbooms (about 12 km / 3-4 hours one way).

A range of other activities were in the planning stages, so phone ahead and find out what's on the menu. All enquiries can be made through the Tourism Information Centre at Eksteenfontein: 027 851 7108.

Just as you leave Eksteenfontein, the road splits. The right-hand fork will take you in a north westerly direction towards Kuboes - this is the shortest route to that town (65km). The left fork will take you south to the village of Lekkersing. About 37km down the latter road, you'll see a turn-off to the left for Koerdap campsite. Keep right and drive for another 5km to reach Lekkersing.

Lekkersing

With a charming name meaning 'beautiful singing', Lekkersing is small settlement established in 1926 by the farmer Ryk Jasper Cloete (who once tried to claim the entire Richtersveld as his own). Originally named *!Xaing !Xnai* in the Nama language, Lekkersing's Afrikaans name comes from either the sweet 'song' made by water bubbling out of a nearby spring or the literal singing of local villagers, overheard by Cloete.

Although the landscape is less mountainous than in the eastern part of the conservancy, Lekkersing is striking; surrounded by stark black hills covered in white quartzite pebbles. It's an alien scene, made even more uncompromising by tall dumps from the neighbourhood quartzite mine. Established in 1964, this quarrying operation produces many beautiful patterned slate slabs in shades of red and gold, which have been exported around the world.

In terms of facilities, Lekkersing is even less developed than Eksteenfontein. There is no petrol station, restaurant or ATM, just a small general store. You might be able to arrange traditional Nama food from the local Cultural Group if you book in advance. The Protea Elderly Club Food Garden won best garden in the Northern Cape, twice, and is hopefully still growing strong (sorry).

There isn't an official guest house in Lekkersing, although they were planning to build one, but you could arrange an overnight room through the municipal office (027 851 8580).

The community-run campsite of Koerdap, about 15kms south of the village, has chalets and several hiking trails (027 851 8136). A nearby farm, Kalkfontein, also offers hiking and horse riding with dormitory-style accommodation (073 507 4301). It's self-catering, but meals can be arranged - bring your own sleeping gear.

Lekkersing has a few cool activities on offer. Horse rides and donkey cart trips can be arranged if you book them in advance. A hike to the Skurwehoogte Caves sounds interesting, and the Rusoord Club for the Elderly may be selling arts and crafts from its small shop.

From Lekkersing, continue driving north for 67km, as the road runs parallel to a row of bare mountains a short distance to your right. After passing the turn-off for Tierhoek camp site and cave, you'll reach a junction with the Alexander Bay-Kuboes road. Turn right and drive for another 5km to arrive at Kuboes.

Kuboes

Originally founded as a Rhenish mission station, the quintessential Richtersveld village of Kuboes (also spelled Khubus or */obes)* takes its name from a Khoikhoi term meaning 'round fountain or spring'. It's a lovely, idiosyncratic town built around the elegantly simple whitewashed church complex, established in 1893. The granite pluton of Ploegberg cocoons the town in a silver-grey fastness, while the lofty Vandersterr Mountains to the north form a natural boundary with the National Park.

Kuboes is considered a stronghold of the Nama people and their culture. Local choirs still sing songs in the soft, clicking Nama tongue, and dance groups perform the traditional *Nama-stap* or Nama-step dance at ceremonial events. If you ask ahead, a cultural programme can be performed. You may even get to hear an ancient folktale narrated by one of the local story tellers.

The Community Property Association that owns and administers RCC land on behalf of local communities has its headquarters in the centre of town and, when I was there, groups of people were gathered around the steps of the municipal offices, chatting in the late afternoon sun. I don't know if the vibe has changed since the CPA fractured (a result of in-fighting triggered by their successful land claim), but I found Kuboes a very friendly place. I particularly enjoyed taking photos of the wonderful faces who came over to say hello - but always ask permission first.

Even if you don't speak Afrikaans (the lingua franca of the town) some basic sign language will suffice in this regard. Here's my personal procedure: I hold my camera in a non-threatening position, with the lens pointing away from my prospective subject. I then gesture at my camera and at the person who I am stalking, I mean propositioning, I mean asking. If they shake their head, I smile and walk away. If they nod, I'm in! And I usually do get a nod. Sometimes, a token of thanks is expected in exchange for a snap. Sometimes, you'll be asked a question about copyright! But you'll have to feel all that out for yourself.

One advantage of having an obvious camera is that some people call you over and ask you to take their pic, often with an alarming shout of 'shoot me!'. In Kuboes, I was positively swamped by kids and young adults who wanted their portrait taken and I spent some time showing everyone their photos on my camera screen, each new pic causing fresh shouts of hilarity.

There is no petrol in Kuboes (the nearest place to get fuel is - maybe - the Baken mine at Sanddrift, about 25 km away). But there is cell phone reception and internet. There are no banks or ATM facilities.

Accommodation for guests is available at the Mountain Valley Guest House, which consists of 4 stand-alone whitewashed cottages built in a lovely river valley on the outskirts of the town. Each cosy cottage has 3 bedrooms and is fully equipped. You can also stay in a traditional *matjiehuis* if you want a real Nama experience. Costs were from R100 per person per night, with conservancy fees of R30 per person per day. The guest house is self-catering, but traditional Nama meals can be arranged if booked in advance. The guest house has electricity and hot water geysers.

A variety of activities are on offer and field guides are available to help you make the most of your time in the town. For more information, contact the RCC Tourism Office in Eksteenfontein, the Kuboes Tourism Office: 027 831 2375, or the Kuboes Municipality: 027 831 1041.

From Kuboes, head back towards Alexander Bay. After about 10km, you'll see a turn-off to the right that leads towards the entrance gate of the Richtersveld National Park, 40km away (that's where we're heading in the next chapter). For now, keep going straight another 8km until you see the turn-off for Sanddrift/Baken. Turn right and continue about 10km on soft sand until you see the turn-off for the Baken mine. A short distance further on you'll find the town of Sanddrift.

Sanddrift and Baken Mine

The first settlers arrived at Sanddrift in the early 1900s, when Nama people along the coast were moved out and relocated to these sandy dune fields. Later, in the 1970s, the Transhex Corporation established a diamond mine at nearby Baken and many Xhosa and Sotho workers were brought in to work on the deposits.

Sanddrift therefore contains a strong Nguni influence which mixes with Nama cultural traditions, creating what is sometimes called the District 6 or Rainbow Town of the Richtersveld. For example, due to its multi-cultural heritage, both *Nama-stap* dance groups and the Sanddrift Youth Forum Basotho Stars are regular features at local functions.

Despite the obvious impoverishment, I found Sanddrift a very cheerful place and spent some time driving around, taking pictures and having a *gesels* (chat). One of the guys I spoke to, by the name of Kosie Fredericks, told me a bit about his life. At school, he said, he was forced to learn Afrikaans and then, as soon as he could read and write a little bit, he was kicked out and made to find work. He described these days as 'swaar jare' (heavy years), but he went on to say that things were better under apartheid because there wasn't so much murder and crime. This isn't the first time I've heard this sentiment from someone who was persecuted by that iniquitous system, and it's always disconcerting - especially in such a remote area.

The Baken mine, a few kms away, was a mainstay of the town when I was there. It was is the only place in the area where you could get petrol and diesel. And there was a well-stocked convenience store for supplies (they even had copies of the Sowetan newspaper when I was there). Back then, the mine complex included an extensive residential settlement with neat little houses, a school, an ATM and a sunburnt miniature golf course.

Unfortunately, Transhex closed the mine in 2017 due to dwindling output and rising costs, putting over 300 people out of work. The state of the facility today is unclear.

As far as I can tell, there is no official guest house at Sanddrift. There's a camping site, Stofbakkies, but this isn't always operational. South African National Parks has built an interpretation centre in the town that does valuable community outreach work, encouraging local people to get involved in their national park up the road.

Other activities include walks to the Hangklip (which offers great views over the Orange River) or the Island Trail (which lets you hop across the small, reed-covered islands that pepper the watercourse). Fishing and other water sports may be available.

For more information, contact the RCC Tourism Office in Eksteenfontein or the Sanddrift Municipal Office: 027 831 1457.

From Sanddrift, head back to the Kuboes-Alexander Bay road. You can now turn left and head east to the Richtersveld National Park (about 47km - see next chapter), or right to Alexander Bay (55km). As you drive towards Alexander Bay, the road rises over several ridges that offer views across the Orange River, with bright strips of verdant farmland fighting against the surrounding desert. Most of these farms were established by Alexkor and now belong to the *Sida !Hub* CPA. A short distance before Alexander Bay, you'll see the turn-off to Oranjemund, on the Namibian side of the border. The road to this Namdeb-owned diamond mining settlement crosses the Orange River on the Ernest Oppenheimer bridge - but you'll probably need a permit as this is a restricted area. Nevertheless, there are guest houses at Oranjemund, and the town is tentatively opening to tourism. Check out www.oranjemunder.com or the Namdeb website for more info: www.namdeb.com.

Alexander Bay and the Orange River Mouth

Located at the mouth of the Orange River, Alexander Bay is a typical company town. Built entirely by and for the state-owned Alexkor diamond mining operation, the town was once heavily restricted and you needed a permit to gain entry. Now, with the onshore diamond mines almost exhausted and Alexkor on the ropes, the town is a shadow of its former self and very much open to tourism. When I was there, all you had to do was stop at the boom gate, sign in, show your ID, and they let you right through.

Once inside the settlement, it all looks very institutional. Rows of low brick houses vary in size, according to the status of the employees who live (or lived) inside. There are several churches and schools, and a couple of walls are painted with murals in an attempt to lighten the mood. But it's a rather sombre place. Tall wire fences that separate the town from mining areas along the beach are omnipresent, and ugly, semi-abandoned industrial structures tower over the scene. It's also said to be the driest town in South Africa, with just 11 days of rain per year. Temperatures in the height of summer can top 40 degrees.

The one big attraction of Alexander Bay, however, is the Orange River mouth. This vitally important Ramsar Wetlands site can be reached by following a series of hand-painted signs (marked 'Riviermonding') through the town and down a long sand road to a small parking area on the beach. On the left, a rusty fence is covered with severe signs that say 'Warning. Mine Area. No Entry'. Beyond the wire barrier, you can see enormous utilitarian buildings, now abandoned, crumbling slowly into the sand. The lifeguard's hut on the public part of the beach is similarly neglected, and even the muddy ocean seems forlorn and angry.

You now have to leave your car and walk along the beach to your right (no beach driving without a permit). It's a wild strip of coastline, with long strands of seaweed and huge pieces of driftwood strewn across the blackened sand. The actual river mouth is a couple of kilometres away, but you can clamber up one of the sand dunes to get a good view over the beautiful wetlands, which sprawl back from the narrow mouth. An old bird hide may be seen but is hard to reach.

Here, the longest river in South Africa meets the sea in a delta of shifting sandbars, reedbeds and marshes, with multiple channels making it hard to pinpoint the exact 'mouth'. Sometimes, the river's water doesn't even reach the Atlantic, despite its 2200km length. Other times, it comes down in flood.

Nowadays, however, by the time it reaches the sea, the Orange is a shadow of its former self. It is estimated that natural inflow to the estuary has halved due to the many dams and irrigation schemes that hamper the Orange's run from the highlands of Lesotho to the ocean. Increasing drain-off has already caused the saltmarsh component of the wetlands to collapse, and a proposed dam on the Fish River tributary in Namibia threatens to exacerbate the situation.

Still, considering all the mining activity, I suppose we're lucky to have any kind of wetlands at all. And, despite its degraded state, it's still a beauty; supporting as many as 20 000 birds from some 60 species. Rated as one of the most important estuaries in South Africa, the Orange River Mouth was declared a cross-border Ramsar Wetlands of International Importance in 1991.

Unfortunately, land ownership remains an issue. Originally the property of Alexkor and now controlled by the Richtersveld CPA, the river mouth has been left largely to its own devices, effectively unmanaged for many years. As such, there isn't any established infrastructure that allows visitors to access the wetlands directly, and you either have to organise a local guide to unlock one of the gates in the fence or find yourself a good vantage point from the beach. One hopes that the various parties in question can find a way to sensitively develop and rehabilitate this natural wonder.

When I was there, Alexander Bay had several guest houses and other tourist facilities including a small shopping centre with a convenience store, post office, clothing shop, and the Koffiekan coffee shop. There was also the Dunvlei sports club with a golf course and the Zonneblom restaurant and ladies bar. However, with the general collapse of Alexkor and governance issues plaguing the Richtersveld CPA, it seems that the town is in a dire position - I hope reports of the settlement's imminent demise are overstated.

There is a museum in A-Bay and it looks like tours of the mine are still being conducted on Thursday mornings (bookings essential). I'd suggest phoning ahead to check on the status quo. A 24-hour petrol station with an ATM machine and a workshop can be found just outside the boom gates. There are hospital and emergency services, in case you run into trouble.

In terms of camping, Patchvlei is located on the banks of the Orange River, about 8km out of town along the Kuboes road. It has a picnic spot and a braai area, but facilities are limited. Farther along the same road, you'll find Brandkaros (27km from Alexander Bay). This is a more established campsite, with chalets, ablution facilities, a restaurant and a swimming pool.

Finally, if you're a fun guy, don't miss Lichen Hill. This little rise is covered with dozens of species of lichen and is the only one of its kind in South Africa. It's located a short distance to the south of Alexander Bay, along the main road to Port Nolloth.

For more information, contact the Alexander Bay tourism office on 027 831 1330 / www.alexanderbay.co.za / www.alexkor.co.za.

From Alexander Bay, turn right onto the tarred R382 towards Port Nolloth (85km). This stretch of road leads across the undulating plains with rolling koppies leading down to the dark green Atlantic waters. The coastline, parts of which are still restricted, is dotted with dumps and other detritus from the decaying mining industry. Rehabilitating the landscape once the mines are finally shut is going to be a major project. Oh, and keep an eye on the telephone poles running along the roadside where hawks, owls and other birds of prey can be seen hanging out, just waiting to swoop down and scoop up a bug or some roadkill from the tarmac. In spring, this is a pretty drive with dustings of bright purple and yellow flowers brightening up the dusty palette of brown and khaki.

Port Nolloth and McDougall's Bay

I arrived at Port Nolloth during the golden hour before sunset and a warm light fell softy across the quiet seafront, making the scene quite irresistible. I was sold! The town also has a well-developed tourism infrastructure so it's a good place to start or end your Richtersveld adventure, with a range of guest houses, inns, hotels and motels from which to choose. And several restaurants specialise in fresh seafood, straight off the fishermen's boats.

The small harbour, which was once the bustling terminal of the copper-era O'okiep-Port Nolloth railway, is now filled with bobbing boats. There's an excellent museum on the beachfront, alongside the old lighthouse and a delightful, baby-blue Catholic Church. The museum is a good place to get tourist information about the town and surrounding area. It also has extensive displays on the natural and cultural history of the region and an internet café. It's housed in the old Cape Copper Company's Officials Club, dating from the 1880s.

You may also want to check out the Richtersveld Experience, which offers information on the area, a restaurant, a pub, a guest house, river rafting excursions, hiking trips, 4x4 hire, tours, you name it. Several other tour operators also run trips in the area.

A few kms down the coast, you'll find the holiday resort of McDougall's Bay, with more guest houses and a well-known caravan park that is literally on the beach - an untouched Blue Flag shingle that's perfect for a late-afternoon stroll. Just don't try to swim in the visually inviting water because it's bloody freezing!

McDougall's was once also a diamond area and thus out of bounds. It was opened to the public around 1986 and slowly blossomed, with several estate agencies and numerous residential developments springing up in the early 2000s. Long-time residents told me they couldn't believe how much the town had grown in the past few years, with property prices rising steadily.

Port Nolloth's best-known eatery is Anita's Tavern, located in the centre of town. This warm bistro is decorated with a cosy clutter of nautical paraphernalia, and it's a great place to spend an evening. The hosts are welcoming, the atmosphere convivial, and the food is excellent (it's even been featured on several TV shows). I tried the house speciality, a Calamari Carpetbagger - two calamari steaks (breaded and deep fried) stuffed with mussels and cheese sauce. It was a bit much, TBH, but they serve a wide range of food so you should find something that appeals. Advance booking is recommended in season.

In terms of nightlife, there ain't much to speak of. But curiosity got the better of me and I did check out a little disco at the back of the Scotia Inn. It turned out to be a rather enticing pool bar, clad in face brick and blaring loud *sokkie* music. The crowd was nicely multi-racial and I quite enjoyed myself.

Between Port Nolloth and MacDougall Bay, there's Sizamile township (meaning 'we have tried'). While driving through this location, I took some pictures of two kids riding their homemade go-cart down the sand dunes. As I was about to leave, they came over to me and, honestly, I was expecting them to ask for money. Instead, they wanted to know if I had a screwdriver or a hammer to fix their buggies. I hope they grew up to become mechanics.

On the outskirts of town, you'll find petrol stations, motor workshops, panel beaters, auto-electricians, hardware stores and tyre fitment joints. So, this is the place to go for mechanical repairs either before or after your Richtersveld odyssey.

Port Nolloth is renowned for having 4 seasons in one day. It also has the highest number of fog days for any town in South Africa. Apparently, the easterly wind brings the sunshine and the westerly wind brings the fog and mist. Either way, it's an enchanting place that is sure to delight visitors.

For more information, contact the Port Nolloth Municipality : 027 851 1111 / www.portnolloth.co.za.

From Port Nolloth, continue on the tarred R382 towards Steinkopf (92km). This returns us to our starting point and completes the circular route through the Richtersveld Community Conservancy.

Steinkopf

Another former mission station, Steinkopf is a small town huddled around an old Rhenish church (built in 1840). There isn't much of a tourism industry here, but the petrol station on the outskirts of town is a good place to fill up before entering the fuel-less expanse of the RCC. The adjoining convenience store and café also made a surprisingly good chicken burger.

For those who do wish to spend some time in town, there are several things to check out. The Immanuel Succulent Nursery and Tea Garden, run by the local home for the disabled, has succulent displays as well as arts and crafts. And the Steinkopf Art Gallery, located inside the old Rhenish Mission Church, features paintings donated by the Brecher family.

4x4 enthusiasts can take a trip into the mountains to see the old Anenous station and Nonahams watering point (both part of the old O'okiep-Port Nolloth railway line). Historically minded visitors may also want to pop in at the Kinderlê memorial or visit the ruins of the old Klipfontein Hotel, which has several gravesites dating back to the Anglo-Boer War.

Overnight accommodation at Steinkopf is limited but you can try the community-run Kookfontein Rondawels and Info Centre (027 721 8841). Traditional Nama food, such as roosterbrood, chicken noodle potjie, lambsneck potjie and 'curry tripe', may be available at the Kookskerm food stall.

The Richtersveld National Park

The landscapes of the Richtersveld National Park (RNP) are often described as 'desolate' and 'forbidding', which they are. But the RNP is much more besides. Administered by South African National Parks (SANParks) on behalf of the Richtersveld community, this is a place out of time, out of the ordinary and out of this world.

Here, in the most mountainous part of the Richtersveld, the rocks are laid bare. No soil or ground cover grows on the mountain slopes, and the dry desert plains are barren and beautiful in equal measure.

That means the roads in the park are variable; some wind along sandy riverbeds, others climb rocky mountain passes, and some wander through the plains on corrugated gravel tracks. So, you need a 4x4 to drive in this rugged reserve (or at least a tough SUV with good ground clearance).

Accommodation in the park is mostly geared for camping, with a couple of self-catering chalets also available, but it's very much a 'bring your own' kind of place. Nevertheless, improvements to the park's infrastructure have made it relatively easy to explore.

For rates, gate times and other information, get in touch with SANParks or visit their comprehensive website.

Contacts

- RNP Reception: 027 831 1506
- SANParks Central Reservations: 012 428 9111
- www.sanparks.org/parks/richtersveld
- www.richtersveldnationalpark.com
- www.transhex.co.za

Getting there

From Steinkopf, take the tarred R382 towards Port Nolloth. Once the Anenous Pass has been navigated, you can either head north through the Richtersveld Community Conservancy, via Eksteenfontein and Kuboes, to reach the entrance gate of the RNP at Sendelingsdrift (about 200km - all gravel). Or you can follow the tarred road that does a big horseshoe from Anenous to Port Nolloth and Alexander Bay, then along the south bank of the Orange River to Sendelingsdrift (a total of 262km, the last 83km on gravel).

Both these routes are described in the previous chapter on the RCC. So, we'll pick up from the point where you turn off the Kuboes-Alexander Bay road (about

50km outside Alexander Bay) and head up to the park itself. The distance from this intersection to the main gate at Sendelingsdrift is about 45km.

The Wondergat

The first intriguing sign you'll see is the turn-off to Cornellskop and the Wondergat (Mystery Hole). The latter is a deep, dark sinkhole that drops straight down for more than 20 metres before angling off and descending even further. It was formed by ground water that percolated through a fault in the rocks, dissolving the limestone as is trickled ever downward.

Nama legends have it that the Wondergat is home to *Heitsi Eibib*, the great spirit. Other stories say it's the lair of the 'Great Snake', a serpent that swims through underground tunnels to the nearby Orange River, where it transforms itself into a young maiden who lures men to their death. There's also a legend that anyone who swims in the black water of the Wondergat will emerge with grey hair and terror in their eyes.

While that may be an over-estimation, the sinkhole is indeed very dangerous and should be approached with extreme caution. The Wondergat can be visited as part of the walk up Cornellskop (a rocky hill named after the well-known prospector, Fred Cornell). This trail is neatly marked out by a line of white stones that begins from the parking area. I must confess that I somehow missed the Wondergat itself, but the view from the koppie's summit was astounding.

Bloeddrif

Shortly after the Wondergat, you'll see a turn-off to Bloeddrif (Blood Drift). I'm not sure what happened at this river crossing, but it must have been pretty damn sanguineous. Bloeddrif mine, once part of the Transhex mining company's holdings, was shuttered in 2017 but there are several ancient stone petroglyphs in the area, which can be visited with permission (contact RNP reception for details).

From the Bloeddrif turn-off, keep driving north as a sharp line of mountains rises up, close on the right. A tenuous string of power lines runs alongside the road, the only sign of civilisation for miles around, until you come to a neat-looking visitors centre. This is the entrance to Helskloof Gate (not to be confused with Helskloof in the adjacent Nababeep Nature Reserve). However, it's strongly recommended that you start your visit at the main reception office at Sendelingsdrift and try to exit the park via the amazing Helskloof Pass.

Reuning Diamond Mine

So, keep driving for another 20km until you get to the Reuning Diamond Mine, home of the fabled 'glory hole' - a 43-metre deep splash pool formed by the Orange River that collected gems worth a modern equivalent of R4 billion.

The Reuning Mine ceased operations in 2015 and, a few years later, Transhex sold its three Richtersveld mines (Bloeddrif, Baken and Reuning) to a 'junior' mining company called Lower Orange River Diamonds for R72 million. They also put aside a trust fund of nearly R100 million, earmarked for land rehabilitation after years of mining, but many industry insiders say that this isn't nearly enough.

Today, the small settlement at Reuning - cluttered with the detritus of heavy machinery, conveyor belts and No Entry signs - is the unlikely location of the RNP's Sendelingsdrift reception office and gate. There are still a couple of mines operating inside the park (some of them perhaps illegally) but you'll see no visible signs, as all current and former mining activity is hidden away down restricted roads.

Planning your trip

In the old days, the RNP was really wild and you had to bring everything with you. Now, the campsites have ablution facilities (albeit with cold water) and there are even a couple of rest camps with proper beds and other luxuries.

Nevertheless, you still need to be prepared and largely self-sufficient. All visitors are reminded to bring along plenty of supplies, flashlights, batteries and an extra spare wheel in case of emergencies. Due to the long distances involved, day visitors are not encouraged. Guests should also note that water from the ablution facilities should not be considered safe to drink.

The only place in the park with cell phone reception is the Sendelingsdrift rest camp. Also, none of the rest camps have electricity outlets except for the cabins at Sendelingsdrift.

So, make sure your vehicle is in good repair and bring along tools and recovery equipment because, if you do break down, you're going to have to wait for a passing vehicle to raise the alarm. During the winter months, the park is relatively busy and help shouldn't be too far away. In the hot summer months, however, the visitors are few and far between and you might be stranded for a while.

The good news is that the roads are generally not as bad as people make out. Don't get me wrong, you still need a 4x4 or a sturdy SUV with good ground clearance (and preferably a diff lock). A low range gear box is nice to have, just in case, but not essential. If you can, take along a portable air-compressor (available at most outdoor suppliers) so that you can deflate/inflate your tyres when the road transitions from soft sand to rocky gravel and back again. Also, plan your day's driving carefully to ensure you make it to your next overnight destination before the sun sets. Driving at night is dangerous and not permitted. Besides, pitching a tent in the dark sucks big time!

In terms of food, take along all the supplies you will need for the duration of your trip. There are no shops inside the park and if you run out, you're either going to have to beg from other campers (not good form) or go hungry.

Fuel is another concern. The store at Sendelingsdrift sells diesel and unleaded petrol but supplies can be erratic. The closest alternative filling stations are at Alexander Bay (90km away), so make sure you top up your tanks and carry some spare fuel in a jerry can or two.

The good news is that distances within the park are moderate (a complete circuit is only about 200km) and you'll be driving slowly, so you can probably make it on a single tank. Personally speaking, I used ¾ of a tank and it was a pretty comprehensive trip (although I didn't use the air-con much, as the outside temperature was quite comfortable). But it all depends on your car and the size of its engine, so use your discretion and err on the side of caution.

Finally, don't be afraid to try out a couple of different camp sites. Each site has its own look, character and appeal. This also gives you the opportunity to explore different parts of the park without having to drive back and forth from one location. Just remember, when you make your booking, you have to specify which campsites you intend staying at each night.

Other things to bear in mind:

- Be careful where you walk. The flora of the RNP is fragile and your big, dumb feet can destroy the plants.
- Always stay on the marked roads and only camp at official camp sites, so that you don't cause environmental damage.
- All rubbish must be taken out of the park with you. Bring along plenty of plastic refuse bags.
- Take a good camera with extra batteries and memory cards. This is an endlessly photogenic reserve and you won't want to run out of storage or juice.
- Pack clothes that are suitable for extreme temperatures, both hot and cold, and dress in layers. Scarves can be used to protect you from dust and wet towels are useful in extreme heat. Heavy dew falls can occur at night.
- Gas cookers are recommended due to evening winds.
- Firewood and kindling may not be collected in the park.
- The picking of plants and the removal of seeds, rocks, crystals or driftwood is an offence.
- Bring a good insect repellent or bug spray.
- This is scorpion country so don't sleep on bare ground and keep your shoes inside the tent.
- No pets, generators or loud music are allowed, obviously.

Sendelingsdrift

The main gate to the RNP is at Sendelingsdrift (Missionaries' Crossing) and it is important that you do a proper check-in at reception before heading off. After all, this is an untamed place and the staff will want to know where you'll be going and how long to wait before sending in the rescue team.

Pick up all the necessary maps and brochures at reception. These are essential for successful navigation through the park, and don't be afraid to ask questions about prevailing conditions. There's also an interpretation centre (still under construction when I was there).

The reception area has a small general store that sells cold drinks and basic supplies (open weekdays only). No other shops or services are available inside the park, so make the most of it. Diesel and unleaded petrol are available. There is no restaurant or ATM. In terms of communications, Sendelingsdrift is the only place in the RNP that has any cell phone reception and there's a coin-operated public phone at reception (when was the last time you used one of those?).

The international border post and pontoon, which ferries vehicles across the Orange River into Namibia, is also located at Sendelingsdrift. Passports are essential if you want to make this crossing.

If you're going to arrive late, it's a good idea to book your first night at the welcoming Sendelingsdrift rest camp. There are campsites with a good ablution block and 10 attractive chalets, which have been recently refurbished. These excellent units (4 x 4-bed and 6 x 2-bed) are fully equipped with an air-conditioner, basic kitchen (fridge and hot plate), bathroom and braai area. Each unit has a covered deck with great views over the Orange/Gariep to Cornellskop. There's also a swimming pool in the camp, and further landscaping and construction work is on-going. If you aren't into camping, you could potentially use the rest camp as a base for day drives into the park, but it's not ideal.

Alternatively, if you want to forsake your last chance of a hot shower and soft bed, push on to the next campsite at Potjiespram, 10km from Sendelingsdrift.

Potjiespram

The road from Sendelingsdrift to Potjiespram runs along a dry riverbed. It's quite rocky and, since I was there at the end of the wet season, there were many water-filled depressions that had to be negotiated with care. Still, it's not nearly as fearsome as I was led to believe.

When you arrive at Potjiespram, you can choose from one of three sections, each with its own ablution block (cold water only). All the campsites are cloistered amid trees along the southern bank of the Orange; the wide, flat waters of which curve serenely through an otherwise blistering landscape of boulders and mountains. Don't be fooled, though, Potjiespram has been closed due to flooding.

Unfortunately, on the north bank, you can see the huge pit of a mining operation, which is a bummer. Having said that, the mountains sides are so shattered and decomposed, it's quite hard to tell what has been mined and what's just collapsed scree. My initial thought was that the mountains reminded me of a broken Flake chocolate sticking out of a soft-serve, but maybe I was just hungry.

The three camps contain a total of 18 camp sites. There's also an environmental education centre, where students can sleep over in traditional Nama huts *(matjieshuise)*.

De Hoop

From Potjiespram, the first intersection you come to is marked for the Oena mine and the Hand of God. Take this road for 200m to see a rather amazing indentation in the rock face, which does indeed look like an almighty handprint - a High 5 from on high, if you will. The mine itself was retired in 2015 but little rehabilitation has been done, so there's no need to continue any further down the restricted road (although there are some Stone Age archaeological sites in the area, which are currently being investigated).

Continue a bit further along the 'main' road and it's time to tackle the Akkedis (Lizard) Pass. This is a rather rough, twisty track with lots of loose rocks and a bit of scrambling may be required to get your car over the steeper sections. Take it slow so that you don't spin your wheels and degrade the road further. And keep an eye out for some rare Halfmens trees that grow along the roadside (I must confess that I missed them completely). It should take you between 45 minutes and an hour to complete the ascent.

Upon cresting the pass, you come out onto a wide plain. I was there during spring, so the ground was blanketed in bright yellow and purple wildflowers. This incongruously fertile bowl is ringed by fierce, naked, steel-grey mountains, and I found the contrast to be profound.

In the middle of the plain is a small homestead that was surrounded by goats. This incongruous structure is sometimes used as a base for the research teams that visit the park each year.

The road to De Hoop campsite now leads along a dry, wide riverbed, and I had to drive carefully so that I didn't get stuck in the soft sand. It was worth it, though, because De Hoop is a heart-stopper.

Set out along the banks of the Gariep, it's a popular campsite with open access to the cool river. The silence is tangible, broken only by the sound of birds and the careless splash of water as it rushes over some small rapids. As with the other campsites, the relatively new ablution blocks are both beautiful and functional. Although do remember that there's neither hot water nor flush toilets.

There are 12 camp sites at De Hoop but these are not clearly demarcated, so pick a spot on the sandy banks and pitch your tent. You can swim in the river, go fishing or just relax, the choice is yours. And don't worry about crocodiles or hippos. The water's too cold to support crocs and the last hippo in the Orange River, Humphrey, died near Alexander Bay in 1921.

Richtersberg and Tatasberg Wilderness Camps

From De Hoop, you used to be able to follow the riverbank to Richtersberg camp site. But the sand on this road is very deep and too many cars were getting stuck, so the route is now closed. Instead, you must head back to the hard road and drive through the mountains, which is fine by me.

Once you get out of the riverbed, the road leads up a low rise, which crests a saddle to reveal a spectacular panorama across the plains, with row upon row of red-hued mountains heading off into the distance. About 10km further on, you'll see a road marked for Richtersberg/Tatasberg. This track is also closed due to sand traps, and passage barred by rocks and a big 'no entry' sign.

Instead, just keep going as the road dips down into another riverbed with some patches of deep sand. Keeping to the left, you'll soon turn down into a narrow canyon that squirms between parallel walls of russet rock. It seems impossible that there's anything at the end of this track, apart from some hungry vultures waiting for their next meal, but the rocky path eventually turns a corner to reveal yet another pristine waterfront campsite.

Richtersberg is similar to De Hoop, with 6 campsites and ample space to pitch your tent along the riverbank. The eternal mountains form a serrated backdrop against the blue sky, reflecting imperfectly in the rippling water.

The Tatasberg Wilderness Camp is located a short distance away from Richtersberg, along a soft sand road. The camp consists of 4 x 2-bed self-catering reed cabins with hot water, a 12- volt lighting system, and a gas fridge and stove. Paraffin lanterns are supplied in case the lights fizzle out and a resident caretaker is on site if there are any other problems. Although the units are kept clean by the park's staff, guests must do their own washing up and make their own beds.

Kokerboomkloof

Back on the main road, after the turn-off to Richtersberg, you'll head up a long rise until the track squeezes around an outcrop of rocks to emerge in an enchanted valley. This is Kokerboomkloof, located on the top of the Tatasberg pluton – a large granitic dome slowly weathering into large boulders, which are in turn slowly weathering into a gallery of weird and wonderful rock formations. As humans tend to do, many of these features have been given fanciful names like the Toe, the Witches, and Queen Victoria - a profile of the great monarch that is indeed uncanny.

Then there are the eponymous kokerbooms growing in haphazard profusion across the plateau. Walking between these bizarre aloe trees is an otherworldly delight that somehow defies any attempt to put down in writing. Needless to say, I sat for hours watching the setting sun soak the colony of quiver trees in a golden light, until it was quite dark. And that night, I sat among the silhouetted kokerbooms, staring sagaciously at the canopy of stars shining bright in an inky, moonless sky. Just wish I knew more about astronomy...

The next morning, I delighted in the peace of watching the sun rise as I absent-mindedly fed my breakfast to fearless starlings who hopped about at my feet. It was all quite marvellous.

There are 8 camp sites at Kokerboomkloof, nestled among the colossal boulders. They are serviced by several dry ablution blocks (you'll need to bring in all your own water).

Gannakouriep and Hakkiesdoring

Driving back from Kokerboomkloof, the rocks seem exposed and raw. Here, the geological processes that formed the landscape are laid bare, with distinct streaks of colour layered along the mountain slopes, clearly indicating the transition from one rock suite to another.

After a while you'll see a turn-off for the panoramic Gannakouriep valley, located in the heart of the RNP.

Overlooking Mount Terror and Rosyntjieberg, the Gannakouriep Wilderness Camp offers comfortable accommodation in 4 x 2-bed cabins. Similar to Tatasberg, there are hot showers, a battery-powered lighting system, and a gas fridge and stove. A resident caretaker is on hand to sweep up the unit, but guests must do their own cooking and cleaning.

The Gannakouriep valley is also the location of the Hakkiesdoring hiking trails base camp. This facility sleeps 9 people, and contains gas stoves, fridges and hot showers. Various hiking routes have been laid out in the RNP, including the 3-night Vensterval Trail, but there is currently a shortage of qualified guides so this offering is not available. Nevertheless, groups can overnight at the base camp and may be allowed to hike, if they bring along a suitably informed trail leader.

Helskloof

The time has now come to, reluctantly, leave the RNP. So, either backtrack through the park to Sendelingsdrift, or take alternate exit route via De Koei and Helskloof Pass (which I wholeheartedly recommend).

De Koei was one of the original campsites in the park but is now closed and overnighting is not allowed. The road, however, is magnificent. It leads along a pretty, well-watered valley before climbing into the mountains and rambling across a high ridge. The road is rough but somehow still charming and, in flower season, this part of the park is bursting with colour. A windmill and a stock pen indicate that this valley is favoured by the registered community herders, who graze their herds inside the park's boundaries.

Then, quite suddenly, the road rounds a spur and a cleft in the mountains appears, in all its precipitous glory. This is Helskloof, home of the rare Pearson's Aloe *(Aloe pearsonii),* which grows abundantly down the slopes on either side of the road. The rocky pass isn't difficult, but there is a sheer drop off to the left and, in the distance, rows of serrated ridges recede gradually into the desert sands. It's a thoroughly appropriate ending to your grand RNP adventure.

At the base of the pass, the road leads along the banks of a dry river and a large herd of goats swarmed around the car as I trundled along (I couldn't see the herder responsible but I'm sure he was there). Finally, I reached the Helskloof Gate on the main access road between Sendelingsdrift and Alexander Bay, whereupon I signed out of the park and sadly turned my back on the RNP. Until next time.

|Ai-|Ais-Richtersveld Transfrontier Conservation Area

The wondrous |Ai-|Ais-Richtersveld TFCA straddles South African and Namibia, covering nearly 6000 square kilometres. This vast aegis includes the Richtersveld National Park, the Ai-Ais Hot Springs, and the colossal Fish River Canyon (one of the largest in the world).

Since it was officially established in 2003, the |Ai-|Ais-Richtersveld TFCA has established a joint park management committee and approved an integrated development plan and operations strategy. Training programmes have been implemented and several unique cross-border adventures have been launched. These include the 5-day Desert Knights mountain bike tour, guided Desert Kayak trails, and the 5-day Richtersveld Wildrun (an insane 200km race through the inhospitable desert).

So, if you've got the means, take the opportunity to cross over from the RNP into the Namibian side of the TFCA. This can be done in grand style at Sendelingsdrift, thanks to an international border post and pontoon that ferries vehicles and pedestrians across the Gariep. From the north bank, you can access a long road that follows the river from Oranjemund to the B1 highway.

A pontoon service had previously been in intermittent operation for years. It ceased operations in 1988 but was resurrected in 2007 to service the new TFCA. Occasional flooding on the Orange River may temporarily close the pontoon, however, so check whether it's operational before you head off.

Without the pont, if you want to go from Sendelingsdrift to Ai-Ais, you have to backtrack all the way to Steinkopf and then continue north on the N7 to cross the border at Vioolsdrift (a trip of nearly 350km). From the border, it's another 125km to reach the entrance of the hot springs. Using the pontoon, the whole trip is just 160km door to door.

For more information about the TFCA, visit the Peace Parks website: www.peaceparks.org/tfcas/ai-ais-richtersveld

Ai-Ais Hot Springs and the Fish River Canyon

The two big highlights in the Namibian part of the TFCA are undoubtedly Ai- Ais Hot Springs and the Fish River Canyon. These are conveniently located within easy driving distance from one another and, collectively, they make one helluva destination.

Located in a barren valley surrounded by black mountains, the hot springs at Ai-Ais bubble out of the ground at a scalding 60° Celsius. The mineral-rich water is then channelled into a large outdoor pool and a rather ritzy indoor complex with fountains and thermal baths. The resort offers a range of accommodation options, a bar, restaurant, and a menu of spa treatments.

Ai-Ais (meaning 'scalding hot') is open throughout the year, although it does get very warm in the summer months. I was there many years ago in mid-December and the temperature hovered around 40 degrees, even at night (which was a problem as we opted for the cheap rooms without air conditioning). Nevertheless, it was awesome to swim in the burning water with a searing sun beating down relentlessly on my head. I couldn't tell where the water ended and the air began. For more information about the hot springs, visit www.aiaisresort.com.

A short drive north of the springs is the Fish River Canyon. According to some sources, this is the second largest Canyon on Earth, after the Grand one in the USA. Although, to be fair, the specific criteria for measuring canyons is up for debate (depth vs. width vs. volume, etc.).

Located on the lower stretches of the Fish River, before its confluence with the Orange, the canyon is 161km long and up to 27km wide - although it's much narrower for most of its course. The inner canyon reaches a depth of almost 550m, revealing rocks that are up to 2.6 billion years old. The river that runs along the canyon floor is quite small and often dries into isolated pools amid the boulders, but flash floods are not uncommon during the rainy season.

All in all, it's a genuine spectacle of nature that deserves to be seen by more people. At Hobas, there are several viewpoints along the main section of the Canyon, allowing you to peer over the lip and into the abyss carved out by the deceptively puny river. I spent a whole day there, just looking out over the scene, chatting to various people as they came and went.

Predictably, my old camera's battery chose that particular moment to go flat and I had to cadge some spare CR2s off a passing German tour group who were thankfully (if stereotypically) well prepared. This was in the days of film, when cameras used disposable batteries, in case you were wondering.

Later that same day, I met another German, Moogie, who was driving an old Mercedes truck from Berlin to Cape Town - a trip that took him two years to complete. Months later, I met Moogie at a totally unrelated party in Joburg - one of those crazy coincidences that make travel so rewarding.

The Hobas viewpoint is also the start of the famous (or infamous) Fish River Canyon hike - a 90km, 5-day odyssey along the canyon floor that ends at the hot springs. I haven't done the trail (yet) but I'm told its rough, tough and utterly unforgettable. Obviously, hikers need to be entirely self-sufficient as there are no facilities whatsoever along the route. Due to the harsh climate, the hike is only open in the winter months (April to September)

In terms of accommodation, apart from the hot springs resort, there's a campsite at the main entrance gate to Hobas, and the Gondwana group runs several lovely 'Cañon' lodges nearby. Their roadhouse is also an excellent place for a meal and a cold drink.

Although it was many years ago now, I still clearly recall leaving the viewpoint as night fell. We were hungry and running low on fuel, despairing that we'd never find supplies in the middle of the darkling desert. Then, just as the fuel light came on, we stumbled across the Canyon roadhouse. We pulled up under a large tree sprinkled with fairy lights, and I was flooded with a sense of delight mixed with extreme relief. The hearty meal we enjoyed on the deck under the stars was one to remember. For more information, visit www.gondwana-collection.com

The Fish River Lodge is another accommodation option, offering various hiking packages, 'fat bike' excursions, drives and guided walks along the canyon's rim. For more information, visit www.fishriverlodge-namibia.com.

Exploring Namaqualand

In this section, we'll have a look Namaqualand south of the Richtersveld. Since the region is famous for its spring flowers, special attention is given to flower spotting routes and destinations. Then, just to be complete, we'll also travel south of Namaqualand proper to briefly discuss some popular wildflower havens in the Cederberg and along the West Coast Peninsula, closer to Cape Town.

Getting There

The N7 highway that leads from Cape Town to Springbok is the major transport corridor through Little Namaqualand (in Afrikaans, *Klein Namakwaland).* Those who've been paying attention will remember that this diminutive appellation applies to the region south of the Orange River, while north of the Orange (in modern Namibia) it's called Great Namaqualand or *Groot Namakwaland* - no relation to Marvel's 'Guardians of the Galaxy'.

So, since we're already in the area, let's start at Springbok and work our way south. I say this knowing that most people will be starting in Cape Town and driving north, so they are going to have to read this part of the book backwards!

Suggested itineraries

As always, it all depends on how much time you have available. The total distance from Cape Town to Springbok is about 560km, but this can be broken up in a number of ways.

Briefly, the two main centres for flower watching are Springbok and Nieuwoudtville (315km from Springbok and 350km from Cape Town). The Namaqua National Park (near Springbok), the west coast around Elands Bay and the Cederberg (near Nieuwoudtville) are also good places to catch the flower show. So...

If you want to do a day trip from Cape Town: the closest flowers to the Mother City are in the West Coast National Park at Langebaan (about 90km). You can then return via Yzerfontein and/or the pretty town of Darling, with its small wildflower reserve - a round trip of roughly 200km.

If you have 2-4 days: there is plenty of floral action in the hills and dales around both Springbok and Nieuwoudtville, so pick a town, choose a nice place to stay and drive around a bit. The Skilpad Wildflower Garden at the Namaqua National Park near Kamieskroon is a definite must (the reserve is also a great overnight destination in its own right, if you can get in).

If you have 5-7 days: after a couple of nights in Springbok, drive the 300-odd km to Nieuwoudtville - or vice versa. Just make sure you book accommodation well in advance as flower season gets busy.

If you have more than 7 days: after a few nights in both Springbok and Nieuwoudtville, extend your trip by spending some time in the Richtersveld (see above), somewhere on the West Coast Peninsula and/or in the Cederberg mountains, just south of Nieuwoudtville. On the West Coast, I would suggest Lambert's Bay, Elands Bay and Paternoster (the Cape Columbine Nature Reserve is a real gem).

If you are driving from Joburg: Due to the distances involved, I would suggest doing an ambitious road trip from Joburg to Springbok on the N14, then Springbok to Cape Town on the N7, before returning to Joburg via the N1 through the Karoo and Bloemfontein (or do the circuit the other way around). This grand tour is about 3150km. Alternatively, you can just drive from Joburg to Springbok and back (about 2200km in total). A side-trip from Springbok to Nieuwoudtville, returning to Springbok, will add about 640km onto the journey. Personally, I hate driving back the way I came so, if you are planning to visit both Springbok and Nieuwoudtville, I would say that it's worth the extra 300-odd kms to complete the Joburg-Springbok-Cape Town circuit. If these distances are too much for you, your only other viable option is to fly to either Cape Town or Upington and rent a car. Chartered flights to Springbok may be available, but this would be beyond the means of most wage-bound mortals.

When to go

This, my friends, is the million-dollar question. And it's not an easy one to answer because the damn spring flowers are unpredictable little buggers.

To be clear, there are actually flowers blooming throughout the year in Namaqualand. Summer-flowering succulents (such as Crassulas) add a dash of colour during the hot months from November to February. Many geophytes and bulbs (such as the Amaryllis family) bloom as temperatures start to drop, in late autumn-early winter. The Scented Candelabra Lily, *Brunsvigia bosmaniae,* puts on a particularly spirited display, flowering three weeks after late-summer rains (although this doesn't happen every year). Then, in winter, many aloe species start to bloom. As such, some experienced Namaqualand flower-spotters actually prefer the March-June season for the specialised blooms on display.

The main event, however, kicks off when the weather starts getting warmer in late winter-early spring and, broadly speaking, the famous spring flowers come out between early August and mid-September (give or take a couple of weeks on either side). Mid to late August is usually considered the peak season, but there are several variables to consider.

Firstly, different types of wildflowers come into bloom during the spring season, including annuals (such as daisies), *vygies* (mesembs), perennials, geophytes, and shrubs. These various species have different life cycles and will bloom and die at different times.

Secondly, you have to find out when the winter rains fell. The flowers will start to appear a month or two after the main rains, and these may occur at different times in different parts of the region. The intensity of the rain is directly related to the intensity of the inflorescence - the more rain, the better the display.

Next, you must ask yourself: where am I? The flowers tend to bloom as temperatures start to rise. This usually occurs first along the coastal areas and in the north, before moving in an easterly direction across the interior of Namaqualand. Altitude also plays a role as the higher up you are, the colder it's going to be and the later the flowering will begin. The heights of the Kamiesberg mountains may have flower displays as late as October.

You also have to consider the vagaries of the spring climate. If there is a sudden shift from a cold winter to a hot spring, the flowers will die faster. If the spring temperatures are low, with cold nights, the flowers will stick around a lot longer. Local conditions are another factor as strong, hot berg winds blowing down the mountains can wipe out an entire colony of flowers overnight.

So, you have to be on your toes and, depending where you are and what type of flowers you want to see, the season can start as early as mid-July and last until the end of September. August is the safest bet, though, especially in Nieuwoudtville and Springbok.

But there's a catch. You cannot just wait around for the flowers to start blooming, then jump in your car and race off to Namaqualand.

This is because during flower season, the entire region goes from somnolent to swamped, with everything booked up months in advance. I found this out first-hand when I arrived in Vanrhynsdorp without pre-booked accommodation (the only night of my trip that I'd left open). I just assumed that I'd easily find a place to crash in this usually sleepy *dorp*, so imagine my outrage when I discovered that every single hotel, guest house and campsite was totally full, and I mean full to bursting. The nearby towns of Vredendal and Nieuwoudtville were also choc-a-bloc.

It's a horrible feeling to be stuck in a strange town, at night, making desperate phone calls, only to find that there is literally no room at any of the inns. I eventually drove to Klawer (20km away) and found the last available room at Oasis Country Lodge, which had been - until very recently - an agricultural high school. Next morning, as I sat eating cornflakes in the barely-converted gymnasium, I realised it was foolish to think that I could just rock up at the height of the season and waltz into a room. But I took solace in the fact that I had made this rookie mistake on behalf of my readers.

Perhaps the main reason for the general shortage of accommodation is the tour groups. You see them everywhere - huge busses hauling hundreds of autumnal pensioners across Namaqualand on guided flower expeditions. The hotel at Vanrhynsdorp was crawling with them, all wearing name tags pinned to neat leisure suits and floral frocks; big teeth and bigger hair glinting in the lamp light. Honestly, it was great fun to watch the procession of happy *ooms* and *tannies* descend the staircase and throng in the lobby, chatting excitedly with their celebrity hosts on the way to the buffet.

Now don't get me wrong. For many people, organised tours are the best way to access Namaqualand and its flowers, and who am I to deny them just because their busses get in the bloody way. A good tour offers security, expert knowledge and convenience, and can also be cost-effective. So, if this is your kind of thing, Google around for a list of operators who specialise in flower tours - there are plenty. If you can, though, I'd avoid this kind of freeze-dried, vacuum-packed tourist experience and travel under your own steam. Or is that too mean?

Flower-Watching Tips

OK, you've checked into your advance-booked accommodation and you're ready to see some flowers. What do you do next? Here are a couple of tips:

Ask questions, speak to people, get recommendations. Conditions change almost daily, so chat to both local residents and fellow visitors to get feedback on where they've been and what they've seen. The staff at tourism offices can also give you the latest info on promising flower-spotting roads and sites. Or try calling the Namaqua Flower Line on 079 294 7260.

Don't go out too early. The flowers respond to the sun and only open as the day gets warmer (just like me). They will also withdraw as the sun starts going down. So, plan to do your peak viewing between 11:00 and 15:00 - depending on how brightly the sun is shining that day. And do note, many flowers will not open at all if it is too rainy, too overcast or too windy.

The flowers face and follow the sun. Place yourself between the sun and the flowers to see them at their best. In the mornings, for example, the flowers on the left-hand side of the road may be open and vice versa in the afternoon. When driving, try to keep the sun at your back.

Look at your feet. There are a vast number of flower species in Namaqualand, so don't just look down on the masses from a distance. Some of the rarer and smaller plants are much more interesting than the common-or-garden daisies that form the famous 'carpets'. So, go down on your hands and knees and get up close.

Don't drive too fast. Many of the most interesting species are hard to spot, so slow down and smell the flowers. It's also important that you drive considerately as cars will be pulling over constantly for photographs and walkabouts. Remember, many of the flower roads are gravel and dust kicked up by a speeding vehicle can make it unpleasant for plants and humans alike.
Do some homework. Get a good flower spotting book, such as the relevant volume of the National Botanical Society's Wildflower Guide series, and familiarise yourself with the plants you'll be seeing. As one harried hotel manager told me, the local people are too busy to hold your hand.

Come with the right attitude. The flowers are disobedient and no-one can (or should) offer any guarantees. So, don't arrive with a sense of entitlement or arrogance in this regard. And don't blame your service provider if the display is less impressive than you had hoped.

Be conservation minded. The plants are very delicate so be careful where you step and always keep to demarcated roads. And don't pick any flowers to show your mates back at the bar.

Bundle up. Take warm clothes as temperatures can drop to below zero at night. If you're camping, an extra sleeping bag is a good idea.

Keep it local. Since there is a paucity of guest houses and hotels in the region, many residents open their homes and farms to overnight guests during peak season. Contact local tourist information centres for a list of private accommodation options.

Get a private flower guide. Some towns in Namaqualand have specialised guides who will usher you around the various sites. This will add greatly to your appreciation of the 'daisies'. Several organisations are also working to train local community members as guides - an initiative that is well worth supporting. Ask at the tourist office for details.

Springbok

At first glance, there's not much to Springbok. It's a hot and dusty place, surrounded by granite outcrops of the Klein Koperberge (Little Copper Mountains) draped in dark vegetation. There are a couple of nice sandstone churches and a pretty rock garden built around a boulder in the centre of the town. But that's about it.

Nevertheless, Springbok has subtle charm and a laid-back atmosphere, and there are several very worthwhile attractions nearby that make it a good place to spend a couple of days. It also offers easy access to some excellent flower-spotting sites, a wide range of accommodation options, and an excellent info centre with well-informed staff.

In terms of food, there isn't much fine dining to be had but most of the hotels and guest houses have a restaurant attached. You'll find plenty of fast-food places, though, including a very popular KFC, a Wimpy and a couple of dodgy hamburger joints on the main road. There are also several independent restaurants operating in a variety of genres.

The architecture of Springbok tends towards the utilitarian; low buildings with corrugated-tin roofs that beat back the summer heat. The main church is very attractive, however. The Edwardian-style Springbok Hotel and art-deco façade of the Masonic Hotel are also notable (both run by the JC Botha Hotel Group - www.namaqualandflowers.co.za).

While you're in town, check out the local museum housed in the old Jewish synagogue, next to the Springbok Hotel. This was the centre of Namaqualand's once-influential Jewish community, most of whom came into the area after fleeing the Pogroms in central Russia, starting around 1880. Initially, they earned their living as *smouses* - travelling salesmen who sold pots, pans, cloth and other useful merchandise from the back of their ox-wagons. A few of these itinerant peddlers eventually settled in Springbok to service the mines in the area and established a small but solid community (peaking at a little over 200 in the 1930s). By the 1970s, however, the last Jewish families had left for greener pastures in the bigger cities of South Africa and abroad.

The museum contains an appealing clutter of artefacts, including old books, typewriters, documents and dresses, while fading info boards take you through the town's history. Next door, the old Jewish festival hall sometimes hosts a community-run art gallery and tea shop, where you can buy paintings and embroidery made by local artists and craftworkers - an initiative that is well worth supporting if it's open.

Another great place to visit is the Springbok Lodge and Café. This unlikely establishment doesn't look like much from the outside but step through the door and a large, wood-panelled emporium beckons. Apart from the usual snacks and assorted crap, the Café has an excellent selection of books on Namaqualand and Namibia, some of which are out of print and hard to find. They also have an extensive gemstone collection on display and a fun semi-precious scratch patch for the kids. The knowledgeable staff at the lodge are a great source of information and can arrange tours to the old Blue Mine - the first substantial copper mining site in the region. The burgers from the attached retro-restaurant are good too (tel. 027 7181 832 / www.springboklodge.com).

Originally named Springbokfontein, the town was first laid out on the farm Melkboschkuil in 1862 by the Phillips & King copper company. The discovery of rich copper deposits at nearby O'okiep in the late 1870s nearly saw Springbok abandoned but the perennial spring continued to run sweet and the town grew into a commercial, educational and administrative centre.

For more information, contact the Namakwa Tourism Centre in Springbok on 027 712 8034/5/6. The Springbok Municipality can be reached on 027 718 8100 / www.namakhoi.gov.za.

Flower Routes

The flowers in Springbok burst out in the most unlikely places. The verges along the N7 highway often contain bright sprays of daisies, for example, while the townships north of town are veritable wildflower extravaganzas with all sorts of colourful blooms transforming the humble plots into impromptu horticultural delights. The people in the townships are usually welcoming to visitors, as long as you approach with respect and ask permission before traipsing through their backyards.

Outside of town, several farms also have large flower fields. The gravel roads around the Kokerboom Motel (about 5km south on the N7) are usually quite reliable in this regard. Just remember that these are private properties so respect closed gates and 'no trespassers' signs.

Another good 'oldfield' display can be found about 12km down the Messelpad road towards Hondeklip Bay (accessed by turning off the N7 about 15km south of Springbok).

Many other flower sites around Springbok are described in the sections that follow. For more up to date information, you can try calling the Namaqua Flower Line on 079 294 7260.

Goegap Nature Reserve & Hester Malan Flower Garden

One of the most popular wildflower destinations in Springbok is the Goegap Nature Reserve, a conservation area covering about 15 000ha. It was first established when the O'okiep Copper Company donated 4600ha of agricultural land to the Cape provincial administration for the development of a wildflower reserve. This was duly opened as the Hester Malan Wildflower Garden in 1966 (named by Nico Malan, Administrator of the Cape Province, in honour of his wife - which must have scored him some points).

Later, the farm 'Goegap' (meaning 'waterhole') was bought by Cape Nature and added to the reserve. A total of 581 plant species have been recorded at Goegap, along with 45 mammal, 25 reptile, 3 amphibian and 94 bird species.

Today, this well-established facility has a tea garden and succulent nursery with interpretive signs and attractive rock gardens. There's also a 13-17km gravel route that leads through a lovely landscape of boulders and koppies, with the bulk of Carolusberg looming in the background. When the flowers are in bloom, the plains along this road are swathed in orange and yellow cloaks, making it popular with photographers and TV crews. It's an easily accessible drive suitable for most cars and highly recommended.

If you wish to explore further, the reserve has about 65km of rougher 4x4 roads for those with appropriate vehicles. There are also trails for walking, hiking, horse rides and mountain bikes. Tourist facilities are rounded out by picnic spots, camp sites, overnight huts and bush camps.

To reach Goegap, head out of Springbok towards Pofadder. Just after you cross the N7, take the turn-off for the tarred R355, which is marked for Goegap, the airport, and the Springbok caravan park. A short distance later, you'll pass the golf course and country club. In season, the greens and fairways of this establishment are surrounded by beautiful dollops of daisies. About 10km from Springbok, you'll see a turn off for the Reserve. Head through the entrance gates and keep going for another 5km on gravel to reach the reception (tel. 027 718 9906).

Spektakel Pass, Komaggas and Kleinzee

From the centre of Springbok, follow signs for Kleinzee. This tarred road (R355) offers great views over Springbok before levelling out and heading west across the plateau. Here you'll see several large stands of flowers, especially in the township of Matjieskloof where the wildflowers bloom indiscriminately among the shacks. The people of Matjieskloof were very friendly the day I visited, and the late-afternoon light was beautiful, so I took many pictures of the local community playing appreciatively in their transient flower gardens.

From Matjieskloof, you can continue down the Spektakel (Spectacle) Pass, which offers expansive vistas over the hilly plains that lead to the sea. The intriguing Naries Namaqua Retreat can be found in this area, with a range of accommodation options and activities (076 238 2934 / www.naries.co.za).

About 40km from Springbok, there is a turn-off to the settlement of Komaggas (about 20km away). This pleasant village, with its pastel-coloured houses, was founded by the London Missionary Society in 1829 before being taken over the Rhenish Church in 1843 and then the Dutch Reformed Church in 1936. The name is said to translate to "place of many wild olive trees'.

Most of the people in Komaggas were employed by now-defunct De Beers diamond mine at Kleinzee, and it's unclear if, when and how new jobs will be generated. For more info on Komaggas, try contacting local area guide Rodville Adams: 076 642 0868.

If you forsake Komaggas and continue straight on the R355, you will arrive at the aforementioned mining village of Kleinzee (about 100km from Springbok). The first diamonds on the farm Kleyne Zee were discovered in 1927 and De Beers established the town itself in 1942. When mining at Kleinzee ceased around 2009, the population dwindled to about 1000 and the formerly restricted settlement began welcoming visitors keen to explore the miles of untouched coastline (although you still have to show your ID and sign in at the boom gates).

Several campsites, guesthouses and restaurants are now established, along with the Molyneux Reserve (tel. 027 877 0028) that boasts over 100 indigenous plant species and a 5km walking route. The abundant birdlife in the Buffels River estuary and the country's largest on-land seal colony will also appeal to nature lovers (local guides are available). Meanwhile, De Beers is still working on rehabilitating the land and developing alternative industries, such as an oyster farm.

The Kleinzee Mine Museum is well maintained and may offer tours through the old mining operations if you book in advance. Hikers will enjoy the self-guided Boulder Heritage Walking Trail and the multi-day Diamond Coast slackpacking trail between Kleinzee and Koingnaas. Guided 4x4 routes include the Dune Route (which offers sandboarding) and the Shipwreck trail that takes in the remains of the Border, which ran around in 1947. You can also try out the formerly restricted road between Kleinzee and Koingnaas, which is now open to the public. The Noup rest camp offers idiosyncratic accommodation on the coast along with other activities (079 877 8859 / www.noup.co.za).

For more information, contact the Kleinzee Tourism Centre on 027 807 2999 or 027 877 0028.

The Messelpad and Wildeperdhoek Pass

Drive about 15km south of Springbok on the N7 and take the turn-off marked for Hondeklip Bay and Soebatsfontein. This is the old Messelpad (Mason's Road), which was once the main thoroughfare used by copper riders to transport ore from the Springbok mines to the harbour at Hondeklip. Today, this somewhat neglected gravel road still cuts a tawny strip through majestic mountains, offering a wonderful stretch of gravel travel. The extensive dry-stone retaining walls, which gave the road its name, can still be seen. It's a breathtaking drive but you probably won't glimpse many daisies, apart from a particularly impressive display on a farm about 12km from the highway. The succulent displays, however, are excellent.

About 20kms down the Messelpad, you'll see a small turn-off that leads back to the N7. This will return you to Springbok in a round trip of about 100km. But don't be hasty. The best part is still to come, so continue driving until the road begins winding down a steep valley covered in succulents and aloes.

This marvellous stretch of track then leads along the banks of the muddy Buffels River, lined with deep-green trees, before rising up again to wend its way through the scrubby mountains once more. On this part of the road, you'll see a sign for a 'historic prison' where the convict labour that built the pass was housed. Park your car in the demarcated area if you want to walk down to the prison and wander around the ruins.

The road now continues as the Wildeperdhoek Pass (Pass of the Wild Horses) until it reaches a large cleft in the mountains. From here, there is an amazing view over the Namaqua National Park below. Keep following the road as it clings to the sheer edge of the cliff face, with a precipitous drop-off to your left; slowly swooping down the contour lines until you arrive on a wide, shrub-covered plain. From here (about 55km from Springbok), you can either follow signs to the Namaqua National Park reception area (which eventually connects to the N7 at Kamieskroon), or you can follow signs for Koingnaas / Soebatsfontein and then turn north towards Komaggas to return to Springbok via Spektakel Pass. Either way, it's a very worthwhile round trip of about 160km.

Okiep, Concordia and Carolusberg

Head north from Springbok on the N7 for about 7km and then turn off towards Okiep (originally spelled O'okiep). The name is Nama in origin and is said to mean either 'the place of the big tree', 'the little fountain' or 'brackish spring where copper occurs'. Whatever the case, this was once the location of the world's richest copper mine.

Okiep's mining heritage is still clearly in evidence. The old smelter smokestack and Cornish pump are both extant and will interest those with a mineralogical bent. You'll also find the remnants of old ore bins, mine houses and granaries, along with a few stone-built churches that serviced the many Cornish tin miners and masons who came to Namaqualand during the copper boom.

The mine closed around 2009 and the town is now experiencing a dearth of employment opportunities (although there are murmurings that a new wave of mining entrepreneurs is looking at reviving the diggings). Nevertheless, the flowers bloom cheerfully along the roadside as kids stroll amiably through the orange fields on their way home from school. Spend some time taking in the scene, then continue on the road out of town towards Concordia.

A short distance outside of Okiep, the tarmac rises over a low saddle between two koppies and dips across a shallow valley. The fields on either side of this stretch of road are often covered with swatches of yellow, white, purple and orange flowers. A wire fence will prevent you from walking through the floral wonderland but it's a lovely scene nonetheless.

Keep going for another 8km or so until you reach Concordia. This section of the road was once fortified by a row of block houses intended to keep the Boer forces at bay during the Anglo-Boer War of 1899-1902. But to no avail. Boer General Jan Smuts captured Concordia, Springbok and Steinkopf, and mounted a month-long siege on O'okiep. Despite these heroics, the war ended in defeat for the Boers shortly thereafter. The remains of some of the block houses, as well as Fort Shelton, can still be seen.

Concordia itself is another former mission station and mine that has now become a humble settlement, made glorious for a few months each year by a spontaneous bounty of wildflowers.

It is also the location of an outcrop of orbicular diorite - a rare rock texture that is "the result of granitoid magmas separating while in a fluid state, with one granite type forming ovoid 'orbs' showing concentric internal banding, within a ground mass of slightly different composition". Whatever that means...

For more information, contact the Namakwa Tourism Centre in Springbok (tel. 027 712 8034/5/6) or visit www.okiep.co.za.

From Concordia, you can continue on gravel roads to Carolusberg, the location of Simon van der Stel's original 'copper mountain' from 1685. Or just retrace your steps to Springbok via Okiep.

Nababeep

From Springbok, head north on the N7 for about 7km, take the marked turn-off and drive another 12km until you reach Nababeep. The name is Nama in origin, although the precise meaning is obscure. Depending on your pronunciation and your source, it is said to translate as either 'the place where the giraffe drinks', 'the water behind the little hump or hill', 'where the rock is carried', 'rhinoceros place' or 'bad road'. Take your pick.

The main attraction here is the mining museum - an interesting facility with installations on the old copper mines that were once the lifeblood of the region. It also has photographic displays of the siege at O'okiep and other documents from the period. A rusting steam locomotive named Clara, which once plied the narrow-gauge railway between O'okiep and Port Nolloth, has pride of place in the courtyard, along with several large pieces of mining equipment. The quarry site itself is closed to the public but you might be able to organise a tour.

Sadly, since the mine closed in 2004, this once-prosperous village has become largely moribund. The houses are neat, however, and the dark, dry mountains that surround the town are starkly beautiful.

There are several eye-catching flower sites in the area, including one great location on the outskirts of town that combines kokerbooms and daisies for a floral landscape that is uniquely Namaqualand (and the cover of this book). The nearby country club and golf course has also been known to boast some deeply impressive flower displays.

In terms of walking the multi-day Schaaprivier (Sheep River) Hiking Trail sounds intriguing. And a network of mountain bike routes can be accessed from the Jakkalswater farm (www.jakkalswater.co.za).

For more info, contact the Namakwa Tourism Centre in Springbok (tel. 027 712 8034/5/6).

Vioolsdrift

If you want to take a plunge in the Orange River, there are a bunch of riverside camps and lodges around Vioolsdrift (115km north of Springbok on the N7). This is the starting point for a range of multi-day white-water rafting excursions on the Orange, which are very popular. Google around to find a suitable tour operator (www.thegrowcery.co.za is one such provider and their website has some good content on the region to boot). Other water sports and adventure activities are also available.

If you have a 4x4, you can drive from Vioolsdrift through the Helskloof/Nababeep Nature Reserve and into the Richtersveld Community Conservancy - see above.

Vioolsdrift is the location of the main border post between South Africa and Namibia (open 24 hours). Legend has it that the site was named after a Nama named Jan Viool (violin), who operated a ferry across the river in the days before a bridge was built.

Cross the border here to visit the astounding Ai-Ais Hot Springs and Fish River Canyon (about 125km away). Passports are required. Bear in mind that the Namibian dollar is pegged to the South African Rand at one to one, and the rand is legal tender within Namibia.

Kamieskroon

Once you've wrapped things up in Springbok, head south on the N7 and drive about 68km until you reach the little town of Kamieskroon. This is the centre of the Kamiesberg mountain range that extends for 100kms, with peaks reaching heights of 1500 metres. It's the coldest and highest part of Namaqualand and is named after the Khoikhoi phrase 'Tjamies', which translates as 'jumble of rocks'.

Kamieskroon itself is a rather ramshackle *dorp* consisting of about 100 unassuming homes arranged along a rough grid of gravel roads. It's a dozy, dreamy place and the enveloping mountains seem to cradle the town in an adamantine embrace, with the 'crown' of a nearby summit providing the village with its title. Electricity only reached the settlement in the 1990s.

In season, the gardens, yards and even drainage ditches of Kamieskroon are adorned with delightful sprays of wildflowers that poke up carelessly from the ground. I even found an adorable group of baby goats gambolling amongst the blooms in an open plot next to one of the houses - I kid you not (hah!). But be careful - those little buggers nip!

In terms of tourist facilities, the town has an attractive church that's worth a look, a convenience store that sells fuel, and a couple of coffee shops (which may or may not be open when you visit). There's also a caravan park and campsite, and the local hotel hosts photographic workshops that promise to improve your flower pics (027 672 1614 / www.kamieskroonhotel.com). Depending on the time of year, a traditional *kookskerm* (outdoor cooking area) may be open, offering guests a Nama-influenced dining experience (tel. 076 902 5488).

The first settlement in the Kamiesberg began in the 1860s on the farm Wilgenhoutskloof, located in a narrow valley about 8km north of present-day Kamieskroon. It was soon renamed Bowesdorp, after the local district surgeon Henry Bowe. Apparently, Bowe's son, Allan, went on to become a partner in the Fabergé jewellery firm - not bad for a country boy.

The Dutch Reformed Congregation chose Bowesdorp as its Namaqualand headquarters in 1870, and a school, hostel, post office, hotel, shops and houses soon grew up around the small church. By 1924, however, the water supply had become insufficient for the growing population and the church was relocated to the nearby village of Kamieskroon. The eerie ruins of Bowesdorp can still be seen, slowly collapsing in the silence of their lonely valley.

Kamieskroon is also the centre of the !Kimmies Tourist Route that incorporates a handful of tiny villages hidden away in the surrounding hills and plains. For more information, contact the Kamieskroon Municipality: 027 672 1627 / www.kamiesberg.gov.za.

Namaqua National Park & Skilpad Wildflower Garden

A popular stop on the flower-spotting map, the Namaqua National Park (NNP) is a very special place indeed. The main entrance is located about 22km to the west of Kamieskroon, on good quality gravel roads. Alternatively, it can be accessed from the somewhat rougher but very scenic Messelpad road heading down from Springbok. The small Groen (Green) River Mouth Gate, offering access to the coastal section of the reserve, can be reached from Garies.

The well-known Skilpad (Tortoise) Wildflower Garden is situated next to the main gate, near Kamieskroon. Originally established by the World Wildlife Fund for Nature, who bought a section of the farm Skilpad as a wildflower reserve in 1988, this is a reliable place to view some flower 'carpets' since it is located in a topographical bowl that effectively captures the moisture blowing in off the sea. The park works to keep the garden blooming by bringing in sheep and goats to graze away the secondary vegetation every couple of years.

A nice circular driving route around the Skilpad garden has been laid out, suitable for all vehicles, and the park manager posts regular flower updates on the park website. A 5km walking trail through the flowers has also been established. The 3km Korhaan Walking Trail that leads through the bush behind the reception office is also worth checking out.

There are several accommodation options in the NNP, which was formally established in 2002.

The Skilpad Rest Camp has 4 chalets, each with two single beds, a sleeper couch, and an open-plan dining room / kitchen. Units have electricity and come with a ceiling fan, indoor fireplace and outdoor braai area. Located a short drive from the main gate, the units all look out over a breathtaking valley. It's an amazing location that offers tremendous views in any season.

The Luiperdskloof (Leopard's Ravine) Guest Cottage is a rustic unit, only accessible with a 4x4 vehicle. There are three bedrooms, a bathroom, kitchen, fireplace and braai area. The cottage has no electricity but is supplied with candles and gas appliances. From the office at Skilpad, it's a 2-3 hour drive to reach the unit, which offers access to several short hiking trails and picnic sites for the exclusive use of residents.

If you're looking for an extra-special experience, try spending a couple of nights at one of the two Flower Camps (one is inland and the other on the beach). These are privately-run luxury camps that are only open during the Spring flower season. Featuring fully serviced *en-suite* canvas tents with full amenities, this is glamping at its best with duvets, carpets, electric blankets and other creature comforts on hand. A full English breakfast, high tea and three-course dinner are included in the package, all served in a heated communal dining tent complete with white linen and glassware. Picnic baskets and cheese boards may be purchased, and a cash bar is available. For more information, visit www.flowercamps.co.za.

Last, but by no means least, there are 9 coastal camp sites. These are very basic and guests need to bring everything with them. There is no water, cell phone reception or ablution facilities (although some have enviro-loos). But the camps are located right on the beach and there's no better way to get up close and personal with the rugged shoreline. The coastal camps are best accessed from the Groen River entrance gate and 4x4 vehicles may be required to reach some of the sites.

There is no shop, ATM, fuel or restaurant within the NNP, but there might be a couple of country kitchens or farm stalls operating outside the main gate. In season, the local community sometimes operates a traditional 'kookskerm' at the reception area that offers visitors a taste of traditional Nama-style cooking. Otherwise, bring along your own food and enjoy an al-fresco lunch in the picnic area. Overnight guests are reminded to bring their own firewood.

Educationally speaking, the park has a resource centre with good displays on the reserve's flora and fauna. Dormitory accommodation for school groups is available and this facility is used for community education and conservation initiatives. Outreach programmes are an integral part of the park's activities, and good progress has been made in this regard despite the park's far-flung constituents.

Although the NNP is not rich in big game species, there are several iconic animals to be spotted within the reserve. These include the Namaqua Speckled Padloper (the world's smallest tortoise), the Namaqua dune molerat, the bat-eared fox and the elusive caracal. Birders will be in their element with over 100 species recorded and a breeding pair of Booted eagles nesting in the tall trees opposite the main reception block. The website also reminds twitchers to look out for Black Harriers. Resident mammals include klipspringer, aardvark, baboon, steenbok, duiker, porcupine, black-backed jackal and leopard.

Other activities in the NNP include mountain biking (bring your own bikes) and the 6km Heaviside Hiking Trail that starts from the Abjoel viewing deck, about 15km north of the Groen River gate. This walk takes you on a rocky path along the coast, from where you might spot humpback whales and Heaviside dolphins.

4x4 enthusiasts won't want to miss the Caracal Eco Route that leads from the Skilpad gate, down the Soebatsfontein Pass, across the Wildeperdehoek plains and along the coast to the Groen River gate - a distance of between 175 and 200kms (allow 6-8 hours, plus another 2 hours if you need to return to the Skilpad gate). The trail is described as easy to moderate with some steep sections and the occasional sandy stretch. 4WD is essential. Get your permit and booklet at Skilpad Reception.

All in all, this beautiful reserve is one to watch. In the last 15 years, it has expanded dramatically from a small landlocked enclave of just 1000 hectares to an extensive conservation area that covers 140 000ha, stretching from the Kamiesberg to the sea. This growth was enabled by an amicable partnership between SANParks, local farmers and the De Beers mining company (who have contractually handed over a 50km stretch of un-mined territory along the coast, between Spoeg River mouth and Groen River mouth). Plans for future expansion (including the establishment of a large marine reserve extending into the sea) are also on the cards.

For more information contact the Namaqua National Park on 027 672 1948 / www.sanparks.org/parks/namaqua.

Leliefontein, Paulshoek, Rooifontein and Vaalputs

To the east and south of Kamieskroon, there's a network of gravel roads that lead through the mountains, past a scattering of small settlements. If you want to escape the relative bustle of the main flower routes, this little-explored area (once a large 'coloured reserve') makes for an excellent day trip with great scenery, intriguing towns and several good flower sites. Many of the local farms also offer hiking, horse riding, mountain bike trails and other country comforts.

If you want to avoid the N7 for a bit, you can also use these back roads to travel north to Springbok (via Gamoep and the gravel R355), south to Garies (via Leliefontein), or south-east to Loeriesfontein and Nieuwoudtville (via Platbakkies and the R355).

The town of Leliefontein (Lily Spring), located in the middle of this unseen corner of Namaqualand, is an interesting place to spend an hour or two. It was originally the kraal of a Nama chief named Jantje Wildschut (Johnny Wildshot) by the colonials. Unusually, the land was granted to Wildschut by the Dutch Governor Van Plettenberg in 1771, who turned down a claim from a white farmer named Hermanus Engelbrecht in favour of the indigenous people.

Missionary work began here under the London Missionary Society in 1809 but an attack by a troublesome raider named Jonker Afrikaner caused the station to be abandoned in 1811. In 1816, the reigning chief asked for another station to be established and the challenge was accepted by Rev. Barnabas Shaw of the Wesleyan Missionary Society. Several church buildings were subsequently built and remain in use today. A ceremonial sundial donated by Rev. Shaw still passes away the hours in the parsonage garden.

But it wasn't all peace and light. During the Anglo-Boer war, the Afrikaner general Manie Maritz reputedly killed 35 Basters at Leliefontein, because he thought they were conspiring with the British. This massacre is little-known today but there is a plaque with the victims' names displayed in the Leliefontein church hall.

Leliefontein is about 30km away from Kamieskroon. For more info, contact the Leliefontein Municipal Office (tel. 027 672 1808) or the Leliefontein Kookskerm, which offers traditional meals (tel. 027 672 1972). Pedroskloof Guest House and Restaurant is located on a working farm a short distance out of Leliefontein. Mountain bike and hiking trails are available (tel. 087 095 0523 / www.pedroskloof.co.za).

Paulshoek, a settlement nestled in the heights of the Kamiesberg, is another nice place to visit. It has a cultural camp where visitors can enjoy traditional meals and spend the night in a *matjieshuis*, but prior booking is required (contact the Sonop Guest House on 027 541 1341). Paulshoek is about 70km away from Kamieskroon. For more info, contact the municipal office on 027 541 1077.

Rooifontein, about 50km away from Kamieskroon, offers hiking trails and a Kokerboom Forest with several unusual quiver tree houses. Hiking trails are available at the nearby towns of Tweerivier, Klipfontein and Spoegrivier. Contact the municipal office on 027 672 1221.

If you are so inclined, you can also visit the nearby town of Vaalputs, near Gamoep, which is South Africa's main nuclear waste disposal site. As the official National Radioactive Waste Disposal Institute Of South Africa website confidently proclaims, "in this area the annual evaporation exceeds the annual rainfall, which means that even if radioactivity should escape, it could not contaminate ground water that might find its way to the surface." Well, that's reassuring.

The website goes on to allay fears by saying that "the Vaalputs site, allocated for the disposal of our low and intermediate-level waste, was chosen for its extreme isolation and dryness. This area is sufficient for storing the nuclear waste of three power stations the size of Koeberg for 40 years. The waste is stored in trenches 10 m deep and radiation at the surface is almost at natural levels and does not constitute a health hazard. However, for safety reasons, the site is fenced off and monitored. On average 500 steel drums and 100 concrete drums are shipped to Vaalputs every year." Amazingly, visits to the site can be arranged - it sounds like a great place to take the kids.

The settlement of Kharkams, 25km to the south of Kamieskroon on the N7, is a good flower spotting site. The name means 'gathering place of the Nama near abundant water' and is part of the old stock farmers' route between Leliefontein and Bethelsklip (an archaeological site which shows evidence of human occupation dating back over 800 years). The huge boulders at Bethelsklip were once used as a pulpit from where Rev. Shaw gave sermons to the local Khoikhoi. This has given the site its alternative name, 'Preacher's Rock'.

Hondeklip Bay to Groen River Mouth

The gravel roads that lead west from Kamieskroon to the sea give the adventurous traveller an opportunity to visit to some remote and unusual places. This area can be accessed by following signs to Soebatsfontein and Hondeklip Bay from various points along the N7. Alternatively, for a more dramatic experience, follow the 4x4 route through the Namaqua National Park towards Soebatsfontein and then wiggle your way along obscure back roads until you reach the ocean.

The roads in this area are quite rough but it's a magnificent journey that trundles through several uninhabited river valleys before reaching the little *dorp* of Soebatsfontein (50km from Kamieskroon). The name translates as 'the spring of pleading', apparently because a Nama shepherd was captured by Bushman while drinking at the spring and had to beg for his life (to no avail).

Despite its rather melancholy title, this small cluster of houses exudes a gentle appeal. It has a post office, a couple of stores (where you can buy a refreshing cold drink to wash the dust from your throat) and a deeply abiding sense of peace and quiet. The short Boesman's Uitkyk (Bushman's Lookout) and Panorama hiking trails are close to the town. Permits and maps are available from the post office.

From here, continue south and east to Hondeklip Bay (although you will need to speak Afrikaans if you want to ask for directions). The road now leads through an undulating landscape, dotted with koppies and rocky outcrops. Occasional farmsteads offer the only visible reminder of human occupation, while herds of goats and sheep can be seen grazing gracefully on the shrubby slopes.

About 30km south of Soebatsfontein, you'll come to the Spoeg River (Spittle or Saliva River) which bubbles between small islands, covered with bright spurts of spring flowers. You'll now head east, past the ruins of the briefly prosperous village of Wallekraal, towards Hondeklip Bay. The river soon veers off to the left where it enters the sea near the Spoeg River Caves, now part of the 4x4 trail through the Namaqua National Park.

As you continue towards Hondeklip Bay, you'll pass a turn-off for the (formerly) De Beer's-controlled mining area of Koingnaas. The presence of mine dumps and high fences indicate that this was once a heavily restricted area. The mine, like many others in the area, is now closed and De Beers handed the town to the local municipality in 2016.

Finally, about 90km from Kamieskroon, you'll reach the sea at Hondeklip Bay.

Maybe it was the grey, inclement weather, but my first impressions of Hondeklip Bay were not good. The sea was angry and grey, the sky was brooding, and the ramshackle collection of houses, plonked haphazardly on a sandy plain, were singularly unlovely. But then the sun came out, the atmosphere shifted, and I began to be won over.

Hondeklip Bay (Dog Stone Bay) gets its name from a small, canine-shaped rock that looks out to sea. The 'ear' of this formation was chopped off in the 1850s and set to Cape Town as the emblem of the spurious 'Dog's Ear Copper Company', which only succeeded in fleecing investors of their money before closing down. The rock was further damaged in 1970 when lightning struck off the 'nose', leaving behind a rather amorphous blob of gneiss. The rock is situated on the edge of town, behind the police station.

Although this was once a bustling copper port, Hondeklip Bay is now a somewhat desolate place notable mainly for its wild and rocky coastline, excellent fishing, and rusting shipwrecks that sprawl across the boulders like enormous steel carcasses.

In terms of accommodation, I would recommend the self-catering Honnehokke Resort. Run by Attie and Esme, a wonderful couple who know the area well, it's a friendly establishment and, when I was there, the well-stocked bar was enlivened by an ice-eating parrot who liked to drop his metallic beaker to get attention. Their jaffles filled with springbok meat were also delicious. Please note, the resort has no ATM nor credit card facilities.

Incidentally, the resort is currently up for sale due to the owners' health concerns, so if you're on the lookout for a new career... For more info, contact the Honnehok on 082 564 5471 / www. honnehokke.co.za.

Other popular places to stay include Visbeen Lodge(027 692 3993 / www.visbeenlodge.co.za) and Flower Power Farm (021 854 7417 / www.flowerpowerfarm.co.za).

Hondeklip Bay is also a rich fossil site and several teeth from the prehistoric Megalodon shark have been unearthed along the beach. Crayfishing is popular in season (if you have a permit) and there are several 4x4 routes along the untouched coastline (note that there is no fuel available in Hondeklip Bay, so arrive with a full tank).

All in all, this wind-tossed little settlement offers the Namaqualand coast at its most unusual. However, the biggest surprise in Hondeklip Bay was the Villain. Allow me to explain...

The Villain

When I was there in 2007, the Villain was local artist who painted "oils, portraits, seascapes, landscapes, flowers, animals, others". I have no idea if he's still there, or even still alive, but I hope he is and will continue referring to him in the present tense...

The Villain's real name is Dion and he described himself as an adrenaline junkie. Unfortunately, this penchant for excitement got him involved in armed robbery and he was sent to jail for 10 years. In prison, he started painting as a hobby and, when he got out, he and his wife packed everything they owned into an old Ford Sapphire station wagon and travelled around the country, looking for a place they could call home. One day, they arrived at Hondeklip Bay and decided to stay.

When I met him, the self-effacing 'villain' lived in a tiny shack in what he called the 'plakkerkamp' (squatter camp) on the outskirts of town. An adjacent caravan served as his studio where he painted compulsively, either from memory or by copying images from the pages of magazines and newspapers. To my big city eyes, it looked to be a very meagre and difficult life, but the Villain had embraced his destiny with an honesty and enthusiasm that I found quite inspiring.

I first noticed the Villain when I saw a row of brightly coloured paintings neatly arrayed on the sandy ground in front of his home, propped against the low, barbed wire fence. The Villain's subjects ranged from attractive flower-themed landscapes to wildlife scenes to gothic hard-rock icons to portraits of celebrities (which included an eclectic collection of luminaries such as Cher, Sophia Loren, Katherine Zeta-Jones and Amor Vittone). He also painted nudes, posing provocatively as they gazed out into the veld.

The residents of Hondeklip Bay seemed quite bemused by the Villain and his art, especially his nudes. Some of the people I spoke to said that he didn't cause any trouble and had become a valuable part of the community; a local celebrity who attracted tourists to this out-of-the-way town.

In return, the Villain loved Hondeklip Bay. He said he could live here for 20 years and still see new things. He loved the sunrises, he loved the land, and he loved the flowers that bloom every spring. Prices at his unlikely gallery ranged from R50 to R100 for his pretty miniatures, while his larger images and 'masterpieces' went for several hundred rand.

I was fascinated by the Villain. He was so open, passionate and positive about his work and life, it made my prosaic neuroses seem petty and irrelevant by comparison. Most poignantly, he called himself the Villain not because of his jail sentence per se, but because he wasn't allowed out to attend his mother's funeral. This, he said, made him feel like a real criminal and his pseudonym is intended as a tribute to his departed mum.

Nazi Invasion!

As you leave Hondeklip, you can either head back towards the N7, or you can turn off to the south and head for the farms of Sarriesam and Soutfontein. This road is blocked by an interminable series of farm gates, but offers an utterly unembellished insight into the life of this rural community with its tiny, isolated homesteads huddling against the winds that blow across the sandy plain. Sparks of wildflowers tickle the eyes, with accompanying shrubs and succulents doing their utmost to attract potential pollinators.

This part of the coast is associated with the strange and sinister story of Robey Leibbrandt, a South African boxing champ who fell under Hitler's spell during the 1936 Olympic Games in Munich. After the competition was over, Leibbrandt returned to Germany for studies and, when the Second World War broke out, he joined the *Wehrmacht.* He was later recruited as an *Abwehr* (German Intelligence) agent.

In 1941, Leibbrandt was sent back to SA under Operation Weissdorn (white thorn). The mission: to assassinate General Jan Smuts, trigger a coup, and establish a new regime that was sympathetic to the Nazis (who already enjoyed the support of many right-wing Afrikaners). As such, Leibbrandt was secretly put ashore by the Germans at Mitchell's Bay, a bit south of Hondeklip Bay, and slowly worked his way down to Cape Town before moving to Pretoria.

Along the way, he tried to form alliances with existing pro-Nazi organisations such as the Ossewabrandwag (ox-wagon sentinel) and their assault troop of 'stormjaers', but only managed to assemble an irregular force of about 60 malcontents. Undeterred, Leibbrandt and his motley crew launched a series of small-scale acts of sabotage, such as dynamiting power lines, blowing up railway tracks, and cutting telephone and telegraph cables.

Against the wishes of his German overlords, Leibbrandt gradually broke cover and began giving fiery speeches around the country. This raised his profile to the extent that, in 1942, he was involved in a shootout with South African soldiers but managed to escape. Now a fugitive, Leibbrandt tried to lie low but was captured in Pretoria thanks to a tip off.

At his trial in 1943, Leibbrandt claimed that had acted 'for Volk and Fuhrer' and proudly gave the Nazi salute. When he was sentenced to death for treason, he shouted, "I greet death!". Nevertheless, keen to avoid a martyrdom, Smuts commuted the sentence to life imprisonment.

After the war, Smuts lost the election in a huge upset (similar to Winston Churchill's contemporaneous defeat at the hands of Clement Attlee), and the newly-enthroned National Party of DF Malan offered an amnesty to all 'war offenders'. Leibbrandt was thus released and continued to dabble in hateful politics until he died of a heart attack in Ladybrand, in 1966.

After about 70km of obscure farm roads, you'll reach an intersection with the 'main' gravel road from Garies to Groen (Green) River Mouth. This part of the road has some fantastic wildflower displays but watch out for the deep cracks that creep across the roadway. If you hit one of these crevices at speed, you could flip the car or twist an axle - neither of which would be pleasant.

The Groen River mouth itself is apparently beautiful but I didn't see it for myself because, when I was there, the river was running high over a low-level causeway and I chickened out from making the crossing. Back then, there were no facilities at Groen River Mouth but there was a long-standing community of hippie-squatters living at a makeshift campsite. Now, the river mouth is the location of a small entrance gate that offers access to the coastal section of the Namaqua National Park,

When you are all done exploring, turn to the east and head back towards Garies and the N7.

Garies

The little town of Garies (pronounced with a hard 'g') is another popular stop on the Kamiesberg flower route. It is named from the Nama word for 'couch-grass' *(Cynodon dactylon),* which grows in the river. The town was first established in 1845 when the land was given to the Dutch Reformed Church by the owner of the farm Goedeverwagting (Good Expectations).

Apart from flower-spotting, visitors can further occupy themselves by tackling one of the walking trails in the area. The nearby Letterklip (Letter Rock) on Studer's Pass is another cool place to visit - a collection of boulders famous for some very old graffiti dating back to 1685, when Simon van der Stel carved his name into the stone *en route* to the Copper Mountain. Other travellers continued the tradition and, during the Anglo-Boer War, British soldiers added their names and regimental insignia to the walls while they were hiding out from Boer commandos. Although the temptation may be strong, please don't add your own initials to this historical site.

For more information, contact the Garies Municipality: 027 652 8000

Vanrhynsdorp and the Olifants River Valley

South of Garies, the N7 highway crosses from the Northern Cape Province into the Western Cape; leading past the huge shunting yard at Bitterfontein, where the main rail line from Cape Town terminates. Bitterfontein is also the centre of the emerging Hardeveld Tourist Route, which takes you through the small villages of Stofkraal, Molsvlei, Rietpoort, Putsekloof, Kliprand and Nuwerus.

Continuing south into the pebbly plains of the Knersvlakte, you'll finally reach Vanrhynsdorp (150km from Garies). This is the centre of the Matzikama Municipal district and the Olifants River Valley tourist region, which stretches down to the coast and incorporates the towns of Doringbaai, Ebenhaezer, Klawer,

Lutzville, Papendorp, Strandfontein and Vredendal. Vanrhynsdorp can also be said to be the southern boundary of the Namaqualand botanical region, on the transition zone with the Cape Floristic Region (i.e. fynbos).

The Olifants River Wine Route runs through the area, which should entertain bibulous visitors with well-known wineries including Lutzville Vineyards, Klawer Wine Cellar, Namaqua Wines and Wilgenhof. Vanrhynsdorp is also the gateway to the Bokkeveld plateau (including the flower-paradise of Nieuwoudtville) located over the mountains to the east - see next section.

But before you rush up Van Rhyn's Pass to see the famous inflorescence of Nieuwoudtville, try spend some time in Vanrhynsdorp itself. This pretty town, built around a relatively grand church, offers a good tourist info centre and a well-appointed museum that's worth a wander. The Old Gaol complex has a couple of enticing coffee and craft shops, while the succulent nursery, just out of town, is another popular attraction (tel. 027 219 1062).

Lovers of retro-electronics should also definitely pop into the Latsky Radio Museum - a private collection of old and rare valve radios, lovingly curated by a loquacious ex-schoolteacher. Toeing the fine line between passion and monomania, this is a must-see for anyone interested in vintage wireless tech. It's the kind of place my eccentric uncle Morris would have loved, but he didn't like to leave his house. Contact the radio museum on 027 219 1032.

Do note though, as I mentioned previously, during flower season this entire region is full, full, full. Every room for miles around is booked up and there's a mania in the air, with all the people frantically asking 'Where the flowers? Where the flowers?'. Book ahead or face sleeping in the car.

But the Olifants River Valley isn't just about flowers and wine. There are several important wetlands along the coast and nature-lovers can spend many happy hours driving through the Matzikama mountains (now being protected in a series of emerging conservation areas, such as the Knersvlakte Nature Reserve).

There's also a range of annual events and festivals to check out, such as the succulent show at Vanrhynsdorp, the Maskam 4x4 Challenge, the West Coast Air Carnival, the cultural Rittelfees, the Vanrhynsdorp agricultural show, the Doringbaai Perlemoenfees (Abalone Festival), and others.

For more info, contact Vanrhynsdorp Tourist Info: 027 201 3371 / www.namaquawestcoast.com. The Matzikama Municipality can be reached on 027 201 3300 / www.matzikamamunicipality.co.za.

Nieuwoudtville

As you head east on the R27 out of Vanrhynsdorp, the road runs dead-straight over the Knersvlakte towards the sheer wall of the Bokkeveld Mountains. At the foot of this massif, you'll start to climb the steep Van Rhyn's Pass, built by legendary road builder Thomas Bain in 1880.

It's a short but dramatic pass, offering fantastic views over the scarred plains below, especially if you are stuck behind a slow-moving truck and have some time to look around. A couple of sharp hairpin bends at the must now be navigated before you crest the summit and enter the Bokkeveld Plateau. The viewpoint at the top of the pass is great for a photo op.

From here, it's a short drive across the plateau to the charming village of Nieuwoudtville (50km from Vanrhynsdorp). Pronounced knee-vote-ville, this delightful *dorp* was established in 1897, on a piece of land bought from a farmer named Nieuwoudt. But white settlers had been resident in the area since the mid-1700s by virtue of the good drainage provided by sandstone rock layers during the wet winter months, which allowed life-giving springs to bubble up to the surface. The sandstone also provided an excellent building material for the charming collection of small houses that began to spring up in the settlement. The gorgeous neo-gothic church in the centre of town dates back to 1906, and farmers from all over the plateau used to gather in the large plot of open ground around the church for their regular *nagmaal* (communion) ceremonies.

Although Nieuwoudtville is considered the heartland of Namaqualand's spring flower bounty, technically it isn't part of Namaqualand at all. Instead, the town is located in the Hantam or Western Mountain Karoo (a subsection of the wider Succulent Karoo biome). Nevertheless, all's fair in love and tourism and, in a good year, the natural floral displays in town and on surrounding farms is nothing short of miraculous.

To cater for tourists (the new lifeblood of the region) many of the old sandstone homes that once housed traders and townsfolk have now been converted into charming B&Bs or self-catering units. Accommodation is also offered on various farms in the area, and there are several campsites in town. But book ahead as things get packed out over the spring season.

Indeed, during this peak time, Nieuwoudtville throws off its sleepy demeanour and turns into a bustling little metropolis. Tour busses chug up and down the main streets, hundreds of people flit in and out of the tourism info centre, and visitors from all over the world meet in coffee shops and restaurants to compare notes.

There are regular talks by flower experts, hosted by the local eco-group, while the Indigo Development organisation offers bio-diversity activities for groups and individuals. They also train up local community members as flower guides and, if you're a novice, hiring one of these spotters is highly recommended as they will make the experience that much more rewarding. Check out the website: www.indigo-dc.org

If you can't make it here for the big spring event, don't despair. Apart from the annual, short-lived displays of daisies and succulents, Nieuwoudtville is the self-proclaimed 'bulb capital of the world'. This is because it has an astounding number of different geophyte species, which bloom at various times of the year starting in March.

A renowned bulb and clivia nursery, run by local enthusiast and regional boffin Hendrik Van Zijl, is located on the outskirts of town. In the evenings, Mr. Van Zijl can usually be found at his Smidswinkel Restaurant, which offers delicious meals and interesting botanical displays to divert diners. He also runs a range of guests houses, so check out his www.nieuwoudtville.co.za website for more details.

Despite the appeal of bulbs and Brunsvigias, the burning question in Spring remains 'where can I see the daisies?'. Well, the small (150ha) wildflower reserve just to the east of town is an obvious place to start. This facility was established in 1974 to protect the district's flora and it contains several endemic species, but the blooms are somewhat erratic. An unstaffed info centre has educational display boards that describe the complex combination of climate, soil, rock and vegetation types that are present on the Bokkeveld plateau, creating the unique conditions that support the region's unparalleled botanical diversity.

The 6300ha Hantam National Botanical Garden (formerly the Glen Lyon Wildflower Reserve) is another excellent destination for both daisies and bulbs. This, the 9th official botanical garden in South Africa, opened in January 2008 and operates under the auspices of the National Biodiversity Institute (SANBI). The gardens are located on the old Glenlyon farm and the original homestead - now the office building - dates back to 1929. Guided walking tours and drives in an open safari vehicle are available (but book in advance). The old bus that used to ferry visitors around the reserve is, sadly, no longer operational.

Sir David Attenborough and the director of Kew Gardens in London are among the botanical luminaries who have visited the farm over the years, and several TV shows have filmed here (including BBC's 1991 series The Private Life of Plants). So, definitely worth a visit. For more info, call 027 218 1200 / www.sanbi.org/gardens/hantam.

Nearby, the 4776ha Oorlogskloof (war ravine) Nature Reserve is another popular natural attraction with a campsite, chalets and 146km of fantastic hiking trails that run along the edge of the mountains and down into the valleys. But do bear in mind that the reserve is dominated by Fynbos, which grows in the poor-quality soil found along the dry rim of the escarpment. So, not too many daisies here. Contact Oorlogskloof on 027 218 1010.

The good news is that, depending on the rains, patches of spring flowers can be seen just about everywhere in Nieuwoudtville and surrounds. Farm fields, roadside verges and open plots in the town itself often boast arresting stands of colour, so all you have to do is keep your eyes open.

For those in the know, however, there are a few special places where you really do get to see the full grandeur of the annual wildflower 'carpets' (including the nearby farms of Matjiesfontein and Papkuilsfontein - see the next section). But remember, it's not just about the number of flowers on display, it's also about the number of species. So, look beyond the fields of common *gous blomme* (marigolds), *katsterte* (cat's tails) and *pietsnot* (literally translated as Pete's boogers, a singularly unlovely name that might refer to the plant's slimy sap), and seek out the rarer endemics.

For more information, contact Nieuwoudtville Tourism: 027 218 1336 / www.nieuwoudtville.com. You can also contact the Hantam Municipality on 027 341 8500 / www.hantam.gov.za.

A Self-drive Flower Tour

Although conditions change all the time, here is a reasonably reliable 2-day itinerary that should take you to most of the important sites. Before you set out, however, get a detailed map from the tourism office and ask around to find out where the flowers are blooming at the moment.

First up, drive south on the gravel road out of town towards Matjiesfontein farm. After about 5kms, you'll pass the Hantam National Botanical Gardens and, a bit further on, you'll see a sign for a 'glacial pavement'. Park your car and walk about 200m to see the grooves and striations carved into the exposed rock by grinding glaciers that passed over this region 300 million years ago.

When you've had your geological jollies, continue on the road until you come to Matjiesfontein (about 20km from Nieuwoudtville).

Matjiesfontein Farm is a marvel. In a good year, the fields are literally blanketed by flowers of every shape, size, colour and description. Apart from the sheer number of plants in bloom, get close to the ground and see how many different species you can identify. It's a mind-boggling display of biodiversity at its most rampant.

To facilitate your exploration, the farm owners have established a series of gravel roads that lead through the property. This circular route is suitable for all types of vehicles and you will happily spend several hours driving slowly through the fields, stopping constantly to take pictures. Bear in mind, though, you won't be alone and the road can get quite congested with all the floral rubbernecking.

So, as is the case in the Kruger Park when a lazy lion causes a traffic jam, you'll just have to be patient. And always be careful where you drive - there aren't many places to pull over and you should never leave the path in case your tyres crush the flowers (or a crouching photographer). If it's been raining, be especially cautious as the gravel tracks get churned up by the heavy traffic and it's easy to get stuck in the muddy patches. I volunteered to tow out one such driver in a VW Polo and all I got for my heroics was an overheated clutch. A tractor was subsequently sent in to complete the job.

Matjiesfontein has a farm stall and a restaurant, which are housed in historic buildings at the entrance gate. Charming tractor-drawn wagon trips through the flowers are also on offer. For more information, contact the farm on 027 218 1217.

The nearby farm of Papkuilsfontein is similarly renowned for its wildflowers and offers an enticing range of country cottages for overnight guests (tel. 027 218 1246 / www.papkuilsfontein.com).

When you're done, turn around and head back to town. I would suggest that you chill for the rest of the day as the flowers tend to close up around 15:00 and it's pointless to try cram too much into a single outing. So, wander the streets, check out the church, grab a bite to eat, and enjoy sundowners on the stoep of your guest house - that sort of thing.

Around 10:00 the next morning, once the flowers have started opening again, leave town and drive north towards Loeriesfontein on the tarred R357. About 7km along this road, you'll see the turn-off for the Nieuwoudtville Waterfall. This is a spectacular sight, where the Doring River cuts through a sandstone rim to drop 100m into a huge natural amphitheatre.

Then, continue north until you see the sign for Gannabos (about 20km from Nieuwoudtville). Turn right onto this gravel road and drive for about a kilometre until you reach the Quiver Tree Forest. This is a remarkable colony of kokerbooms that grow up the craggy, north-facing slopes of a koppie. The farmer who owns this land says he doesn't mind tourists coming to visit but does ask that they stick to the demarcated roads and clean up after themselves.

You can now either turn back to town or keep driving on this gravel road for another 20km until you see the turn-off to the left marked for 'Loeriesfontein and Cavinia oor Naressie' (going straight will take you back to Nieuwoudtville via Nuweplaas). Follow the Naressie road and try not to gawp at the millions of flowers you'll see sprouting from the roadside and up the mountain slopes.

About 15km further along, you'll come to an intersection with the gravel R355. Left will take you up to Loeriesfontein, right will take you down to Calvinia. Turn right and drive for about 5km until you see the turn off for the AP2286 to Toren.

It's quite a long detour through some very rugged mountains to the farm of Groot Toren, which often has excellent flower displays. A road has been laid out around this farm, and I found the setting to be superb. You will then have to turn around and drive back to the R355 before continuing onto Calvinia. The entire side-trip to Groot Toren, including a drive around the farm, is about 45km but allow for a couple of hours.

Once you're back on the R355, drive for another 20km to reach the lovely Hantam Karoo town of Calvinia. Do note that there is nowhere to get food or drinks between Nieuwoudtville and Calvinia, so stock up before you leave on your trip or prepare to arrive in Calvinia parched and hungry. When you're done exploring this historic town, turn right on the tarred R27 and drive the 70kms back to Nieuwoudtville.

The total distance of this round trip is about 200km and the route will take up most of the day, but you won't be disappointed. So, grab your camera and all the memory cards you can find. If your timing is good, I can quite confidently predict that your flabber will be well and truly gasted.

For more up to date information, you can try calling the Namaqua Flower Line on 079 294 7260.

Calvinia

Ecologically speaking, Calvinia is at the far eastern edge of the Namaqualand flower route. Nevertheless, it forms one corner of the triangle between the towns of Nieuwoudtville and Loeriesfontein and, as such, is drawn into the tourism sphere of the Bokkeveld plateau.

Besides, it's a lovely little place. Lying at the foot of the Hantam mountains, this is a classic Karoo *dorp* with tin-roofed houses, *stoeps* dripping with *broekie*-lace metal work, and an impressive neo-gothic sandstone church. The town was founded in 1851 and named after John Calvin, the 16th-century French protestant reformer who set the puritanical tone for South Africa's dominant religious discourse during the apartheid years.

Today, Calvinia is one of SA's largest wool producing centres. It also boasts what is probably the country's biggest post box, converted from an old water tower by the Chamber of Commerce in 1995. Mail that is posted in the box gets franked with a special flower stamp. This kind of quirky humour is similarly evident in the joyous Calvinia Vleisfees (meat festival) which takes place every year towards the end of August. So, if you're a fan of boerewors, lamb chops and *lang-arm* dancing, don't miss this celebration of all things carnivorous.

In terms of activities, the nearby Akkerdam Nature Reserve is the place to go if you want to do some hiking, and several farms offer 4x4 routes. And, for those who are historically minded, a visit to the Calvinia museum is a must. This well-run facility is located in the old Jewish Synagogue, which was built in 1920 and donated to the town in 1967 when the once-prominent Jewish community dwindled. The museum can give you a good walking-tour map that guides you on a pleasant stroll through all the important sites in town, including several of the original town houses that were built over 150 years ago.

For more information, contact the Namakwa Tourism Office in Calvinia: 027 341 8131.

Loeriesfontein

The other notable town on the Bokkeveld plateau is Loeriesfontein, a peaceful place that is well-known for its spontaneous wildflower displays. It also has an unusual windmill museum, one of only a handful in the world, with 27 examples of these aeolian turbines standing tall on the grounds of the Fred Turner Folk and Cultural Museum (tel. 027 662 1023).

A good day trip for 4x4 enthusiasts leads from Nieuwoudtville to Loeriesfontein (64km) and down 'The Hell' pass - a rough track that descends the escarpment and then runs south along the Knersvlakte to rejoin the tarred R27 at the foot of Van Rhyn's Pass. The journey will take you through some dramatic scenery and three distinct vegetation zones: Fynbos, Renosterveld and Succulent Karoo. It's a round trip of roughly 150km.

For more information, contact the Loeriesfontein Municipality: 027 662 8600.

The Cederberg

Continuing south from Nieuwoudtville, you will transition from Namaqualand into the province of the Western Cape. Here, the displays of flowering succulents and annuals are supplemented by the restios (reeds), ericas and proteas that characterise the Fynbos biome.

More accurately known as the Cape Floristic Region (CFR), this is by far the smallest of the world's 6 Floral Kingdoms yet it contains over 9000 plant species, 69% of which are endemic. According to UNESCO, the CFR is "one of the richest areas for plants when compared to any similar sized area in the world. It represents less than 0.5% of the area of Africa but is home to nearly 20% of the continent's flora".

In 2004, the 'Cape Floral Region Protected Areas' was declared a UNESCO World Heritage Site, recognising its significance as 'one of the world's great centres of terrestrial biodiversity'. The protected areas in question originally included 8 representative nature reserves, namely Table Mountain National Park, the Boland Mountain Complex (around Stellenbosch and Gordon's Bay), the Cederberg, the Swartberg, Baviaanskloof, De Hoop, Boosmansbos and Groot Winterhoek, In 2015, the World Heritage Site was extended - doubling its size to just over 1 000 000 hectares in 13 protected areas.

Fynbos vegetation can be roughly divided into the dunefields of the Strandveld along the west coast, the endangered Renosterveld of the Swartland around Darling, and the Mountain Fynbos of the Cederberg.

We'll start with the unsurpassed visual drama of the Cederberg. To enter this mountainous wonderland from the Bokkeveld, you can drive to Vanrhynsdorp and follow the N7 highway to the town of Clanwilliam -gateway to the Cederberg. This route is about 130km.

Alternatively, you can drive south from Nieuwoudtville on the gravel R364 and over the diverting Botterkloof Pass to gain direct access to the sandstone stillness of these amazing mountains. This road eventually reaches the town of Clanwilliam after 150km, and you'll find the turn-off to the flower-rich Biedouw Valley *en route*.

Although the flowers are marvellous, the weird, wind-blown rock formations of the Cederberg are beautiful in any season. Nature lovers will be entranced and could spend many days hiking through the cliffs, swimming in the rivers, or exploring the exhilarating landscape in a 4x4. There really is a lot to do...

The birding is excellent. Stargazers can check out the privately owned astronomical observatory (www.cederbergobs.org.za). The walk to the iconic Maltese Cross is classic Cederberg, as is the more strenuous hike to the Wolfberg Cracks and Arch. And the Stadsaal (City Hall) Caves have been used as a shelter by locals for thousands of years, bearing both bushman rock art and more modern monograms from white settlers and farmers (including some early National Party politicians). But don't even think about adding your own initials to the collection - you're not that important.

There are plenty of accommodation options available, for all budgets, but camping in the Cederberg is legendary. Cape Nature has a range of cottages and campsites at Algeria and Kliphius, and their Cederberg Wilderness Area is crammed with outstanding hikes, mountain bike trails and other activities (www.capenature.co.za/reserves/cederberg-wilderness-area).

The privately-owned Sanddrif Holiday Resort also has a magnificent property with a variety of cottages, camp sites and things to do (try doing the high jump into the deep pool at Maalgat). Plus, it's the location of both a craft brewery (www.cederbergbrewery.com) and a winery that produces 'South Africa's Highest Altitude Wines' (www.cederbergwine.com). For more info, contact 027 482 2825 / www.sanddrif.com.

In previous decades, much of the land in this region was degraded by unsustainable farming practices. The indigenous Clanwilliam Ceder tree, which gives the mountains their name, was particularly hard hit and is currently a threatened species. Thankfully, these unique uplands are now under the protection of the Cederberg Conservancy, a collaborative organisation that is working with private landowners and Cape Nature to protect and restore the Cederberg's natural splendour (www.cederberg.co.za).

In terms of flowers, the most reliable place to see them bloom is in the Biedouw Valley, close to the picturesque mission station of Wupperthal. But do note that a hot berg wind could wither this colony within a couple of days, so try to check ahead before you go.

Even though it generally blooms in the summer months, the rare Snow Protea *(Protea cryophila)* is also worth a brief mention. This narrowly endemic plant is found only along the snow line of the Cederberg, in a small belt about 25 km in length. It grows in the cracks between bare rocks and can survive in both extreme cold and blistering heat, sometimes living for up to 70 years. The white, furry flowers of the Snow Protea take a full year to open and finding one of these floral gems is a mega-tick for flower spotters.

If you are coming from the N7, the Cederberg can be accessed from the town of Clanwilliam by taking the gravel R364 over the jaw-dropping Pakhuis Pass. After about 40km on this road, you'll see a turn-off to the right marked for Wupperthal and the Biedouw Valley. Take this road and, about 13km later, you'll reach an intersection.

17km to your right is the white-washed mission station of Wupperthal, which has changed little since it was established in 1830 by the Rhenish Church (the

Moravians took over in 1965). Once famous for its handmade *velskoene* (literally 'shoes made of hide'), it's an idyllic place tucked away in a tangle of tall peaks, with neat houses and a tranquil air. Tragically, a wildfire ripped through the town on the very last day of 2018, destroying the clinic, community hall and over 50 homes, leaving 200 homeless and one dead. Rebuilding continues and I'm sure they'd welcome a visit if you're in the area (tel. 027 492 3410 / www.wupperthal.co.za).

To your left is the Biedouw Valley route, which extends for about 30km up to the little settlement of Uitspankraal. You will then have to retrace your steps to Clanwilliam or continue northwards to the R355, which leads up to Calvinia (an additional distance of 100km from Uitspankraal).

For more information, contact the Cederberg Tourism Office: 027 482 2024 / www.cederberg.com. Or check out the Cederberg Heritage Route's website: www.cedheroute.co.za. The Cederberg Municipality can be reached on 027 482 8000 / www.cederbergmun.gov.za.

Clanwilliam

Originally established in 1725 as Jan Disselsvalleij, Clanwilliam is one of the 10 oldest towns in South Africa. The name was changed to its current Celtic-sounding title by Sir John Cradock in 1814, who was trying to curry favour with his father-in-law, the Earl of Clanwilliam.

This once-sleepy farming town is the centre of South Africa's rooibos (red bush) tea industry. A fragrantly aromatic brew, rooibos is actually a species of Fynbos that is endemic to the area and there are several farms in the vicinity that offer tours of their facilities. February is harvesting season, according to www.rooibos-route.co.za. Technically, this is the only place in the world where you can grow certified rooibos - kinda like champagne.

Clanwilliam is also the gateway to the northern Cederberg, as has been described above, but it's an increasingly popular tourist destination in its own right with lots of shops, restaurants, guest houses, and a large dam that is highly favoured by water sport enthusiasts.

It's no slouch in the flower department either. The Ramskop Nature Garden on the outskirts of town contains more than 350 species of 'cultivated' wildflowers and there are several paths leading through this little slice of botanical heaven, offering great views over the mountains. During peak season, the local woman's organisation runs a small tea shop at the garden (tel. 027 482 8012).

The big botanical event in Clanwilliam is the annual wildflower show, held in the old Dutch Reformed Church on the main road. Hosted by the Clanwilliam Wildflower Association, this 10-day extravaganza features a variety of enormous arrangements that sees farmers from surrounding districts put their best flowers forward for the edification of townsfolk and visitors alike. The dates of the show vary depending on the vagaries of the season, but it usually takes place towards the end of August and the beginning of September (in times of drought, it may be cancelled altogether). In a good year, though, about 360 different species can be seen inside the small church, and associated festivities include concerts, art and food stalls, and a street carnival. For the full programme, check out www.clanwilliamwildflowershow.co.za.

While you're in the area, you can also pick up a new pair of footwear from the 'oldest shoe factory in South Africa' (www.strassbergers.co.za). Or catch a show at the Bushman's Cave Berg Theatre (www.bushmanscave.co.za).

For more information, contact the Clanwilliam Tourism Bureau: 027 482 2024 / www.clanwilliam.info.

Citrusdal

At the southern end of the Cederberg Mountains, about 60km south of Clanwilliam on the N7, is the attractive riverside town of Citrusdal. As the name implies, there are several large citrus farms in the area and tours can arranged during the harvest season.

Citrusdal offers visitors the usual array of shops, accommodation, restaurants and a wide range of leisure activities. These include hiking trails, 4x4 trails, quad biking, canoeing in the Olifants River, rock climbing, a golf course, and mountain biking. The popular Cape Nature campsites at Algeria can be accessed via the gravel Nieuwoudt's Pass, which cuts a narrow path up the mountains about 20km north of town.

There are several good wildflower routes around Citrusdal, including the 'Bo-Rivier' road that runs between the banks of the Olifants River and the steep flanks of the Cederberg. The road up to The Baths Hot Springs Resort is another popular route for spotters (www.thebaths.co.za). You can also try the road to Paleisheuwel, which can be reached from the top of Pikenierskloof Pass on the N7.

From Citrusdal, you can either head off to the Strandveld region along the West Coast, or you can continue south over the majestic Piekenierskloof Pass to Cape Town, which is 170km away. This pass, named after the Pike Men - soldiers armed with long spears who used to protect this important access route, has been in use since the 1660s.

For more info, contact the Citrusdal Tourism Bureau: 022 921 3210 / www.citrusdal.info.

The West Coast

For the purposes of this book, we're going to say that the West Coast region runs along the sea from Lambert's Bay in the north to the Langebaan lagoon in the south (although some tourist websites extend the appellation to cover the entire shoreline up to Alexander Bay). Either way, it's a lovely part of the world that offers visitors charming small towns, quiet gravel roads, bird-filled wetlands, excellent seafood, and unpretentious hospitality.

Unfortunately, these delicate delights are also attracting ever-increasing numbers of property developers who are slowly spreading their particular brand of holiday-home horror up and down the coast. One only hopes that, going forward, the region is able to strike a responsible balance between development, aesthetics and conservation.

It is beyond the scope of this book to discuss the West Coast in detail (after all, we aren't in Namaqualand anymore). So, instead, I will briefly focus on the tourist hotspots around Lambert's Bay, Elands Bay, Velddrif, Paternoster, Saldanha Bay and the West Coast National Park at Langebaan. Suffice it to say, however, that each town in the region offers its own special combination of historical sites, hiking trails, fishing, whale-watching, boat trips, 4x4 routes and flower-spotting, along with other natural and cultural attractions.

Lambert's Bay

Known primarily as a fishing resort, Lambert's Bay is a nice seaside town with an annual *Kreeffees* (crayfish festival), which has become something of a pilgrimage for West Coast seafood enthusiasts. For flowers, several farms in the area may have good displays, and the road to Leipoldtville is recommended by the locals.

For those who like a bit of history, check out the Heerenlogement (Gentleman's Lodging) Cave near the town of Graafwater. This was a regular stop on the old wagon road to the north, and the walls of the cave are covered with historical graffiti made by travellers of old.

You can access Lambert's Bay by taking the tarred R364 from Clanwilliam. Alternatively, you can follow the gravel roads along the coast, either from Strandfontein in the north or Elands Bay in the South. You can also take the private Sishen-Saldanha toll road, which runs close to the sea alongside the industrial railway line from Elands Bay.

Some other highlights include: Bird Island Nature Reserve, an important breeding and roosting site for Cape gannets and cormorants (www.capenature.co.za/reserves/bird-island-nature-reserve); Bosduifklip - a well-known restaurant and wedding venue tucked under a rock overhang (www.bosduifklip.co.za); and Muisbosskerm - a renowned restaurant located right on the beach (www.muisbosskerm.co.za).

For more info, contact the Lambert's Bay Tourism Office on 027 432 1000 / www.lambertsbay.co.za.

Elands Bay

As soon as drove into Elands Bay, I knew it was something special. A small, untouched resort town built around a magnificent bay, it's everything a West Coast seaside village should be. The beach is wide and pristine, the air is clean, and the atmosphere is tranquil enough to soothe the savage breast of even the most hard-core city slicker. Best of all, no sprawling 'lifestyle' developments - so far.

There are several accommodation choices in Elands Bay including guest houses and the rather old-fashioned hotel, which offers traditional rooms with sea-views. But I would recommend staying at the local caravan park which is quite literally on the beach.

The flowers on the roads around Elands Bay aren't too shabby either. The displays begin shortly outside the town of Eendekuil, which can be accessed from the N7 at the foot of the Piekenierskloof Pass. From here, the road largely keeps to the north bank of the Verlorenvlei River as it flows towards the sea, about 80km away. You can also access this road from the Citrusdal side of the mountains.

In its later stretches, the river spreads out across a series of wetlands that harbour a wealth of avian and botanical life. The farm at Vensterklip (window rock) has a particularly eye-popping location on the banks of a shallow marshland, boasting a dense display of wildflowers that bloom profusely around the headstones in their small family cemetery. Accommodation and a restaurant are also on-site (www.vensterklip.co.za).

The Verlorenvlei itself (one of the largest and most important estuarine systems on the west coast, and a Ramsar Wetland of International Importance) can be reached just outside the town of Redelingshuys.

From Elands Bay, you simply have to do the short drive around the adjacent headland known as Baboon Point. This gravel road leads right along the sea, offering unobstructed views over the ocean. It's also a good place to see the local Strandveld flowers bloom among the fecund, green vegetation that grows right up to the water's edge.

When you've done your time at Elands Bay, you either have to return to the N7 or continue south down the coast on gravel roads that lead to Velddrif. If you choose the latter, you'll pass the popular Rocherpan coastal nature reserve, a 930ha conservation area declared in 1966. A seasonal vlei (marshland) that's usually dry between March and June, Rocherpan is great for birders and beach lovers alike, with cute cottages for overnighters (www.capenature.co.za/reserves/rocherpan-nature-reserve).

Rocherpan is also the start of the Crayfish Trail, a multi-day slackpacking experience along the West Coast (www.crayfishtrail.co.za).

Piketberg and Velddrif

Following the N7 down from Citrusdal, the next large (ish) town you'll come to is Piketberg - an agricultural centre with a range of activities, accommodation, restaurants and markets. Contact Piketberg Tourism on 022 913 2063 / www.piketbergtourism.co.za.

From Piketberg, you can access the low-key coastal conurbation of Velddrif, Port Owen and Laaiplek - an agglomeration of marinas, harbours and holiday homes clustered around the mouth of the Berg River. It's a good place for fishermen and those keen on boat trips or whale spotting, with a full range of tourist facilities and several well-established resorts, but the area around the harbour smells fishy.

The sea itself is rather muddy, as is often the case at river mouths, but I still spent a couple of happy hours sitting on the beach and chatting with some local fishermen who were enjoying the sunset over a box of wine. If you want a change of pace, the outlying towns of Dwarkersbos, Hopefield and Aurora offer some nature-based activities, including flower spotting in season.

For more info, contact 022 783 1821 / www.velddriftourism.co.za. You can contact the Berg River Municipality on 022 913 6000 / www.bergmun.org.za.

Paternoster, Cape Columbine and St. Helena Bay

For me, the highlight of the West Coast Peninsula is Paternoster - one of the oldest fishing villages in the Cape. Unfortunately, over the last decade or so, an anonymous blur of modern housing estates and holiday homes has sprung up, threatening to swamp the character of the original village with cookie-cutter modernity. But the old part of town is hanging in there, with its rough-hewn, white-washed homes still looking out over the broad 8km expanse of Langstrand (Long Beach).

Given its proximity to Cape Town, over the years Paternoster has attracted a collection of chefs, hoteliers, artists, potters and artisans - with the all the shops, restaurants, guest houses and wellness retreats that implies. But the main attraction of the town remains the stunning, silvery shingle, perfect for a sunset stroll as you watch the small fishing boats flit in and out of the bay. The water's bloody freezing, though.

Highlights of any visit to must include the iconic 'Winkel op Paternoster' - a nicely cluttered general dealers with an old row boat stranded in the sand outside - and don't forget to enjoy an authentic serving of fresh fish and chips from the kiosk at the beachfront. There are also several excellent restaurants offering upper-end dining.

But the main attraction in Paternoster, for me anyway, isn't actually in town at all. Instead, head through the village and down the coast a stretch until you come to the transcendent Cape Columbine Nature Reserve - a small, municipal reserve of 263ha, declared in 1973.

Consisting of a series of small bays, flanked by grey boulders, Cape Columbine is a stunning juxtaposition of sea and stone. The waves smash themselves into salty spray on the rocks, while sea birds wheel and screech in the sky above. During spring, the green dunes of the reserve are full of wildflowers, many of which are rare or narrowly endemic.

Several campsites have been established in the various coves and crannies of the headland and, although there are few facilities, intrepid campers will be treated to an unsurpassed seaside location. You can also camp it up at Tietiesbaai Beach, where there's a cold-water ablution block. This famous bowl-shaped bay is indeed shaped like a pair of boobies, but the cheeky appellation is probably a corruption of a person's name, one Mr. Titus, who used to own a farm in the area. For bookings, you can try contact Cape Columbine on 022 752 2718 or just arrive at the gate and hope for the best.

Overlooking the scene is the Cape Columbine lighthouse. This was the last manned lighthouse built in South Africa, in 1936. It is still manned today, and tours to the top of the tower can be arranged. At one stage, the lighthouse was also offering comfortable overnight accommodation in two adjacent chalets, but I can't determine if that facility is still available.

The other place to overnight in the reserve is the extraordinary Sea Shack Beach Camp, where you get to sleep in simple huts perched right on the lip of a small beach. When I stayed there, it was called the Beach Camp and the whole place seemed to be made of little more than canvas and driftwood, but it was magical to sleep just steps away from the waves. The venue now seems to have been upgraded somewhat but the location remains sublime (www.seashack.co.za).

On the way back to the N7 from Paternoster, you'll pass signs that point to the woefully over-developed strip of St. Helena Bay, Britannia Bay, Shelley Point and Stompneus Bay - a cluster of holiday homes and marinas that offers a range of tourist facilities. For those with a historical bent, check out the Vasco da Gama memorial in St. Helena Bay. This is the location where the Portuguese navigator dropped anchor way back in 1497, marking the start of southern Africa's long and complicated colonial era.

For more info, contact the Paternoster Tourism Centre: 022 752 2323 / www.visitwestcoast.co.za.

Saldanha Bay

The Saldanha-Sishen railway line, which stretches 1000kms from the huge iron ore mine in Bushmanland, terminates at the large industrial and commercial fishing complex of Saldanha Bay. This is said to be the only really good natural harbour in South Africa, as all our other ports have required extensive dredging and re-working. Despite its size, though, it's not a particularly dirty or polluted port. The boats bobbing in the blue bay are very picturesque and there is a full range of accommodation and dining options.

The nearby town of Vredenburg offers more of the same, while the nearby sea-side village of Jacob's Bay is an up-and-coming destination that sometimes offers good flower-spotting. The West Coast Fossil Park can be found in the vicinity, a few km down the road towards Langebaan. This 14ha facility was once the part of a phosphate mining operation, which uncovered one of the richest animal fossil sites in the world. 200 different kinds of prehistoric creatures have been found here and are now displayed at the park's interpretation centre (www.fossilpark.org.za).

For more info, contact Saldanha Bay Tourism on 022 772 1515 / www.visitwestcoast.co.za. The Saldanha Bay Municipality can be reached on 022 701 7000 / www.sbm.gov.za.

Langebaan and the West Coast National Park

At the southern end of the large bay, 20kms from Saldanha, is the extensive Langebaan lagoon system. It's a broad waterway that supports a wide range of boating and water sport activities. The town is a popular destination for holiday makers and has all the facilities that you'd expect, including a casino.

The main attraction, however, is the West Coast National Park - a beautiful conservation area that protects both sides of the lagoon from development. For flower-spotters, Postberg mountain is well-known for the spring flowers that bloom on its slopes. This is the closest reliable wildflower site to Cape Town (only 90km away) and makes for a good day trip from the Mother City. You can also stay overnight at one of their appealing cottages or campsites (tel. 022 772 2144 / www.sanparks.org/parks/west_coast).

For more info, contact Langebaan Tourism: 022 772 1515 / www.visitwestcoast.co.za.

Darling

Whether you are heading down to Cape Town on the N7 from Citrusdal, or coming in from the West Coast, the Swartland town of Darling is worth a visit. This lovely little village has a range of art galleries, antique shops, wine farms and other cultural activities. It is also the home of the invaluable Pieter-Dirk Uys and his alter-ego, the unstoppable Evita Bezuidenhout. Together, they hold court at Evita se Perron, a converted train station that's now painted pink and surrounded by an unusual sculpture garden known as Boerassic Park. hese two national treasures have hosted regular performances at their intimate theatre in Darling since 1996, and attending a show is highly recommended (www.evita.co.za).

Darling also has a couple of small wildflower reserves and an annual wildflower show, usually held in September. These reserves, which include the Tienie Verster wildflower site, protect the highly endangered veld type known as Renosterveld and can boast impressive displays during the season.

Other attractions include the !Khwa ttu San Heritage Centre (www.khwattu.org), a Darling Wine Route, and the Darling Museum (www.darlingmuseum.co.za).

For more information, contact Darling Tourism: 022 492 3391 / www.hellodarling.org.za. The Swartland Municipality can be reached on 022 487 9400 / www.swartland.org.za.

From Darling, it is a short trip back to Cape Town (75km) through waves of bright, yellow flowers that bloom in the Canola fields (which are cultivated as opposed to wild). And there, in the shadow of The Mountain, we must leave take our leave. The Namaqualand adventure that began in all the way up in the Richtersveld, 700km to the north, has finally come to an end. Thank you for joining me on this remarkable journey. I'm sure you'll agree that it's a trip well worth taking.

References / Further Reading

Boonzaier, Emile; Berens (Penny); Malherbe, Candy; Smith, Andy. 1996. *The Cape Herders - a history of the Khoikhoi in southern Africa.* David Philip, Ohio University Press.

Bulpin, TV. 2001. *Discovering Southern Africa (sixth edition).* Tafelberg Publishers.

Cowling, Richard and Pierce, Shirley. 1999. *Namaqualand - a succulent desert.* Fernwood Press.

Fleminger, David. 2005. *Back Roads of the Cape.* Jacana Media.

Forbes, VS. 1965. *Pioneer travellers in South Africa.* A.A. Balkema.

Jowell, Phyllis and Folb, Adrienne. 2004. *Into Kokerboom Country - Namaqualand's Jewish pioneers.* Fernwood Press.

Joyce, Peter. 2004. *Flower Watching in the Cape - scenic routes throughout the year.* Struik Publishers.

Le Roux, Annelise. 2005. *South African Wild Flower Guide 1 - Namaqualand.* Botanical Society of South Africa.

Manning, John & Goldblatt, Peter. 2007. *South African Wild Flower Guide 9 - Nieuwoudtville. Bokkeveld Plateau & Hantam.* Botanical Society of South Africa

Manning, John & Goldblatt, Peter. 2007. *South African Wild Flower Guide 7 - West Coast.* Botanical Society of South Africa.

Manning, John. 2004. *Southern African Wild Flowers - jewels of the veld.* Struik Publishers.

Manning, John. 2003. *Photographic guide to the wildflowers of South Africa.* Briza Publications.

Norman, Nick and Whitfield, Gavin. 2006. *Geological Journeys.* Struik Publishers.

Odendaal, Francois and Suich, Helen. 2007. *Richtersveld - the land and its people.* Struik Publishers.

Raper, Peter E. 2004. *New Dictionary of South African Place Names.* Jonathan Ball Publishers.

Ross, Graham. 1998. *The interactive role of transportation and the economy of Namaqualand.* Unpublished PhD thesis.

Ross, Graham. 2002. *The Romance of Cape Mountain Passes.* David Phillip.

Smalberger, John M. 1975 (reprinted 2000). *A history of Copper Mining in Namaqualand.* Struik / Scholtz Trust.

Smith, Gideon. 2003 *Sasol first field guide to aloes of southern Africa.* Struik Publishers.

Smith, G.F. Chesselet, P. van Jaarsveld, E. Hartmann, H. Hammer, S. van Wyk, B-E. Burgoyne, P. Klak, C. & Kurzweil H. 1998. *Mesembs of the world - a complete field guide to the Mesembryanthemaceae.* Briza Publications.

Smith, G.F. van Jaarsveld, E.J. Arnold, T.H. Steffins, F.E. Dixon, R.D. & Retief, J.A. (eds). 1997. *List of southern African succulent plants.* Umdaus Press.

South African National Parks. 2006. */Ai-/Ais-Richtersveld Transfrontier Park - official information guide.* SAN Parks.

Steenkamp, Willem. 1975. *Land of the Thirst King.* Howard Timmins.
Truter, Cornel. 1998. *West Coast Tourist Guide.* UCT Press.

Van Rooyen, Gretel & Steyn, Hester. 1999. *South African Wild Flower Guide 10 - Cederberg: Clanwilliam & Biedouw Valley.* Botanical Society of South Africa.

Van Wyk, Braam. 2000. *A photographic guide to wild flowers of South Africa.* Struik Publishers.

Viljoen, MJ and Reimold, WU. 1999. *An introduction to South Africa's geological and mining heritage.* Mintek.

Williamson, Graham. 2000. *Richtersveld - the enchanted wilderness.* Umdaus Press.

Websites

- www.capewestcoast.org - West Coast Tourism portal
- www.experiencenortherncape.com - official NC Tourism portal
- www.namakwa-dm.gov.za - Namakwa District Municipality
- www.namakwa-info.co.za
- www.ramsar.org
- www.sahistory.org.za
- www.sanbi.org - National Biodiversity Institute
- www.sanparks.org - SA National Parks
- whc.unesco.org - UNESCO World Heritage Sites portal

Acknowledgements

As is always the case, a book of this scope is never the work of just one person. The author therefore wishes to thank all the people of Namaqualand for their friendliness, hospitality and time.

In particular, I am indebted to the communities who make up the Richtersveld Conservancy, as represented by Volenti van der Westhuisen and Gert Links who spent several hours chatting with me about the history and future plans of their organisation.

Bernard van Lente and the staff of the Namaqua National Park were also very generous with their insight and knowledge. Hendrik Van Zijl of Nieuwoudtville was another font of helpful information, as was the wonderfully enthusiastic Hugo Nagel of Springbok.

As picking brains is something of a hobby for me, I would like to offer a collective thanks to the well-informed staff at all the tourism offices and museums I visited during my trip in 2007.

I would also like to tip my hat to a regular contributor, the road-guru Graham Ross who made his excellent PhD thesis on the transportation history of Namaqualand available to me. Graham sadly left us in 2015.

To Kerrin and Chris Cocks, thanks for sending me off on this adventure in the first place.

To Judd Kirkel Welwitch, thank you for doing me a solid and checking the text from a botanical perspective (although any errors which may have crept in remain entirely my fault).

To Ilan Mizrachi, sincere thanks for sitting with me for hours while I kibitzed with the maps and cover. Your patience is very much appreciated.

Finally, as always, I wish to offer sincere thanks to my trusty family and friends who never fail to provide me with all the support I need to see things through - no matter how long it takes!

About the Author

David is a writer and director, working in the media industry for the last 25 years. His passion for travel began as a child, when his family would pile into a motorhome and drive around South Africa for their holidays.

His interest in travel writing grew out of an open curiosity about people, a love of history in all its gory, and an insatiable desire for the open road.

A long-standing film buff, David is currently developing screenplays and sitcoms. And he's going to start working on his novel, tomorrow.

David is a lifelong Joburger but acknowledges that his hometown is an excellent place from which to take a holiday. He walks his dogs in the park every day.

For more info, please visit www.davidfleminger.com or email davidfleminger@gmail.com.